Color and the Moving Image

This new AFI Film Reader is the first comprehensive collection of original essays on the use of color in film. Contributors from diverse film studies backgrounds consider the importance of color throughout the history of the medium, assessing not only the theoretical implications of color on the screen, but also the ways in which developments in cinematographic technologies transformed the aesthetics of color and the nature of film archiving and restoration. *Color and the Moving Image* includes new writing on key directors whose work is already associated with color—such as Hitchcock, Jarman and Sirk—as well as others whose use of color has not yet been explored in such detail—including Eric Rohmer and the Coen brothers.

With sixteen pages of full-color plates, *Color and the Moving Image* is an excellent resource for a variety of film studies courses and the global film archiving community at large.

Simon Brown is Director of Studies for Film and TV at Kingston University, UK. He has published widely on a variety of topics including the development of the early British film industry, early color cinematography and contemporary American television.

Sarah Street is Professor of Film, University of Bristol. Her publications include *British National Cinema* (1997 and 2009), *Transatlantic Crossings* (2002) and *Black Narcissus* (2005). Her latest book is *Colour Films in Britain: The Negotiation of Innovation, 1900–55* (2012).

Liz Watkins is a Lecturer in the History of Art at the University of Leeds and an Honorary Research Fellow at the University of Bristol. She has published on feminism, film/philosophy and the materiality of film in *parallax*, *Paragraph* and the *British Journal of Cinema and Television*.

Previously published in the AFI Film Readers series
EDITED BY EDWARD BRANIGAN AND CHARLES WOLFE

Color and the Moving Image

History, Theory, Aesthetics, Archive

EDITED BY

SIMON BROWN, SARAH STREET, AND LIZ WATKINS

Routledge
Taylor & Francis Group

NEW YORK AND LONDON

First published 2013
by Routledge
711 Third Avenue, New York, NY 10017

Simultaneously published in the UK
by Routledge
2 Park Square, Milton Park, Abingdon, Oxon OX14 4RN

Routledge is an imprint of the Taylor & Francis Group, an informa business

Library of Congress Cataloging in Publication Data
Color and the moving image: history, theory, aesthetics, archive / edited by Simon Brown,
Sarah Street, and Liz I Watkins.
p. cm. – (AFI film readers)
Includes bibliographical references and index.
1. Color motion pictures – History. 2. Color cinematography – History. I. Brown, Simon
(Simon David) II. Street, Sarah. III. Watkins, Liz I., 1972-
PN1995.9.C546C65 2012
791.4301–dc23   2012003464

ISBN: 978-0-415-89263-6 (hbk)
ISBN: 978-0-415-89264-3 (pbk)
ISBN: 978-0-203-11812-2 (ebk)

Typeset in Spectrum MT Font
by Cenveo Publisher Services

Printed and bound in the United States of America by Sheridan Books, Inc. (a Sheridan Group Company).

contents

contents

vi

plates and figures

figures

acknowledgments

We would like to thank those who have contributed to this volume in various ways and in particular the authors for collaborating with us with such good grace throughout the editorial process and for producing such accomplished work. The project originated from the *Colour and the Moving Image* conference which was held in Bristol in July 2009 as part of an Arts and Humanities Research Council-funded project, with additional support from the Universities of Bristol and Kingston. This provided a wonderful opportunity for so many chromophiles (and cinephiles) to gather in one place and we are thankful that the discussion from this conference has been able to continue through this book and will now be shared with others beyond the initial scope of the event. In particular we would like to thank Edward Branigan and Charles Wolfe, co-editors of the AFI Film Reader series, for their continued enthusiasm for this volume from the early planning stages to completion. We would also like to thank the editors at Routledge, Matthew Byrnie, Erica Wetter and Margo Irvin, for all their assistance, and to Vicky Jackson for completing the index.

The images for chapter 2 are courtesy of George Eastman House, Motion Picture Department Collection, Rochester; chapters 5 and 21 the BFI National Archive; chapter 6 courtesy of the collection of Carol and Eugene Epstein and the Thomas Wilfred papers, Yale University Library; chapter 20 courtesy of the EYE Film Institute, Amsterdam.

Simon Brown, Sarah Street, and Liz Watkins

introduction

s i m o n   b r o w n ,   s a r a h   s t r e e t ,   a n d
l i z   w a t k i n s

An enquiry into color can take you just about anywhere.
(Batchelor 2000: 124)

Color is a fundamental element of film form, technology and aesthetics and yet has tended to be overlooked in Film and Moving Image studies. This collection brings together a variety of the most intriguing facets and debates on color as an integral element of the production and circulation of film texts, and of the image itself, and in addition for its impetus as a theoretical concept that links technology and aesthetics. As color technologies develop then new filmmaking practices emerge, so that as the object of study alters it demands an attendant shift in the theories and modes of analysis that have informed our understanding of film (Doane 2002; Mulvey 2006). A study of color calls to a diverse range of disciplines including history, philosophy and literary sources, to indicate the potential of interdisciplinary perspectives for theories of spectatorship.

simon brown, sarah street, and liz watkins

The interdisciplinary nature of color is reflected by the range of connections that the essays in this volume make within an extensive network of technological, philosophical and aesthetic imperatives – color remains open to multifarious interpretations, analytical approaches and pertinent case studies. An examination of color through the perspective of moving image and cultural experience presents multiple challenges and opportunities to focus on the intersections of complex media histories, theories, aesthetics and archives. This volume therefore constitutes a vital contribution to film/color/chromatic studies at a crucial point when some of the most timely and innovative research is being carried out.

While published literature on color and film is significant, it is not extensive. Existing texts tend to fall into four areas: technical histories and surveys; color theory and film; the history and aesthetics of color and particular processes such as Technicolor; and color film restoration and archiving. While technical histories have offered an overview of different color processes (Cornwell-Clyne 1951; Coe 1978; Enticknap 2005), the shifting technological ground of the image has been also been recognized for its effect on the aesthetics of film (Neale 1985; Gunning 1994; Hanssen 2006; Misek 2010). Such studies address a range of issues from the applied color processes (tinting, toning, hand painting) of silent cinema to more recent digital manipulations. This approach, which operates at the intersection of two methodologies – a history of technology and aesthetics – informs an understanding of the significance of three-strip Technicolor design as the advocacy of a specific practice of base notes and color accents (Higgins 2007: 18–19) to organize the spectator's visual engagement with the image and narrative. The interweaving of technology, design and aesthetics persists through the movements and cultures that underlay the specific historical framing of the Technicolor image to foreground the decisions of production as they impact on the reception of the film.

Color theory is a nexus of perspectives as diverse as ontology, phenomenology, physics and the classics. For film, color foregrounds a discourse on light, perception and subjectivity that is an integral, but all too often overlooked, aspect of spectatorship. While the scope of color theory has been noted through an attention to its shifting cultural and material contexts (Gage 1993, 1999, 2007; Batchelor 2000, 2006; Coates 2010) this focus has also impelled the analysis of the participation of color both in the organization of the image and as specific to the textual system of each film. Color meaning unfolds through each film text (Jameson 1995; Branigan 2006) and is informed by the practices common to a genre such as melodrama (Elsaesser 1987; Haralovich 1990) where musical excesses are echoed by color design. Critical readings of the significance of color for feminist theory have also focused on certain sequences where the ideologically complicit system of representation is disturbed, opening a space in which to explore the significance of color for analyses of the gendered image and text (Mulvey

2006; Bellour 2007). As a theoretical paradigm color situates a broader range of social and cultural contexts within cinematic representation.

Issues of color restoration and archiving have included the problem of reconstructing color from faded and fragile nitrate film stock or the variations that occur through transfer to different media (de Klerk and Hertogs 1996; Cherchi Usai 2000). As restoration technologies develop, the selection of which films will be preserved impacts on the archive of materials accessed, underscoring the variables affecting the resolution of the film image. Color fades and balances shift, requiring that the viewer revisits the grounding questions of film history and analysis – what is it that we see when we study a (restored) film image? Restoration practices, policies and the (re)circulation of archival film affect the object studied in film history, technology, theory and aesthetics.

Color and the Moving Image extends the existing body of work by offering a resource encompassing color technology, visual style, theory, the practices of specific filmmakers and the added dimension of color film restoration to introduce a range of new perspectives. This volume is therefore situated in the resurgence of interest surrounding the implications of color for film theory, history and aesthetics and is in part a response to the impact of digital technologies as a mode of accessing the cinematic archive. A focus on archiving and restoration extends the emerging scholarship by conservationists and curators around the complex relationship between digital and photochemical film materials (such as nitrate, celluloid or acetate film stocks) as a mode of questioning the ontology of the cinematic image. This strand of enquiry, which also affects archival practices, can be tracked through the different perspectives offered by the work of Paolo Cherchi Usai (2001) and Giovanna Fossati (2009).

The original essays and case studies in this collection are therefore divided into four key strands: History, Theory, Aesthetics and Archive. These four sections serve as broad organizing structures to explore the use of color in topics as diverse as silent film, Hollywood cinema (including classical and post-classical eras), East European cinema, British cinema, experimental and amateur film. The book includes new writing on key directors whose work is already associated with color such as Hitchcock, Jarman and Sirk, and others whose work with color has not yet been explored in such detail, including Ford, Rohmer and the Coen brothers. Benchmark color processes such as Prizmacolor, Agfacolor and Technicolor are considered alongside digital technologies of image manipulation and the production of colorized versions of classic texts on video. Furthermore, we have included essays by specialists in color restoration as a vital technical activity of global concern as nitrate and some cellulose acetate color originals continue to deteriorate.

Color film history is particularly difficult to research due to the sparse availability of primary source material, the loss of many film titles from the silent period and relative dearth of explicit discourse about color in the pre Technicolor years. The History section nevertheless includes new research on topics that have seldom received extensive analysis. Simon Brown's chapter focuses on the parallel development of Cinechrome and Biocolour, British additive two-color processes that have received far less academic attention than their contemporary rival, Kinemacolor. Brown highlights the role played by patents in the silent period, and presents a revised view of early color experimentation shaped by the idiosyncrasies of the personalities involved. Hilde D'haeyere also revises previous historical accounts in her research by concentrating on the largely unexplored color sequences inserted into the predominately black-and-white world of Mack Sennett comedy shorts, including sequences in early Technicolor.

Early Technicolor is also the backdrop for Charles O'Brien's examination of song sequences in *King of Jazz* (1930), and his proposition of a method for their analysis. O'Brien utilizes a quantitative method of analyzing color in film, whereby color is correlated with music and also with editing. In particular, music–color relations are analyzed in song sequences, considering the extent to which color choices correlate with shot lengths and what this can reveal about color's function. While the analysis focuses on *King of Jazz*, the method has potential for the more general analysis of color film and its relation to music.

In comparison with Technicolor in the USA, the histories of other processes in other countries have received far less attention. Anna Batistová's chapter seeks to redress the imbalance by examining the development of color cinematography in post-war Czechoslovak cinema, focusing on the replacement of Soviet Agfacolor, used since 1947, by Eastmancolor in the 1950s. While there were complaints about the quality of the Agfacolor stock throughout the 1940s, it was the arrival of widescreen in Czechoslovakia that forced the industry to look beyond the iron curtain. The chapter demonstrates how it was the technological requirements of a global industry which overcame the realities of the post-war political situation to drive a modernization in color filmmaking in Czechoslovakia. Bringing the focus back to Britain, Sarah Street's chapter examines the history of the Prizma process, first developed in the USA but then utilized for a British feature film, *The Glorious Adventure* (1922), by J. Stuart Blackton who had made his name working in the American film industry. Based on a surviving restored print of the film, Street's analysis suggests that Blackton was astute in making a virtue of a technical "fringing" problem by exploiting it as a special effect in scenes of the Great Fire of London. The film is an excellent example of the mixing of color styles, demonstrating how applied and photographic methods were not necessarily distinct during this period of "color hybridity". The final essay in the History section by Andrew Johnston is concerned with Thomas Wilfred's early experimental kinetic light projections, or "lumia". Wilfred's work could be differentiated from the projected effects of nineteenth- and early twentieth-century color organs in its formulation of motion without recourse to musical rhythms and conventions. This chapter investigates Wilfred's manipulation of color in his lumia as abstract dramas of light and his theories on lumia's manipulation of the senses and interactions with other arts.

The theme of the second section of the book is Theory, a vast area as far as color is concerned but again featuring authors who write about aspects that suggest new ways of thinking about color and the moving image. Tom Gunning extends his theorization of early color film by isolating black as a color often ignored in analyses. His chapter probes the fundamental paradox: Is black a color, or the lack of color? He argues that the role of black as an image for the lack of light has special power in a medium made up of light, and its symbolic overtones in film mark it as one of film's most powerful tools of expression. Rather than simply the negative of color, Gunning argues that black may be seen in some films as the matrix and source of color, an invisible source from which vision arises. Rosalind Galt seeks in her chapter to illuminate another case of color refusing to be rendered invisible. British artist Derek Jarman engaged explicitly with color throughout his career and Galt argues that the mobilization of color in Jarman's films can be seen as constituting a politics of form. As a crucial component of his queer aesthetics and as a refusal of the chromophobia that has dominated the history of film theory, she concludes that his artisanal activism can be opened out to a broader color militancy.

The final two chapters in the Theory section concentrate on color as sensory experience. Jocelyn Szczepaniak-Gillece examines the flicker of innumerable tints and traces between memory and experience which illuminate the interplay of history and event, occurrence and depiction in Apichatpong Weerasethakul's *Syndromes and a Century* (2006). The film demonstrates a gradual leeching of color from the frame in the movement from the "historical" to the "contemporary" especially evident in shots of washed out corridors between hospital rooms. Szczepaniak-Gillece suggests that this strategy constitutes a bridge between preservation and reproduction which serves to create a feedback loop of memory and experience. Where "memory" is saturated and vibrant, "experience" is whitened and drained, calling into question which images are preserved and which are reproduced, as well as the general role color plays in creating images as illusory sensory moments. Philipp Schmerheim's study is similarly concerned with how film experience involves the interplay of different sensory perceptions, and of visual, aural and haptic perception. He addresses the juxtaposition of color and black-and-white imagery both within the film frame and across different versions of the same film as a potential strategy for eliciting "haptic" film experiences in spectators. Schmerheim's analysis of *Memento* (2000), a film that involves color as well as black-and-white imagery, and Gus Van Sant's 1998 color remake of Hitchcock's *Psycho* (1960), suggests that such shifts in chromatic schema mark a discourse of memory and sensory perceptions. The choice of color is not limited to its effects in the visual field, but also induces a shift in the interplay of the other sensory perceptions.

Section three concentrates on Aesthetics, another theme commonly linked to color form and design in the moving image. Joshua Yumibe discusses Paul Fejos's *Lonesome* (1928), a film that contains three tinted and hand-colored sequences shot in Coney Island. He demonstrates how in these sequences color is deployed in conjunction with topoi deriving from urban mass culture (Coney Island, advertising, neon lighting) and modernism (color abstraction and synaesthesia). To unpack the relation of these categories, Yumibe's chapter explores the aesthetic functions of color in the film by looking at the glimmering and yet terrifying world that color opens for the characters. As a modernist fairy tale, the film marshals a critical ambivalence toward color that places its utopian potential under threat. Fiction feature films like *Lonesome* are normally accorded a privileged position in color analysis, but Charles Tepperman's chapter on amateur color cinema in the 1930s demonstrates how in the early 1930s when "natural" color was still rare in theatres, amateurs claimed color filmmaking as their own terrain for aesthetic experimentation. While attention has been paid to color home movies, equally significant was color's potential value for aesthetic experimentation and defamiliarization. Based on the films and writings of prominent amateur filmmaker John Hansen, Tepperman argues that 1930s amateur filmmakers saw color not just as a tool for recording domestic activities, but also as a means of disclosing the aesthetic experiences immanent in quotidian materials. Returning to fiction, Fiona Handyside considers French filmmaker Eric Rohmer's symbolic and metaphorical uses of color. She makes clear that color is central in spite of the identification of Rohmer's films with neo-Bazinian realism and their concomitant use of natural light. While functioning as an index of the real, color also tells of the existence of a deliberate controlling presence behind the camera, echoing a theological world-view in which design is deliberate and color acquires specific religious meaning.

The remaining essays in this section look towards Hollywood to offer detailed textual analysis of color design. Inspired by a recent restoration, Heather Heckman's analysis of John Ford's earliest Technicolor feature, *Drums Along the Mohawk* (1939), provides the perfect opportunity to situate color in his compositional system. Through a close analysis of two night scenes from *Drums* Heckman argues that Ford not only uses color as an integral compositional strategy from the beginning, but that his practice also offers an innovative color aesthetic. In this sense *Drums* was an experiment in color cinematography that weds Ford's late 1930s high-contrast black-and-white aesthetic to the developing norms of Technicolor mise-en-scène design. Scott Higgins looks anew at Douglas Sirk's aggressively color-coordinated mise-en-scène that is most often viewed through the lens of Brechtian discourse as a distancing device that allowed the director to critically comment on the ideological underpinnings of 1950s melodrama. In a close analysis of *All that Heaven Allows* (1955) Higgins argues that it was Sirk's collaboration with cinematographer Russell Metty, a Hollywood colorist, that enabled a push against the boundaries of reigning conventions without departing from the norms of craft practice. The two final essays in this section focus upon Alfred Hitchcock, a director noted for his remarkable use of color. Firstly, Steven Jacobs examines the role of color and production design in *Rope* (1948), *Under Capricorn* (1949) and *Dial M for Murder* (1953). Jacobs considers how the work of color cinematographers such as Joseph Valentine, Jack Cardiff and Robert Burks contributes to the creation of claustrophobic interiors. He also illustrates how specific color combinations and pictorial light effects help to mark the difference between inside and outside, concluding that colors greatly add to the construction of intrusion, a spatial motif which plays a crucial role in Hitchcock's work. John Belton's chapter analyses red as a mutable signifier in relation to *Marnie* (1964). Although red is initially attached in the film to specific things (such as gladioli, ink and polka dots), it is repeatedly wrenched from these disparate, seemingly unrelated objects and projected upon the face of the heroine. Belton argues that the disruptive, striking red suffusions signify Marnie's repressed childhood trauma so that red becomes a fetish onto which that trauma is displaced. Red becomes associated with the complex fears and desires that obsess the character, suggesting that the meaning of red can change dramatically according to context.

The final section concentrates on Archive from four different perspectives. Jason Gendler focuses on colorization – the process of using computers to apply color to previously produced black-and-white films to create a color video version of a film. He shows how colorizers often have artistic aspirations and create distinctly different products from the original black-and-white films. His comparative analysis of the aesthetics of the black-and-white and the colorized versions of *Casablanca* addresses the effects of the process on the spectator's engagement with the film image and narrative. This analysis employs the general aesthetic principles of Technicolor's integration of color and film as the most successful integration of color into the classical Hollywood mode of production during the studio system era in which *Casablanca* was made. William Brown looks at another area of image manipulation in the context of digital technologies. Using principles of neuroscience which suggest that intense colors naturally attract attention, he argues that *O Brother, Where Art Thou?* (2000), a film that involves much digital manipulation of color, presents intense digital color spaces designed to appeal "naturally" to viewers. Film Archivists Ulrich Ruedel, Daniela Currò and Claudy Op den Kamp discuss how film restoration has developed since the first restoration of silent films in their original colors. Early color can be recreated using procedures such as the Desmet method, which simulates tinting and toning on modern color stock. Although the colors of silent cinema have been brought back, opening up new areas for film studies, color preservation still offers ongoing challenges. Their chapter addresses these challenges and the issues they raise for archives and laboratories, and considers scientific approaches which might lead archives towards a more accurate preservation and presentation of color in the future. The final chapter by Liz Watkins details the case of a recent restoration project. Herbert G. Ponting re-edited his film footage of Scott's fated polar expedition (1910–1913) across an initial twenty-year period in a historiographic practice that was responsive to technological innovations. The 2010 digital color reconstruction of his 1924 edit *The Great White Silence,* which was keyed to color instructions scratched into sections of leader, marked the synthesis of diverse materials sourced from different archives and prints into a new film text. It is in this sense that the 2010 release of *Silence* continues to operate within an epistemology of ontology, realism and spectatorship. Watkins's analysis, which is informed by the alterations that occur across numerous releases of the film, finds that the layering of diverse materials and of interpretation trace the historicity of the film within a social and historical imaginary.

Batchelor's assertion that an enquiry into color can take you just about anywhere is both exciting and highly challenging. It might appear obvious to suggest that color is not black-and-white, but more than a statement of fact this suggestion indicates the complexity of the study of color in relation to the moving image, which is far more than the analysis of technical details or process histories. Ultimately color is a matter of perception, never more so than in the field of moving images. Here, for example, a seemingly simple close-up of a pair of red ballet shoes can carry with it not only a series of intricate aesthetic and thematic meanings, but also the very redness of the shoes themselves is ultimately unknowable, as original copies fade, are transferred from one color process to another, or from a photochemical to a digital platform. An engagement with color therefore invites not only the unearthing of objective facts but rather the search for subjective truths. Embracing this challenge, the chapters collected in this volume offer a series of distinct but interlocking pathways through the rich and complex study of color and the moving image.

references

Batchelor, D. (2000) *Chromophobia,* London: Reaktion Books.

Batchelor, D. (2006) *Colour: Documents in Contemporary Art,* London: Whitechapel Art Gallery.

Bellour, R. (2007) "Marnie Color", in C. Liu, J. Mowitt, T. Pepper, J. Spicer (eds), *Dreams of Interpretation: A Century down the Royal Road*, London and Minneapolis: University of Minnesota: 253–262.

Branigan, E. (2006) "The Articulation of Color in a Filmic System: *Deux ou trios choses que je sais d'elle*", reprinted in A. Dalle Vacche, B. Price (eds), *Color: The Film Reader*, New York: Routledge: 170–182.

Cherchi Usai, P. (1991) "The Color of Nitrate", *Image*, 34, 1–2: 29–38.

Cherchi Usai, P. (2000) *Silent Cinema: An Introduction*, London: BFI Publishing.

Cherchi Usai, P. (2001) *The Death of Cinema*, London: BFI Publishing.

Coates, P. (2010) *Cinema and Colour: The Saturated Image*, London: Palgrave Macmillan.

Coe, B. (1978) *History of Movie Photography*, London: Ash & Grant.

Cornwell-Clyne, A. ([1936] 1951) *Colour Cinematography*, London: Chapman & Hall.

De Klerk, N. and Hertogs, D. (eds) (1996) *"Disorderly Order": Colours in Silent Film*, Amsterdam: Stichting Nederlands Filmmuseum.

Doane, M. A. (2002) *The Emergence of Cinematic Time: Modernity, Contingency, Archive*, Cambridge, MA: Harvard University Press.

Elsaesser, T. (1987) "Tales of Sound and Fury", in C. Gledhill (ed.), *Home is Where the Heart is: Studies in Melodrama and the Women's Film*, London: BFI.

Enticknap, L. (2005) *Moving Image Technology: From Zeotrope to Digital*, London: Wallflower Press.

Fossati, G. (2009) *From Grain to Pixel, The Archival Life of Film in Transition*, Amsterdam: Amsterdam University Press.

Gage, J. (1993) *Colour and Culture: Practice and Meaning from Antiquity to Abstraction*, London: Thames and Hudson.

Gage, J. (1999) *Colour and Meaning: Art, Science and Symbolism*, London: Thames and Hudson.

Gage, J. (2007) *Colour in Art*, London: Thames and Hudson.

Gunning, T. (1994) "Colorful Metaphors: The Attraction of Color in Early Silent Cinema", *Fotogenia*, 1: 249–255.

Hanssen, E. (2006) *Early Discourses on Color and Cinema: Origins, Functions, Meanings*, Stockholm: University of Stockholm Press.

Haralovich, M. B. (1990) "*All that Heaven Allows*: Color, Narrative Space, Melodrama", in P. Lehman (ed.), *Close Viewings: An Anthology of New Film Criticism*, Tallahassee, FL: Florida State University Press.

Higgins, S. (2007) *Harnessing the Technicolor Rainbow: Color Design in the 1930s*, Austin, TX: University of Texas Press.

Jameson, F. (1995) *Signatures of the Visible*, London: Routledge.

Misek, R. (2010) *Chromatic Cinema: A History of Screen Color*, Malden, MA: Wiley Blackwell.

Mulvey, L. (2006) *Death 24× a Second: Stillness and the Moving Image*, London: Reaktion Books.

Neale, S. (1985) *Cinema and Technology: Image, Sound, Colour*, London: BFI.

history

part one

"the brighton
school and the
quest for natural
color" – redux

o n e

s i m o n   b r o w n

> *The generative mechanisms of history operate at a number*
> *of levels and with uneven force, so that it is the historian's*
> *job to understand these mechanisms in their complexity*
> *rather to isolate a single "cause" for a given event.*
>
> (Allen and Gomery 1985: 16)

In his article "The Brighton School and the Quest for Natural Colour" (2004: 205–218) Luke McKernan illuminates the history surrounding early color processes developed in Britain, particularly Kinemacolor and its rival, Biocolour. Kinemacolor was the first commercially successful natural color process, developed by George Albert Smith around 1906, premièred in 1908 and successfully exploited by American entrepreneur Charles Urban through the early part of the 1910s. Biocolour on the other hand was considerably less successful commercially, barely being exploited at all. It was developed by William Friese-Greene who was championed, notably by early cinema historian Will Day (Bottomore 1996: 38) and Ray Allister

(1948), as the founder of cinematography, a view later cemented in popular opinion through the *The Magic Box* (1951), a British feature film starring Robert Donat as Friese-Greene. Yet the historical evidence fails to bear out this romantic and idealized tale. An alternate view is offered by McKernan who mercilessly describes Friese-Greene as "a man of scant technical genius, an opportunist, fantasist, and an incorrigible borrower of others' ideas" (2004: 209).

On a technical level, Kinemacolor and Biocolour were similar additive two-color processes. The principle of additive systems involved using filters to record a particular portion of the color spectrum and then in projection adding that portion of the spectrum to white light. By combining the two additive primary colors of red and green, a broad range of color could be achieved. Both Kinemacolor and Biocolour films were taken the same way, recording successive images through red and green filters at twice the normal speed, resulting in a black-and-white film which was alternately a record of the red and green components of the spectrum. In projection they used the same principle that by projecting at twice the normal speed, persistence of vision would blur the red and green records and thus give the illusion of natural color. The methods by which they achieved this were however different. While Kinemacolor projected through similar filters, Biocolour film was stained red and green and projected without filters. What links these together historically is not only their technological similarities, but the fact that Urban threatened to sue Biocolour for infringement of his patents and after a series of court battles and appeals, Smith's patent was revoked leading to the end of the commercial lives of both processes.

McKernan's research is significant because unlike the majority of studies of color it does not focus upon technological development but instead examines the more complex history of the people involved, how they came together and how their involvement led to technological change. To do this he links the story of Biocolour and Kinemacolor to the invention and activity which grew up in Brighton in the early years of the British film industry, termed by Georges Sadoul as the "Brighton School" (1948: 155–176). While focusing on the figures of Smith, Urban and Friese-Greene, McKernan also highlights the role in the development of color played by lesser known figures including William Norman Lascelles Davidson, Dr Benjamin Jumeaux and Edward Turner, all of whom were involved in various ways in bringing natural color to the screen.

McKernan's focus serves to illuminate the importance of these previously unknown characters and by shining a light on the people rather than the processes he illustrates the complexities behind even the most seemingly straightforward history of inventors and invention. Such an approach has broader implications not only for the history of color cinematography but also film history in general. It is tempting to interpret the growth of cinema as either a series of technological advancements which build upon one another, or as a series of aesthetic developments which similarly move consistently forward. Equally however the development of cinema is an industrial history, and behind each inventor are investors and supporters whose contributions may have little to do with technology but who may have exerted influence or pressures on the inventors. To acknowledge such a thing however risks a necessary engagement with a level of granularity which is potentially counter-productive, since small details may obscure the bigger picture. At the same time however broadening out the focus from the main players, in this case Friese-Greene and Urban, towards those on the periphery, allows us not to lose sight of the fact that film was, and is, fundamentally a business, knowledge of which can establish connections that challenge existing histories, raise new questions and suggest new perspectives.

The research which informs this chapter was provoked by a query about McKernan's statement that with the formation of Biocolour "the intention was to exploit two-color films made using the prism color process from Friese-Greene's 1905 patent" (2004: 213). However, as mentioned on p. 14, Biocolour used a successive frame system which did not involve the use of a prism. In undertaking what appeared to be a relatively simple task of clarification, it became clear that the reality of the situation was more complicated than even McKernan's detailed study reveals, and involved a number of significant figures whom McKernan does not mention. This chapter therefore builds on McKernan's work by introducing new peripheral figures, hence my giving it the same title as McKernan's but with the addition of the word "Redux". My aim is to explore the complexities around the formation of Biocolour while also considering the risks and rewards of the kind of analysis which I am attempting here. If Friese-Greene was as McKernan describes him, and I am inclined to think he was, then he is a useful case study for considering how the character of the people involved in a particular historical moment can serve to complicate the truth of that moment, and to consider the value of that complication to historical analysis.

The key to this history is the patent no. 9465 filed in 1905 by Friese-Greene who at the time was working as an assistant to Captain William Norman Lascelles Davidson at 20 Middle Street, Brighton. Friese-Greene's patent was a version of an earlier one, no. 7179, filed by Davidson and Benjamin Jumeaux in 1903. Which suggested using colored prisms to split the light from the object and direct it through lenses onto a film strip where it registered images side-by-side. Friese-Greene proposed that a prism be placed in such a way as it lay behind and half way across the lens, thus refracting half of the light. The light which was not refracted passed through a yellow-orange color screen whilst the remainder passed through a blue-red color screen, and the two images were registered side by side.

Friese-Greene insisted his 1905 patent was the master for color cinematography, one of the claims which later formed the basis of the legal battle between Biocolour and Kinemacolor. Biocolour Ltd. was formed in 1911 by the exhibitor Walter Harold Speer to commercially exploit the Biocolour process. As part of the formation, Biocolour was granted the rights to the Friese-Greene 1905 patent which was owned by a Brighton furniture dealer named Harry Birch. While he was still working for Davidson, in 1905 Friese-Greene had shown Birch some examples of color films. On the strength of the prism process Birch advanced Friese-Greene £500, and in August 1906 Birch acquired the patent in lieu of an outstanding debt of £150 (URB 7/2-6: 172). Friese-Greene left Davidson's employ in October 1906 and Birch set Friese-Greene up in a photographic shop at 203a Western Road in Brighton. Part of the deal by which Biocolour Ltd. was founded was an agreement made in August 1911 between Speer and Birch that for the sum of one fully paid up share Birch would sell the company the rights to the 1905 patent.

So far the information agrees with McKernan's assertion that the company was formed to exploit two-color films made by the prism system, but it is at this point that the problems emerge. The first is that the company was formed and acquired the prism patent in August 1911, and yet only a month later announced that Biocolour was ready for commercial exploitation. A public demonstration was held at the Piccadilly Cinematograph Theatre and on 8 September a deal was struck with the exhibitor Montagu Pyke for exclusive rights to show Biocolour on the Pyke circuit in all London districts (*Bioscope* supplement, 14 September 1911: xv). An advertisement suggested that showmen in the provinces had already started acquiring rights and that a large factory and studio had been built in Brighton (*Bioscope*, 14 September 1911: 577). There is no record of a Biocolour lab and factory but it is possible that in 1911 Biocolour was granted use of the studio which was being built for The Brighton and County Film Company, later Brightonia. Brighton and County was formed in 1911 by Speer and was funded by the cyclist, boat manufacturer and adventurer Selwyn Francis Edge who in November 1911 would fund Biocolour's battle with Kinemacolor by helping to re-form Biocolour into a new and better resourced company, Bioschemes Ltd.

The second problematic issue, which explains why Biocolour was able to launch so quickly after the company was formed, was that the process was not based upon Friese-Greene's 1905 patent at all. It did not use a prism system registering images on the frame side-by-side using instead, as described above, a rotating disc containing red and green filters through which successive frames were taken at double speed, then stained red and green and projected again at twice the normal speed.

In fact the 1905 patent formed the basis for a completely different natural color system, known as Cinechrome and developed by a company called Friese-Greene Patents Ltd. While working with Davidson on a prism system for natural color, which Davidson and Friese-Greene demonstrated in January 1906 at the Royal Institution and in July at the photographic convention of Great Britain in Southampton, Friese-Greene was also trying to perfect a successive-frame system of color using a rotating filter wheel, which would become the basis of Biocolour. A number of witnesses testified in court during the Bioschemes v Kinemacolor court case that Friese-Greene, both while working for Davidson at Middle Street and shortly after moving to Western Road in October 1906 with Harry Birch, demonstrated color films taken with both a prism system and a rotating filter system using a projector made by Robert Royou Beard which was modified so that the mechanism could be changed to accommodate both (URB 7/2-6: 164-165). Friese-Greene therefore had two color processes in development.

Confusingly, not only was the 1905 patent which Friese-Greene Patents Ltd. developed actually owned by Biocolour, but also it was the only patent registered by Friese-Greene which Friese-Greene Patents Ltd. did not own. In November 1907 Friese-Greene assigned the rights to all his patents, excluding the 1905 patent owned by Birch, to Charles James Morris. This assignation bore the provision that Friese-Greene and George Walter Chapman would subsequently secure the rights of these patents from Morris for an engineer named Allan Ramsay. The deal securing the rights for Ramsay was signed in July 1908 and that same month Friese-Greene Patents Ltd. was formed with a capital of £2,400 and a registered office in Ramsay's premises in Victoria Street in London. Ramsay agreed to sell his rights to the company and became the Managing Director and Friese-Greene was appointed as Technical Director for a period of four years (BT 31/18498/98940, Friese-Greene Patents Ltd., 1908).

Under the auspices of this new company, Friese-Greene continued his experiments to develop a successive frame rotating disc system. Somewhere between 1908 and 1910 Friese-Greene came into contact with the aforementioned Walter Harold Speer. In 1909 Friese-Greene opened a workshop at 130 Western Road in Brighton above Speer's Electric Bioscope Theatre. In December 1909 Speer and Friese-Greene, along with Friese-Greene's head electrician James Clifford Crawley, invited members of the National Association of Cinematograph Operators to his workshop, grandly named the New Scientific Hall, to demonstrate a new process of tri-color stereoscopic cinematography (*Bioscope*, 2 December 1909: 29). Then between November 1910 and August 1911, Speer, who was not involved in Friese-Greene Patents Ltd., took the impetus to build up an infrastructure with a view to forming a company to exploit under the brand name Biocolour the successive frame color system which Friese-Greene was developing whilst working for Friese-Greene Patents Ltd., acquiring at the same time the unrelated 1905 patent presumably because it was the only Friese-Greene patent which was available (BT 31/13680/117253, Biocolour Ltd., 1911).

Friese-Greene evidently had no qualms about taking the money to develop rival processes for competing companies. In 1911 he therefore found himself with his patents divided between two companies and his attention divided between competing color systems, one using a prism to record images side-by-side, owned by Biocolour Ltd. yet being developed by Friese-Greene Patents Ltd., and another using a rotating disc to record successive frame images, owned by Friese-Greene Patents Ltd. but being exploited by Biocolour Ltd. Friese-Greene himself was working for both companies at the same time, patenting a color stereoscopic process in February 1912 under the auspices of Friese-Greene Patents Ltd. while simultaneously involved with Biocolour's court case with Kinemacolor (*British Journal of Photography*, 28 March 1913: 255–256).

It was between 1911 and 1912 that Friese-Greene Patents Ltd. became involved with another significant figure, Colin Noel Bennett, who was a journalist, a photographer and cinematographer who became well known for his regular columns published in the *Kinematograph and Lantern Weekly (Kine Weekly)*, *The Handbook of Kinematography*, published by the *Kine Weekly* in 1912, as well as a 25-page booklet for Kinemacolor operators called "On Operating Kinemacolor" (Bennett 1910). Bennett was also experimenting with color cinematography. In January 1911 he filed patent no. 1642 in association with Conrad Beck, a London optician, for a specially designed camera using two small lenses one above the other behind a rotating shutter with cutaway sections which worked in synch to expose two frames simultaneously. Before the lenses were two filters, one red and one green. Both the red and green images were therefore recorded simultaneously but successively. Bennett's involvement in color experimentation led to his becoming associated with Friese-Greene Patents Ltd. This may have been facilitated by the fact that in late 1911 or early 1912 Bennett granted the rights to his 1911 patent to Friese-Greene (Bennett 1912: 236–237) which seems to have been a move to create links between Friese-Greene Patents Ltd. and his own work. The result was that negotiations began in 1911 to re-form Friese-Greene Patents Ltd. with Bennett as the driving force. In December 1911 the two directors of Friese-Greene Patents Ltd., Ramsay and Morris, resigned and were replaced by R. H. Crooke and F. W. Pendleton, with William Holden appointed as secretary. The registered office moved to Crooke's premises at 7 Little St. Andrew Street in London. In November 1912 a new company was registered, Colin Bennett Ltd., with both Pendleton and Holden as directors, along with Bennett, James Marsden and John Sharp Higham. The company had the financial backing of Sir William Pickles Hartley, owner of Hartley's Jams, who was Higham's father-in-law, Higham having married Pollie Hartley in 1899.[1] Friese-Greene Patents Ltd. continued to operate in name only until around 1917.

So by the end of 1912 both Biocolour and Colin Bennett Ltd. were drawing upon and utilising the inventions of William Friese-Greene with backing from influential figures from the world of business, Selwyn Francis Edge and William Pickles Hartley. Curiously, at the moment that both companies were well financed and had the potential for success, both Friese-Greene and Bennett walked away. Bennett continued his color work into 1913 and then stopped. He filed no more patents and had nothing more to do with his company, returning to journalism and writing a regular technical column for the *Kine Weekly*. In 1915 Colin Bennett Ltd. was re-formed as Cinechrome Ltd., without Bennett but still with Hartley, Higham and Marsden as directors, registering three patents that year adapting Bennett's original ideas under the names of Higham, Frank Twynam and Harold Workman, the latter two being involved with a company called Adam Hilger Ltd. By 1921 the system had developed from the original ideas outlined by Bennett, and used a beam splitter to record two color records side-by-side on an extra-wide film with perforations down both sides and in the middle. It was this version of the process which was used by S. J. Cox to film the visit of the Prince of Wales to India and which was subsequently premièred at The Royal Society of Arts in 1922 and later had a public run at the Stoll Picture Theatre. By this time Hartley was dead and the company was acquired by Cox and Demetre Daponte, who had also worked with Twynam for Adam Hilger Ltd. Cox and Daponte reworked and remarketed the process as Cinecolor, and the patents were ultimately taken over in 1937 by Dufay-Chromex, producers of the Dufaycolor process.

Equally, almost every account of the life of William Friese-Greene stops with the climax of the court case with Kinemacolor, and then jumps to 1921 when he died at a meeting of the Cinematograph Exhibitors' Association. The court case with Kinemacolor dragged on into 1914 without Biocolour being able to exploit its product, which was at best mediocre, and in the end only one fiction film was made in Biocolour after the court case ended. *The Earl of Camelot* was released in November 1914 and produced by Aurora Films, which had been set up by William's son Claude Friese-Greene. The film was not successful and while Aurora was registered as a Limited Company in February 1915 for the purpose of making films in Natural Color using the Biocolour process, the company went into voluntary liquidation in November the same year, by which time Claude had joined up to fight in the First World War.

Rachael Low cites a claim by R. H. Cricks that around 1915 Friese-Greene was experimenting with color at the Cricks and Martin Studio (1950: 101). Certainly by the end of 1915 he was in sufficient financial straits that Will Day made an appeal in the *Bioscope* for funds to help him out (*Bioscope*, 23 December 1915: 1,306, 1,369). According to Ray Allister's unreliable account, Friese-Greene took the money, moved to London and got a job in a government lab doing dye research (1948: 162). In 1918 however he returned to inventing, patenting a number of color related inventions in 1918 and 1919 and going into business with a photographer, John Newlands Thompson. In 1920 they formed Colour Photography Ltd. to acquire, develop and exploit these patents in association with some of the independent investors who had helped Friese-Greene in their development. The company was formed in February with a huge nominal capital of £25,000 which was doubled in July, but after three years of research and development, in which no trading of any kind was done, the company went into voluntary liquidation in November 1924.

This begs the question as to why Bennett and Friese-Greene abandoned their experiments and the companies with which they were involved. Did they decide they had had enough? Were they removed by the boards? Or did they sit back, having done the initial development and leave further research and commercial exploitation to the professionals? It seems evident that Friese-Greene watched his Biocolour process falter and die in 1914 and 1915, leaving him in a woefully impecunious state, but why then did he not get involved with Cinechrome once more? They owned the rights to his patents so owed him nothing, and the process had been moved on considerably from the 1905 patent by the work of Bennett and others, so perhaps there was no room for him there. There might also be a very good reason why Colin Bennett stopped experimenting with color. Perhaps he took his ideas as far as he could and then passed them on, or another possibility is that there was an irreconcilable disagreement between himself and Friese-Greene or with the board of Colin Bennett Ltd.

Such questions may never be answered without the discovery of personal diaries or letters, but I would argue that raising them is nevertheless important because they demonstrate that what seems on the surface to be a simple history hides a great deal of unknowable variables. When considering the history of Biocolour and Kinemacolor it is straightforward to see it as a polarized conflict of two sides with no common ground. Yet Bennett wrote an operating manual for Kinemacolor whilst working with Friese-Greene. It is equally easy to see Biocolour and Cinechrome as separate technological processes, yet they were inextricably linked by common personnel at a management and technical level.

This chapter is very much a micro-study of a small and seemingly insignificant moment in British cinema history; the formation of two companies which did not survive, the development of two processes for color cinematography which did not achieve long-term commercial success, and the stories of a number of people whose impact on the wider film industry is perhaps negligible. Nevertheless, it suggests the chaotic and unstructured nature of technological development during the formative years of the film industry, and that notion of the film *industry* is key to our understanding of cinema's development. The financial dealings behind this story are striking. While Friese-Greene Patents Ltd. was funded by a local Brighton furniture dealer, Colin Bennett Ltd. was backed by

Sir William Pickles Hartley. While Biocolour Ltd. was formed by exhibitor Walter Speer, Bioschemes Ltd. was supported by Selwyn Francis Edge. Ultimately neither backer saw major returns but their presence in this history indicates that both companies were formed and transformed on the cusp of an investment boom which effectively raised cinema to the level of a global media business. This case study ultimately suggests that an examination of the figures on the margins of the technological and aesthetic developments which form the thrust of the history of the development of cinema can offer insightful and provocative new perspectives on histories both known and unknown.

note

1. Adrian Klein states that Hartley and Bennett were involved in the formation of Friese-Greene Patents Ltd. (Klein 1936: 9) but Board of Trade files indicate that they were not involved until at least 1911.

references

Allen, R. C. and Gomery, D. (1985) *Film History: Theory and Practice*, New York: McGraw Hill.

Allister, R. (1948) *Friese-Greene: Close-up of an Inventor*, London: Marsland.

Anon. (1911) *Bioscope*, 14 September: 577.

Bennett, C. (1910) *On Operating Kinemacolor*, London: *The Kinematograph and Lantern Weekly*.

Bennett, C. (1912) *The Handbook of Kinematography: The History, Theory and Practice of Motion Photography and Projection*, London: *The Kinematograph and Lantern Weekly*.

Bottomore, S. (1996) "Will Day (Wilfred Ernest Lytton Day)" in Herbert S., and McKernan, L. (eds.) *Who's Who of Victorian Cinema*, London: BFI.

Friese-Greene, W. (1905) "Improvements in and Relating to the Production of Negatives and Positives for Multi-colour Projection and Improved Means for Projection on to a Screen", Patent No. 9465, 14 June.

Klein, A. B. (1936) *Colour Cinematography*, London: Chapman & Hall Ltd.

Low, R. (1950) *The History of the British Film 1914–1918*, London: George Allen and Unwin.

McKernan, L. (2004) "The Brighton School and the Quest for Natural Colour" in Popple, S. and Toulmin, V. (eds.) *Visual Delights Two: Exhibition and Reception*, Sydney: John Libbey and Co.: 205–218.

Sadoul, G. (1948) *Histoire générale du cinema 2: Les pionnieres du cinema 1907–1909*, Paris: Denoel.

unpublished sources:

"In the House of Lords On Appeal From His Majesty's Court of Appeal (England) In the Matter of Letters Patent no 26671 of 1906 Granted to George Albert Smith and In the Matter of the Patents and Designs Act, 1907 Natural

Colour Kinematograph Company Limited (IN liquidation) v Bioschemes Ltd."
URB7: "Papers, Patent Specifications and Court Report relating to the Urban V
Bioschemes Court Case 1913–1915", Charles Urban Papers Collection, National
Media Museum, Bradford.

Board of Trade Files, National Archives, Kew.

technicolor-multicolor-sennett-color

natural color processes in mack sennett comedies 1926–1931

t w o

h i l d e   d ' h a e y e r e

In the 1910s and 1920s, slapstick comedy shorts were released by the thousand. Nearly all of these productions were filmed in black-and-white, which tallied perfectly with the cruel slapstick world of stereotyped characters and violent and destructive actions. The fact that Mack Sennett was also a pioneer in natural color processes is far less commonly known.[1] In line with so many legends and apocryphal stories about the self-proclaimed *King of Comedy*, color does not fit in easily with the slapstick studio's image of a crude and mocking use of the technology of picture production. This article studies surviving film prints, shooting scripts, and press material to examine Sennett's exploration of natural color through his use of Technicolor and Multicolor, culminating, in 1930, in the launch of his own two-color process, aptly called Sennett-Color. In addition, a filmography listing all the released Sennett shorts containing color film, including the identification of the color process, is added as an appendix.

a technicolor test

The first sign of Sennett's interest in natural color is a note in the produc tion file of *Hubby's Quiet Little Game* (1926) (MSC 1926).[2] A "Company Forecast Sheet" dated April 24 mentions director Del Lord planning to shoot some scenes on resensitized Technicolor film. This was evidently a test of the process, since no Technicolor footage is featured in Sennett shorts from this period. As Lord was Sennett's top director, known for his effects-laden cinematography, it is not surprising that it was he who eagerly tried out this technical novelty. The date of the test indicates quite an early interest in natural color, right after the release of the critically successful, but tech-nically problematic feature film *The Black Pirate* (1926), filmed and printed in Technicolor's two-color process #2.

Significantly, a discussion was going on within Technicolor's board of directors around this time between founding father Dr. Herbert T. Kalmus and Head of Research Dr. Leonard Troland. In letters written between February and April 1927, it appears that Technicolor was planning to court short subject producers to prove the quality and cost efficiency of the improved printing process #3 to the bigger producers in the movie indus-try. Troland, however, disagreed with Kalmus' suggestion to produce short historical dramas in a series of *Great Events*, stating, "People want a laugh or a kick, and not tears or historical instruction" (Troland 1927a: 2). In a paper delivered before the Society of Motion Picture Engineers, he gave an over-view of the types of scenes that, according to him, were enhanced by the use of natural color. He mentioned "seascapes and landscapes," "flesh tints in their normal hues and saturations," "feminine beauty," and "the latest fashions," on the grounds that color added to sex-appeal (Troland 1927b: 686–690). Troland therefore suggested making "a series of two-reel come-dies of a very ordinary type so far as action goes, but Ziegfeldized to the absolute limit that the censorship will stand" (Troland 1927a: 2).[3] He con-cluded: "I should strongly recommend that we experiment with at least one subject which is distinctly of the type which we as a high-brow group would shun and would blush to sign our names to" (Troland 1927a: 3).

Troland did not identify any actual Ziegfeldized comedy short that was technicolored, but in Mack Sennett's production files Technicolor was credited for color sequences in eight two-reel *Bathing Girl* comedies released between December 1927 and March 1929 (see Appendix). Thus, this series of comical subjects ran perfectly parallel with Kalmus' twelve historical shorts in the *Great Events* series produced by Technicolor Inc. and released by M-G-M between October 1927 and May 1929. Both series tried out the sub-jects and film forms best suited for color application. Whereas the *Great Events* focused on full-color shorts for historical dramatizations of high-brow subjects, the color inserts in Sennett *Bathing Girl* comedies aimed at the surprise appearance of a novel technology into slapstick comedy.

Both test cases shaped the position of (Techni)color in the heretofore monochrome movie world, and provided Sennett with a template he would expand on for his comedy-novelties in Sennett-Color.

technicolor sequences: sennett *bathing girl* comedies (1926–1929)

The first official day of Technicolor filming at the Sennett Studio was scheduled for July 16, 1927, more than a year after the first Technicolor test. Technicolor sequences were to be inserted into the lavishly produced *Bathing Girl* comedy *The Girl From Everywhere* (1927). This time, Technicolor's chief cinematographer Ray Rennahan and second cameraman Roy Musgrave were behind the camera. Ray Rennahan also shot the color footage for *Love at First Flight* (1928); *Run, Girl, Run* (1928); *The Swim Princess* (1928); *The Campus Carmen* (1928); *The Campus Vamp* (1928); and *Matchmaking Mamas* (1929) – all filmed between August 1927 and January 1928, resulting in color sequences varying in length between 120 and 295 feet. Only *The Girl From Nowhere* (1928), featuring a tiny 17 feet of Technicolor footage, did not credit Ray Rennahan or any other Technicolor cameraman.

When announcing the new series of *Bathing Girl* comedies on July 2, 1927, Sennett's publicity department distributed the following press release:

> SENNETT USING NEW TECHNICOLOR IN COMEDIES:
> Bathing costumes of a highly abbreviated nature are again in vogue around the Mack Sennett Studio. The reason for the seashore atmosphere is that Mack Sennett has revived the bathing beauty comedies that made him a world famous producer. There are sequences in the new series of girl films done in technicolor [*sic*], this being the first time technicolor [*sic*] film has been used in short comedy films.
>
> The new faces and new figures will be seen in the lavish though scanty costumes designed by Madame Violette, internationally known modiste. [...]
>
> The combination of technicolor [*sic*] film and unique lighting effects will give the films an artistic touch never before known in two-reel comedies. (MSC 1927)

The announcement of bathing beauties in costumes designed by a modiste, enhanced with the artistic touch of color and lighting effects, points at concepts that Sennett was trying out for color application. First of all, the press text mentioned the *revival* of the *Bathing Girl* comedies, indicating an awareness that color might add new box-office attraction to the old chorus of feminine beauty. Oddly enough, Sennett relaunched a signature motif that he was only slightly earlier considering getting rid of (D'haeyere 2010: 219–222). Correspondence between the New York office and the Los

Angeles-based publicity department demonstrates that Sennett was looking for ways to *dispose of* the *Bathing Girl* pictures. A letter stated that Sennett is "not very keen about bathing girl publicity any longer – says he is tired of being called a beauty expert – wants more dignified publicity" (MSC 1927). It was probably Sennett's instant recognition of color's potential to "dignify" his slapstick comedy pictures that accounted for this swift change of mind. In October 1927, the simultaneous launch of the series of Sennett *Bathing Girl* shorts and the monthly publication of the illustrated newspaper the *Mack Sennett-Pathé Studio Review* fully foregrounded the bathing girls as their main attraction and exploited them in their promotional campaigns. Color played an important part in the updating of the bathing girls and indicates how they were repositioned to convey contemporary appeal.

technicolor tableaux

The Technicolor sequences in the shorts articulate two concepts for color treatment, both focusing on feminine beauty and on sexy ways to display flesh tints in seascapes and landscapes, precisely as Troland suggested.

The color sequences in *The Girl From Everywhere*; *Run, Girl, Run*; *The Campus Carmen*; and *The Girl From Nowhere* all are announced by a shot of a velvet curtain, bordered by a gilded picture frame at the edges of the film frame. The following shot is a Technicolor composition of girls and props representing a *tableau vivant* with historical, mythical, or pictorial references, re-enacted by Sennett girls. For instance, *The Girl From Everywhere* ends with a lost Technicolor shot of a girl posing with bow and arrow as Diana the Huntress, while at her feet, in majestic pose, is the lion that shortly before, in black-and-white, caused havoc in the studio. In *Run, Girl, Run*, the Technicolor sequence precedes a race between two all-girl college teams filmed in black-and-white. Two heralds on either side of the frame formed by Grecian pillars pull the cords to open a curtain. Among the unveiled Technicolor scenes, representing "the evolution of athletics," is a gladiator scene modeled after the famous painting *Pollice Verso* by Jean-Léon Gérôme (1872) with a female gladiator in tied drapes.

Using the practice of legitimizing nudity by citing classical art, established in film by Pathé at the turn of the century (Brown 2002), color was definitely treated as a token of a pictorial tradition in which poses, compositions, light effects, and color harmonies referred to grand historical painting and artistic tableaux vivants (or at least to their Ziegfeldized versions). Consequently, the choice and application of color was confided to an artist. From July 1927 onward Sennett hired the talented art photographer Edwin Bower Hesser for his advice on artistic color effects. He was credited as "art effects supervisor" in four *Bathing Girl* shorts. Hesser's fame as an art photographer was based on *plein air* studies of movie actresses and Ziegfeld girls in which he used natural backlight to outline their bodies through the veils in which they were draped. Sennett selected Hesser especially for his pictorial style that fully exploited the associations between art and nudity, hoping that Hesser would add a touch of class and culture which were never before considered necessary in slapstick comedy. In addition, Hesser was also hired to take still photographs of the girls, a selection of which featured on the back cover of the first and the second issue of the *Mack Sennett-Pathé Studio Review*. By means of artistic backlight, a larger amount of undress and more sophisticated poses, these photographs were far more glamorous and erotically charged than the otherwise playful poses and smiling faces on the other Sennett stills of the same period. However, Hesser disappeared from Sennett's movie credits in mid-1928 and the *Mack Sennett-Pathé Studio Review* ceased publication after its December 1927 issue (Walker 2010: 179).[4] In addition, for the last four *Bathing Girl* comedy shorts, the concept of the Technicolor sequences changed from a photographical idiom, exploiting the stillness of a pose in a tableau setting, to a more modern and mobile approach.

mobile technicolor

This new approach can be found in the Technicolor sequences in *The Swim Princess*, *Love At First Flight*, *The Campus Vamp*, and *Matchmaking Mamas*, which depict the bathing girls in athletic movements such as diving from a spring board, playing baseball on a beach, or rehearsing a ballet for a charity dance. In these shorts, we find active flappers in collegiate settings engaged in contemporary activities performed with youthful energy by healthy bodies wrapped in brightly colored costumes. Again, the color inserts show feminine beauty, and the natural hues and saturations of flesh tints in seascapes and landscapes, this time completing Troland's suggestions with the sporting of beach attire of the latest fashions. Whereas the appearance of a butterfly dance in *Love At First Flight* still allows for a Ziegfeldized color insert with sophisticated nudity through elaborate costuming, the trend towards highly athletic color sequences in the later shorts called for more up-to-date, but equally undressed, outfits.

The credit for costume design was given to "Madame Violette, internationally known modiste." "Madame Violette" was the rather parodic name of Violet Schofield, wife of Sennett cinematographer George Unholz. While she was widely advertised as designing the costumes for all the *Bathing Girl* stories with color sequences, she had been working in the Sennett studio as a dressmaker since at least 1921. Titles such as "madame" and "modiste" linked her to French ancestors, referring to Paris as the world's capital for fashion in the 1920s. The term "Madame Violette" also invoked Madeleine Vionnet, the French fashion designer whose famous bias-cut dresses lay at the heart of the sleek look of 1920s fashion. In so doing,

Sennett positioned the movie costumes as exemplary fashion items and proposed color as an up-to-date commercial asset.

Madame Violette designed brightly colored bathing suits and matching accessories in loud colors and patterns for the bathing girls and a few male co-actors. The nearly monochrome settings of a sandy beach, a garden lawn, or a swimming pool were used as backgrounds against which color patches of suits, caps, socks, shoes, cardigans, parasols, and pennants stood out in a multitude of shades, hues, and graphic designs. Remarkably, sometimes the two colors which made up the color process – red and green – were isolated into color patches: pom-poms and pennants in *The Swim Princess*, and paper lanterns and costumes in *Matchmaking Mamas* were either Technicolor-viridian-green or Technicolor-scarlet-red. This foregrounding of the technical and material aspect of the color process remained a staple of Sennett's treatment of color subjects. In later shorts filmed in Sennett-Color, the color spectrum was also separated into its composing elements. For instance, in *Movie-Town* (1931) the all-girl water polo teams are wearing either Sennett-Color-cyan or Sennett-Color-orange-red suits and caps. In so doing, Sennett unveiled color cinematography as a mechanical reproduction rather than as a natural rendition of reality.

Again, the athletic actions in the color sequences were restrained by showstopping film techniques. This time, not a frozen pose but slow-motion analysis through Ultra Speed cinematography stylized the sporting interventions of the bathing girls. The demonstrations of dives in *The Swim Princess* and *The Campus Carmen* were even enhanced by slow-motion *underwater* color photography to transform the girls into dreamlike visions of unearthly creatures (and, again, to show off the technical prowess of the production).

It is remarkable that, in differentiating the pace, tone, and cinematographic style between the slapstick actions in black-and-white and the spectacular display of girls and fabrics in the color inserts, the Sennett shorts actually were early examples of color coding, which would become an established practice in the late 1930s. In films such as *The Wizard of Oz* (1939), *Hollywood Cavalcade* (1939), and *The Moon and the Sixpence* (1942), color and black-and-white sequences acted as opposites. As Richard Misek argues, these chromatically separated sequences communicated narrative information, while chromatic switches from black-and-white to color indicated shifts from the cinematic reality to a world of dreams, desire, fantasy, insanity, art, and history (Misek 2010: 31–35). The musical revues of Technicolor's first boom year 1929 did not yet ration their limited color footage dependent on color motivations or codes, but inserted color stock according to the available budget, with a preference for musical numbers (Misek 2010: 28–29). Already in 1927, Sennett clearly assigned to color cinematography the power to suspend the comic drama of slapstick actions for the entertainment value of show-stopping color display, adding a dreamy quality to girls and costumes in motion.

It is also interesting to note that, while Dr. Troland referred to color in comedy as a low-brow test-case, natural color for Sennett was a technical novelty boosting production values and adding high-class appeal. Natural color was applied to revive the bathing girls, injecting them with a touch of fine art and updating them as role models of fashion and desire, in an attempt to target slapstick comedy more precisely at the increasingly female audiences of the late 1920s (Stamp 2000: 6–7). Moreover, foregrounding the technicality of picture production by inserting color in a monochrome movie and by isolating the two colors of the process is a trick appealing to an educated audience that appreciated this kind of self-referential humor. This strategy of uplifting and updating comedy through color application would find even more personal and practical ways in the full-color shorts which followed.

multicolor: all color, all-talking comedy jazz mamas

In June 1929, Educational Film Exchanges released the Mack Sennett Special *Jazz Mamas* with a promotional campaign presenting the film as the first all-color all-talking comedy to reach the screen (Educational Film Exchanges, Inc. 1929). Unfortunately, the short is not known to exist today. Very recently, however, a short surviving section of a nitrate positive print was identified in the Frames Collection at George Eastman House.[5] (**See Plate 1.**) As a result, we can ascertain that the short is photographed in the Multicolor process, printed on double-coated positive film stock which was toned orange-red on one side and blue on the other, and with a very characteristic blue variable-area soundtrack recorded by the RCA Photophone system.

Shooting scripts, a press sheet issued by Sennett's publicity department, and some newspaper reviews give us an idea of the color treatment in *Jazz Mamas*. Most of the buzz was about the International Detectives, a collection of gaily-costumed detectives who dress "in international fashion – the chief dolls up like a Swiss, his chief lieutenant sports Scotch garb and a Hebrew accent and the assistants look like Spanish bullfighters" (Mack Sennett Comedies 1929). The short opened with a shot of "a group of burlesqued flags of various countries, none definite, waving as they move forward in the breeze" (MSC 1929). Obviously, the folkloristic costumes and banners in the national colors of various countries were inserted to ridicule the desire for accurately reproduced colors. The association of color film with the proud display of national colors tallies with numerous examples of flags that were used to prove the veracity of new color processes. Examples include the hand-colored flag in *Three American Beauties* (1906), *The Coronation of George V* filmed in Kinemacolor in 1911, Technicolor's first entry in the *Great Events* series *The Flag: A Story of the Tradition of Betsy Ross* (1927), and the American flag broadcast by Bell Laboratories in the first U.S. public demonstration of color television in New York, on June 27, 1929.

The script was written for a one-reel talking picture "if possible in color" (MSC 1929) because Sennett's technicians were still working hard to overcome the technical difficulties of combining sound technology with color film. Sennett had been preparing for sound in his new state-of-the-art facilities in Studio City between the spring of 1928 and late October, when his first talking comedy *The Lion's Roar* (1928) was previewed in the RCA Photophone process (Walker 2010: 184–185). During the first half of 1929, Sennett had already produced eight two-reel talking comedies with improving sound quality and increasingly complex sound tracks, although even the first short already displayed a clever use of sound effects and snappy dialogues. But *Jazz Mamas* was his first sound short in natural color.

Remarkably, William T. Crespinel, the inventor of the Multicolor process, was working in Sennett's brand new studio between November 1928 and January 1929, around the time of the filming of *Jazz Mamas* (Walker 2010: 433). In contrast to the procedure for shooting with Technicolor film, which imposed the services of a Technicolor cameraman to operate the specially constructed camera with a beam splitter and a claw mechanism to pull two frames after each exposure, it was not necessary for a Multicolor cameraman to supervise the color shooting. Using a fairly simple bi-pack process, Multicolor even advertised the fact that every standard camera could be transformed into a Multicolor camera at the slight expense of an adjustment to the film gate and that the bi-pack negative did not require any special lighting (Multicolor Films Inc. 1929). In short, there was no real need for Crespinel to be around. But *Jazz Mamas* was not only Sennett's first experience with color-on-sound film, it was also Multicolor's first encounter with sound-on-color film. Crespinel had enormous experience in color film development, previously having worked on Kinemacolor, Prizmacolor and Harriscolor, but he had little experience with sound (Crespinel 2000: 57–71). So, most probably, Crespinel and Sennett cooperated in a gentlemen's agreement: Crespinel assisted Sennett's sound technicians in their experiments with sound-on-Multicolor film, and Sennett provided Crespinel with a practical test-case and studio facilities to complete the Multicolor process with sound-on-film. In March 1929, Crespinel announced that the Multicolor process was ready for sound-on-film: "sound is an integral part of the film itself, is colored and is protected with a transparent coating," he reported (Crespinel 1929: 7). With this technical feat, and the release of *Jazz Mamas* to prove it, small-timers Mack Sennett Comedies and Multicolor Inc. were keeping in step with the Warners-Technicolor cooperation who released *On with the Show* in May 1929 as the first all-color, all-talking feature, with Vitaphone's sound-on-disc technology.

The short itself was a "musical comedy in tabloid form" (Mack Sennett Comedies 1929) in which Virginia Lee Corbin demonstrated her skills as a dancer and a singer. This miniature musical led the parade of musical comedies in natural color that swept the movie houses from mid-1929 on. Numerous song-and-dance revues or show-within-the-show backstage stories were released by every major studio in 1929 and 1930, until the depression hit hard and the public temporarily grew weary of musicals in color. *Jazz Mamas* was also one of the last films to advertise the bathing girls as a signature motive. When color and sound were joined on film, the costumed chorus of bathing girls disintegrated, soon replaced by marine life of a very different kind.

sennett-color: full-color comedy-novelties (1930–1931)

By inserting Technicolor sequences into the *Bathing Girl* shorts, constructing one of the best equipped soundstages in early Hollywood, and successfully combining sound with Multicolor film, Sennett had already proven that he was not afraid of technical challenges. With his keen eye for commercial opportunities, Sennett was inclined to try his hand at a natural color process under his own name. This research was facilitated by several key introductions in the industry, including the special dye-filtered negative for bi-pack filming developed by Eastman, and the commercial availability of duplitized film from Kodak and Dupont. After more than six months of testing, a huge investment in a color lab with printing machines and a chemical room, and the salaries for the cast and crew of an unsuccessful test film (*Bulls and Bears*, 1930 filmed in color but released in black-and-white), Sennett was finally able to release *Radio Kisses* (1930) with sequences in Sennett-Color. The subdued quality of the color rendition was favorably reviewed in the *Los Angeles Times* despite remarks about a certain blotchiness (Schallert 1930). Around the same time, Sennett's chief technician Paul Guerin filed a patent application for a contact printer with two light sources on either side of the film gate, typically to enable printing on two sides of duplitized film (Guerin 1930). Inspection of one of the few surviving original nitrate prints, *Strange Birds* (1930), confirms that Sennett-Color was a two-color process printed on double-coated film. The film was toned cyan-blue on one side and orange-red on the other, and finished with a protective varnish on both sides. The soundtrack was a RCA variable-area track, but not toned blue as in the Multicolor process.

Between September 1930 and November 1931, Sennett released ten shorts in Sennett-Color: six one-reel *Mack Sennett Brevities*, two one-reel *Cannibals of the Deep* shorts, and two two-reel *Mack Sennett Comedies* (see Appendix). These full-color shorts share a novel approach to color, employing the expanded realism of color and sound film for comic effect. The advertisement announcing the *Mack Sennett Brevities* put it in catchy phrases: "Light comedy-novelty stories that hit the high spots of our hectic modern life. Our sports, our hobbies, all our crowded interests. And always girls, girls, beautiful girls" (Educational Film Exchanges, Inc. 1930a).

Contemporary subjects as diverse as airplanes, speedboat races, exotic animals, and tourist outings comprise the colorful settings, matching the technology that captured them. Using these sports and hobbies as subjects also invited unusual camera angles. *Speed* (1931), for instance, deals with a race between two girls to marry a football star. One of the contenders tries to win the race by airplane, and the beauty of the scenery below is filmed through the airplane windows. *The World Flier* (1931) features shots of a speedboat race as seen from an airplane, and *Movie-Town* and *Strange Birds* open with aerial images establishing the film's locations. *Wrestling Swordfish* (1931), *The Bluffer* (1930), and *Movie-Town* have underwater color shots filmed by the Sennett submarine camera, depicting exciting marine life such as fighting swordfish, a game of water polo, Olympic swimmer Buster Crabbe, and a blushing fish.

While the stories still deal with the familiar comical incidents surrounding love triangles and silly aristocrats, the backgrounds are virtually travelogues promoting novelty settings. *Strange Birds*, for instance, pictures colorful birds in the Catalina Bird Aviary, and *Who's Who in the Zoo* (1931) introduces the animals in the Selig Zoo. Both locations provided exotic escapism at an affordable price, "as modern as television, and as homely as the average American husband," to paraphrase a tagline (Educational Film Exchanges, Inc. 1930b). Also, the embedding of comic actions in timely topics and actual locations harks back to the early Keystone days, when film crews rushed out to exploit the spectacle of an actual event and a crowd of onlookers for a slapstick short. Sometimes even pure non-fiction shorts were released, if the footage permitted or the release schedule necessitated this. Of course, releasing the non-fiction *A Glimpse at the San Diego Exposition* (1915), along with the comedy short *Fatty and Mabel at the San Diego Exposition* (1915), also provided an original to spoof and to make fun of. When, in 1930–1931, the most popular short formats were the travelogue and the newsreel (both greatly enhanced by natural color and synchronized sound) (Ramsaye 1931: 59), Sennett could easily cash in on movies mocking those film forms, by adding comic elements that burlesqued them. The tone of the shorts was educational, even instructional, but a funny accent, a song, or a color joke undermined the seriousness of the information. When, in *Movie-Town,* a girl wearing a red dress falls in the swimming pool, she resurfaces wearing a blue one. Since *Movie-Town* is also a movie about the making of movies, the switch between the two colors of the color process functions as a self-referential comic device on a technical as well as on a narrative level. Furthermore, when the tagline announcing the *Mack Sennett Brevities* claimed that they depict "*our* sports, *our* hobbies, all *our* crowded interests" (Educational Film Exchanges, Inc. 1930a), this might very well have been referring to Sennett himself, who documented his own hobbies and sporting activities and released them as novelty subjects. Two Sennett-Color shorts in the *Cannibals of the Deep* series,

The Trail of the Swordfish (1931) and *Wrestling Swordfish* (1931), depict Sennett on a fishing trip in Baja California. With his typical flair for business, the Sennett-Color process was also made available for the straight commercial field with the formation of the short-lived *Mack Sennett Industrial Film Division* in 1930 (Anon. 1930).

Unfortunately, *Wrestling Swordfish* was the very last short in Sennett-Color. It was released only one month before Sennett Color Film Ltd. ceased all color activities in December 1931. The bill of sale stated that "color proved an unwise venture" (MSC 1932) but the discontinuation of the color work was more probably connected to the very stringent patent situation in 1931, when the Technicolor Corporation won a major patent victory in preparation of its three-color process, paralyzing all methods of manufacturing color film in its wake (Anon. 1931).

Perhaps it is ironic that Mack Sennett, the king of silent slapstick comedy, won an Academy Award for 1931–1932 with the documentary all-color sound short *Wrestling Swordfish*. But winning his first Oscar in the category 'Short subject – novelty" reassured the audience that Sennett was still up-to-date after nearly twenty years of filmmaking, and still spoofing the technicalities of picture production.

appendix: film list

TECHNICOLOR: *Bathing Girl* comedies: silent Sennett shorts with sequences in two-color Technicolor #3 (IB), distributed through Pathé Film Exchanges:

- *The Girl From Everywhere* (Eddie Cline, Dec. 1927)
- *Love At First Flight* (Eddie Cline, Jan. 1928)
- *Run, Girl, Run* (Alf Goulding, Jan. 1928)
- *The Swim Princess* (Alf Goulding, Febr. 1928)
- *The Girl From Nowhere* (Harry Edwards, May 1928)
- *The Campus Carmen* (Alf Goulding, Sept. 1928)
- *The Campus Vamp* (Harry Edwards, Nov. 1928)
- *Matchmaking Mamas* (Harry Edwards, March 1929)

MULTICOLOR: full-color sound short, produced by Mack Sennett Comedies, distributed by Educational Film Exchanges:

- *Jazz Mamas* (Mack Sennett, June 30, 1929) *Mack Sennett Special*

SENNETT-COLOR: full-color sound shorts, produced by Mack Sennett Comedies, distributed by Educational Film Exchanges:

- *Radio Kisses* (Leslie A. Pearce, May 1930) (color sequences)
- *The Bluffer* (Eddie Cline, Sept. 1930), *Mack Sennett Brevity*
- *Take Your Medicine* (Eddie Cline, Oct. 1930), *Mack Sennett Brevity*
- *Strange Birds* (Nov. 1930), *Mack Sennett Brevity*
- *A Poor Fish* (Mack Sennett, Jan. 1931), *Mack Sennett Brevity*

- *Speed* (Mack Sennett, May 1931)
- *Movie-Town* (Mack Sennett, July 1931)
- *The Trail of the Swordfish* (Sept. 1931), *Cannibals of the Deep #1*
- *The World Flier* (Del Lord, Sept. 1931), *Mack Sennett Brevity*
- *Who's Who in the Zoo* (Babe Stafford, Oct. 1931), *Mack Sennett Brevity*
- *Wrestling Swordfish* (Nov. 1931), *Cannibals of the Deep #2*

notes

1. I would like to acknowledge the professional assistance and kindness of the experts at the following archives for their invaluable help in making a lot of rare, precious, and fragile material available: Barbara Hall and Jenny Romero at the Academy of Motion Picture Arts and Sciences, Margaret Herrick Library in Los Angeles; George Willeman at the National Audio-Visual Conservation Center of the Library of Congress, Culpeper, VA; Nancy Kauffman, Anthony L'Abbate and James Layton at George Eastman House, Rochester, NY; May Haduong and Melissa Lovesque at Academy Film Archive, Los Angeles; Marc Quigley at the UCLA Film & Television Archive, Los Angeles; and sennett experts Brent Walker and Rob King.
2. All the consulted production papers are in the Mack Sennett papers in Margaret Herrick Library, Academy of Motion Picture Arts and Sciences, Beverly Hills, and will be referred to as: MSC plus the date of the paper or file when available.
3. The term "Ziegfeldized" refers to theatrical producer Florenz Ziegfeld, Jr. (1867–1932) who staged Ziegfeld Follies revues on Broadway from 1907 to 1931. He was famous for "glorifying" the American girl by selecting beauties to appear in elaborate – though scanty – costumes in choreographed production numbers.
4. This might be connected with some legal trouble: Hesser was arrested and charged with suspicions of narcotics peddling, battery, and impersonating a police officer, in connection with the alleged suicide of a film actress (see *Weekly Variety*, 18 April 1928: 9). The discontinuation of the *Mack Sennett-Pathé Studio Review* was most probably caused by difficulties surrounding the negotiations for a contract renewal between Pathé and Sennett at the end of 1927. The negotiations eventually broke off with Sennett changing his distribution channels to Educational Pictures at the end of 1928.
5. The George Eastman House Frames Collection is a collection of short clippings charting different processes and formats, donated by Kodak Research lab to George Eastman House, Motion Picture Department Collection. In the spring of 2010, I mailed scans of the film frames reproduced in the full-color promotional campaign for *Jazz Mamas* to film archivist James Layton, which resulted in his identification of the clip.

references

Papers in the Mack Sennett Collection in Margaret Herrick Library, Academy of Motion Picture Arts and Sciences, Beverly Hills, will be referred to as: MSC followed by the date of the individual file or paper (see also endnote 2).

Anon. (1930) "Mack Sennett's Color for Industrial Films", *Variety*, 35, 4 October: 1.

Anon. (1931) "Technicolor Wins Big Patent Victory", *Motion Picture Herald,* 10 October: 37.

Brown, S. (2002) "The Spectacle of Reality and British National Cinema". Online. Available at http://www.bftv.ac.uk/projects/dufaycolor.htm#_ftnref66 (accessed 17 February 2011).

Crespinel, W. T. (1929) "Color Photography, Yesterday, Today and Tomorrow", *American Cinematographer*, March: 4–7.

Crespinel, W. A. (2000) "Pioneer Days in Colour Motion Pictures with William T. Crespinel", *Film History*, 12, 1: 57–71.

D'haeyere, H. (2010) "Splashes of Fun and Beauty: Mack Sennett's Bathing Beauties" in King, R. and Paulus, T. (eds.), *Slapstick Comedy, AFI Film Reader*, London and New York: Routledge: 207–225.

Educational Film Exchanges, Inc. (1929) "Mack Sennett presents Jazz Mamas", *Exhibitors Herald – World*, 31 August, inserted page.

Educational Film Exchanges, Inc. (1930a) "11th Annual Announcement 1930–31: One Big Comedy Program", *Exhibitors Herald – World*, 2 August: 6 of 8 page promotional insert.

Educational Film Exchanges, Inc. (1930b) "Mack Sennett Talking Comedies: As Modern As Television", *Exhibitors Herald – World*, 16 August: back cover.

Guerin, P. J., Mack Sennett Color Film Co. Ltd. (1930) *Printing Machine for Cinematograph Films*, US Patent 1,880,087 (filed May 9, 1930, patented September 27, 1932).

Klein, Major Adrian B. (1936) *Colour Cinematography*, London: Chapman & Hall: 165–166.

Mack Sennett Comedies (1929) "Jazz Mamas" (Press sheet) in New York Public Library for the Performing Arts, Dorothy and Lewis B. Cullman Center, New York: 3.

Misek, R. (2010) *Chromatic Cinema: A History of Screen Color*, Chichester: Wiley-Blackwell.

Multicolor Films Inc. (1929) "Multicolor: The Final Answer To The Color Problem, Says Alvin Wyckoff", advertisement in *International Photographer*, December: 14.

Nowotny, R. A. (1983) *The Way of All Flesh Tones*, New York; London: Garland Publishing, Inc.: 271.

Ramsaye, T. (1931) "The Short Picture – Cocktail of the Program", *Motion Picture Herald*, 14 March: 59.

Ryan, R. T. (1977) *A History of Motion Picture Color Technology*, London: Focal Press: 98.

Schallert, E. (1930) "Cast Good In New York Narrative; 'Young Man Of Manhattan' Tells of Newspaper Folk; Sennett Color Film Shows", *The Los Angeles Times*, 17 May: A7.

Stamp, S. (2000) *Movie-Struck Girls: Women and Motion Picture Culture after the Nickelodeon,* Princeton, NJ: Princeton University Press.

Troland, L. (1927a) "My Dear Herbert" (letter to Dr. Kalmus), Technicolor Collection, Correspondence Files September 1925 to December 1927, Motion Picture Department, George Eastman House, Rochester, 3 March.

Troland, L. (1927b) "Some Psychological Aspects of Natural Color Motion Pictures", *Journal of the* Society of Motion Pictures Engineers, XI, 32: 686–690.

Walker, B. (2010) *Mack Sennett's Fun Factory: A History and Filmography of His Studio and His Keystone and Mack Sennett Comedies, with Biographies of Players and Personnel,* Jefferson, NC; London: McFarland & Co.

color as image schema

technicolor number 3 in

king of jazz (1930)

three

charles o'brien

King of Jazz, the big-budget film directed by John Murray Anderson and featuring the music of Paul Whiteman and his orchestra, illustrates how a familiar film-color motif was re-worked for two-color Technicolor. The motif involves movement toward what can be called red-dominant moments, when red (or a cognate hue like reddish orange, pink, or magenta) ends up taking up more surface area of the frame than any rival hue. Such moments typically occur in the final third or quarter of a shot, scene, or the film as a whole – as they do in *King of Jazz*. The practice in question suggests a variation on what philosopher Mark Johnson identifies as an "image schema" whereby musical motion is figured as analogous to the experience of the movement of one's own body through physical space (Johnson 2007: 243–262). The following analysis conceptualizes the movement-to-red in *King of Jazz* as an image schema in which music, vocals, the physical gestures of the performer, cutting, camerawork, and color, at key moments, combine to suggest increased proximity of viewer to performer. As viewer and performer come closer together, the image reddens and figuratively becomes warmer. This particular schema is evident through-out the history of motion picture color, from the applied color shorts of the late 1890s up through the digital features of the present.[1] To construe the movement-to-red in *King of Jazz* as an image schema thus opens the way for comparing and contrasting color technique in this unusual revue musical with that in a great many other films – regardless of how they may differ from *King of Jazz* in other respects.

color and music

A full-length all-Technicolor revue comprised of various musical and comedic performances, a mega-budget Hollywood film with no narrative arc, *King of Jazz* is an unusual motion picture in important respects. But its music-defined style is continuous with the aesthetics of mainstream film-color practice, where color often performs an aesthetic function linked to musical accompaniment. In this regard *King of Jazz* anticipates the Technicolor films of the late 1930s, in which intense, eye-catching hues frequently coincide with musical flourishes (see Higgins 2007: 40, 101–104, 127–133, 142). In a great many color films, from the 1930s up through the present, chromatic changes, like music cues, underline dramatic twists, signal the arrival of characters, mark transitions from scene to scene or act to act, and draw parallels or contrasts between one narrative event and another from a different part of the film. For Natalie Kalmus, Technicolor's chief "consultant" to the film industry, the "color chart" that her team produced for each Technicolor film was comparable to "a musical score [that] amplifies the picture in the same manner" (Kalmus 1935: 145). For Kalmus and countless other film-color experts in the 1930s and since, deciding on when in a film specific colors appear is like deciding when music is to be introduced.

The color/music analogy was by no means unique to the culture of synch-sound cinema but stemmed from "a tradition dating back to antiq-uity," Joshua Yumibe points out (Yumibe 2009: 164). This rich history of speculation on synaesthetic affinities between color and music was crucial to Hollywood's adoption of Technicolor Number 3, which coincided with the film industry's conversion to sound and the emergence circa 1930 of the musical as the major commercial film genre of the time. The musicals of the early 1930s provided the main vehicle for introducing the new Technicolor process into Hollywood cinema, which created for the movie-going public an association between the new sound-era genre and color cinematography (Anon. 1929a: X6; Anon. 1930a: 38). "[I]t seems likely that [the 'musical comedy'] will increasingly become associated in the public mind with color, so that a film musical without color will not count as a film musical," *Fortune* magazine reported (Anon. 1930b: 124). The Jolson vehicle *Mammy* (1930) and RKO's *Dixiana* (1931) are among conversion-era musicals currently available on DVD that use Number 3 in one or more song sequences. *King of Jazz* was among the films of the time to employ Number 3 throughout, from beginning to end.

What made Number 3 a major technical breakthrough in movie-color history was its dye-transfer process, which involved applying two layers of color onto the same side of the filmstrip (Haines 1993: 8–13). The color layers when printed appeared as magenta and cyan, the subtractive primaries. The dye-transfer system provided excellent registration of the separate color layers while eliminating the warping and other defects of the positive prints from earlier, laminate systems – including preceding versions of Technicolor. Since Technicolor films were shown with ordinary projectors, they were distributed far more widely than films made with any other photographic color system. Used in some eighty films of the late 1920s/early 1930s (Haines 1993: 15–16), Number 3 helped spur Hollywood's shift away from the applied color methods of the preceding thirty-five years of cinema history – tinting, toning, hand coloring, and stenciling – and toward the photographic systems that became standard in cinema worldwide beginning in the 1960s and continuing up through the advent of digital color in the early twenty-first century.

image schemas in film

The color/music analogy was highly relevant to *King of Jazz* given the latter's extensive use of popular songs. Song sequences in cinema exhibit techniques of editing, cinematography, acting, and mise-en-scène whose music-defined character is evident the instant the song begins, when the image changes, with editing, motion in the frame, and camera movement reconfiguring to fit the song's pulse and meter (see Buhler et al. 2010: 181–187). John Murray Anderson, the director of *King of Jazz*, captured the essence of this approach by observing that in his film, "the jump from one 'shot' to another is accomplished always on the downbeat of the accompanying music, or at a break in the phrasing" (quoted in Scheuer 1930: 19; see also Anderson's comments in Anon. 1930c: 122). A single close viewing of *King of Jazz* is enough to support Anderson's claim that its song sequences are cut to the musical pulse. Tap your finger to the beat and note where the cuts occur. Of the twenty-four cuts encompassed by the "A Bench in the Park" song number, fourteen, by my count, occur on the downbeat, i.e., the first quarter note in a measure, which theorists of music cognition identify as the strongest of metrical accents (Huron 2006: 184–185). A similar pattern concerns camera movement, such as the crane shot in "A Bench in the Park" that reveals the series of lovemaking couples, and whose tracking motions likewise start and stop on the downbeat.

Enabling the music/image alignment in *King of Jazz* was bandleader Whiteman's insistence on recording the music separately from the image in a proper music-studio setting prior to shooting the film. Besides ensuring a high-quality recording, the independent music track enabled the construction of a music-based image, with music serving as the dominant formal parameter, the pivot for the film's overall form and style (Schallert 1930a: B13). Indicative here are the similarities of Anderson's staging of "A Bench in the Park" and other song numbers in *King of Jazz* to the work of musician Ferde Grofé, famous in the 1920s for having arranged many of the hits performed by the Whiteman band. Grofé's method of arranging involved dividing up the band into sectional choirs of strings, reeds, brass, and so on, and then rotating the music through the sections, each positioned to contrast with adjacent sections in timbre and voicing (see Berrett 2004: 35, 41). Exemplary is the film's third sequence (see sequences list), whose introduction of the band via a series of vignette-like solo performances led critics to claim that Anderson had created in *King of Jazz* a visual equivalent for the sound of the Whiteman orchestra (Bell 1930: 11).

The 28 Sequences of *King of Jazz:*[2]

1. Opening credits (1 minute and 29 seconds)
2. The Walter Lantz cartoon "How Paul Became Known as the King of Jazz," introduced by emcee Charles Irwin (3 min. and 17 sec.)
3. Whiteman, introduced by Irwin, goes on to introduce the band via a series of solo performances (4 min. and 59 sec.)
4. The Russell Markert Girls dance (1 min. and 51 sec.)
5. The "My Bridal Veil" number (7 min. and 22 sec.)
6. "Ladies of the Press" comedy sketch with Laura LaPlante (43 sec.)
7. The Rhythm Boys sing "Mississippi Mud" and "When the Bluebirds and Blackbirds Get Together" (2 min. and 37 sec.)
8. "Monterey" song number starring John Boles and Jeanette Loff (5 min. and 50 sec.)
9. "In conference" skit with Laura LaPlante (43 sec.)
10. Jack Wright crazy comedy act, introduced by C. Irwin (3 min. and 22 sec.)
11. "A Bench in the Park" musical number (6 min. and 9 sec.)
12. "Springtime" comedy sketch with Slim Summerville (18 sec.)
13. "All Noisy on the Eastern Front," introduced by Irwin (1 min. and 38 sec.)
14. Wilbur Hall performs "The Stars and Stripes Forever" (2 min. and 55 sec.)
15. "Rhapsody in Blue" number, introduced by Whiteman (9 min. and 19 sec.)
16. "Oh Forevermore" skit featuring William Kent (3 min. and 34 sec.)
17. "My Ragmuffin Romeo" number (3 min. and 29 sec.)
18. The two-people-inside-a-horse-costume gag (1 min. and 23 sec.)
19. The comedian-in-baby-costume gag (25 sec.)
20. "Happy Feet" number with rubber-leg specialty dance (4 min. and 23 sec.)
21. Paul Whiteman (impersonated by double) dances! Introduced by Irwin (1 min. and 37 sec.)

22. Suitor-meets-dad comedy sketch (1 min. and 25 sec.)
23. "I'd Like to Do Things for You" (4 min. and 25 sec.)
24. "Has Anyone Seen My Nellie" song slide parody (2 min. and 45 sec.)
25. "Song of the Dawn" number (3 min. and 28 sec.)
26. "Melting Pot" number (8 min. and 49 sec.)
27. Paul stirs the pot, thus introducing the closing medley (3 min. and 4 sec.)
28. Finis (34 sec.)

A revue musical comprised of twenty-six self-contained song and comedy sequences (excluding the opening and closing titles) connected together via formal patterning rather than narrative causality, *King of Jazz* differed from the majority of the Hollywood films employing Technicolor, its structure more characteristic of a musical revue or vaudeville program than an ordinary feature film. The choice of the revue format entailed big risks in the fall of 1929, when Universal Pictures, wary of the waning popularity of revue musicals, decided to change course and script *King of Jazz* around a backstage story about a famous bandleader; Whiteman, however, vetoed the idea, protesting that his status as a celebrity musician made him incapable of playing a fictional character – even one modeled on his own public persona (Babcock 1929: 13, 24). The absence of narrative causality in *King of Jazz* – or put positively, the formal autonomy of its individual sequences, the show-stopping singularity of each act – allowed Universal in 1933 to release a re-cut version of the film that juggled the order of the sequences to shift the emphasis away from Whiteman, whose popularity had faded over the preceding three years, and toward Bing Crosby, now a major star.[3] Like a stage revue, *King of Jazz* is modular in construction, its constituent acts capable of addition, deletion, and other reorderings. Nonetheless, *King of Jazz* "holds together," director John Murray Anderson insisted, given the role in structuring the film played by "certain contrasts and continuities" in form: "The actual plan is bound to be an indefinable thing; but it is there nonetheless. One senses its presence in the audience. It is the design, the pattern of the production" (quoted in Schallert 1930b: B11). In sum, formal continuity via what Anderson called the film's design compensated for the absence of narrative structure.

color in *king of jazz*

How does Technicolor Number 3 factor into the film's design? Like other aspects of style, color in *King of Jazz* varies from one act or number to the next per the revue format, in which individual acts are ordered to maximize the contrast between them. Thus, the ethereal "Bridal Veil" dance number is followed by Laura LaPlante's comedy sketch, which is in turn succeeded by the Rhythm Boys, a singing trio; and so on, each act displaying a genre-appropriate color scheme. Some sequences showcase what can be called naturalistic color, with the filmmakers exploring Technicolor's capacity for simulating real-world color experience, especially flesh tones, which had been difficult to achieve with earlier color technologies. An example is the sketch "All Noisy on the Eastern Front," with its bombed-out chiaroscuro setting (see Hall 1929: 30). The naturalistic aesthetic, however, is not typical of the film as a whole, which, by and large, favors the abstraction achieved through a reduction of the color design to Number 3's constituent hues of magenta and cyan along with the liberal use of colored-light special effects. The formal "contrasts and continuities" that serve to "hold together" this film thus include an experimental use of color.

Making the color challenge critical for *King of Jazz* was the need for an extravagant set piece devoted to George Gershwin's "Rhapsody in Blue" – a famous concert piece associated with Whiteman since its gala première in New York in 1924. The "Rhapsody in Blue" sequence, put simply, had to look blue. That is, it had to feature a unitary blue, unmixed with red or yellow – the hue recognized as the prototypical blue in diverse cultures. But Number 3, with its cyan/magenta base, was unable to produce a straight blue of this sort (Anon. 1934: 94). Anderson recalled in his memoires that he and set designer Herman Rosse, aiming to overcome Number 3's limitations, made tests of "various fabrics and pigments, and by using an all gray-and-silver background, finally arrived at a shade of green which gave the illusion of peacock blue" (in Anderson 1954: 124). The result was not enough, however, to keep critics from labeling the color in question as green rather than blue or from referring to *King of Jazz* as a "rhapsody in turquoise" (Scheuer 1930: B11; Sime 1930).

Song sequences in *King of Jazz* are staged and lit to foreground the bi-chromatic basis of the color technology, with the result that the already limited palette of Technicolor Number 3 – a two- rather than three-color system – is further reduced down to magenta and cyan, with minimal mixing of the two.[4] The two-color scheme carried over to film-related illustrated sheet music editions, whose red and blue design emulated the clean, modernist, poster-art graphics of the film's mise-en-scène (see G. 1930: 4). Adding to the binary aesthetic was Anderson's use of colored lights during filming.[5] In *King of Jazz* beams of filtered light strike actors and sets in ways that juxtapose separate and distinct renditions of magenta and cyan. The film's third sequence, for example, where the band is introduced, includes numerous shots in which Number 3's two fundamental hues are placed side by side so that magenta covers one half of the frame and cyan the other – as in the striking medium close-up of the clarinet player, his face bathed half in "red" and half in "blue." "Futuristic" is how one critic described the overall effect (Anon. 1930a: B13). At the same time, the two-color motif, sustained across an entire feature film, spurred the complaint that "[b]y the end of *King of Jazz* one is tired of particular kinds of red and blue" (Herring 1930: 60).

In combining Technicolor with special effects stage lighting, Anderson and his team invoked what had been a hallmark of their Broadway shows and movie-palace prologues. With, certain of the film's musical numbers and black-out sketches, critics noted, adapted from Anderson's stage revues. The epic "Bridal Veil" sequence, for instance, had already been introduced in Anderson's revue "What's in a Name?" and then reworked as a movie-house prologue for "the entire circuit of Publix Theatres" (in Lusk 1930: B9). Ensuring continuity between the previous stage work and *King of Jazz* was the involvement in the film of Anderson's key stage associates, set designer Rosse and cartoonist and graphic artist Wynn Holcomb (Anon 1929b: 8, 20; Anon 1929c: 18). The modernist aesthetic linked to these artists was in keeping with Universal's boast that *King of Jazz* had inaugurated a new era in entertainment. At the same time, *King of Jazz*, in a pattern familiar to media history, invoked the old-media contexts capable of highlighting its novelty. Exemplary is the film's grotesque song-slide parody (sequence 24), whose farcical rendition of the singing quartet, with their awkward demeanor and tuneless vibrato, both mocks the movie-house song-slide shows of twenty years before while acknowledging these shows as *King of Jazz*'s predecessor in the entertainment field. With its futuristic vision mobilized for a re-staging of color cinema's own past, *King of Jazz* implies a kind of self-awareness regarding its own place in entertainment history.

the movement to red

Signaling the centrality of the movement-toward-red motif to *King of Jazz* is its introduction over the opening credits, whose listing of titles and names compels the viewer to scan the frame as if reading a page – from right to left and top to bottom. With the frame's upper half entirely blue while the lower half displays blue mixed with red highlights, the viewer/reader takes in the text by encountering first blue and then a red-blue mix. The movement-to-red pattern plays out over the remainder of the credits as the blue, cloud-like swirl acquires additional red accents. The "Melting Pot" musical number, the last major sequence in the film, exhibits the same schema. Toward the end, the massive pot "heats up" as Paul Whiteman, facing us in medium long shot and wearing a cook's hat, stirs with a stick. Ultimately he leans over the stew in close-up, red light floods his face from below. Soon after comes the coda, where the pattern is reversed. Beginning with a blue and red swirl pattern (much like that of the opening credits), the sequence evolves so that the degree of redness gradually diminishes prior to the final "Finis," thus enacting a progression toward blue rather than red. The exception proves the rule, however, since the sequence occurs at the end of the film, where it works as a closure cue, sealing off not only the "Melting Pot" sequence but everything that has happened since the opening credits.

The movement toward red defines six additional sequences comprising roughly one-third of the film's total running time, by my reckoning. The epic "My Bridal Veil" sequence ends with the seemingly endless reddish-pink wedding train gradually filling the space of the shot, even as the camera cranes back, away from the set. The "Song of the Dawn" sequence concludes with singer Boles and his chorus of backing vocalists striding toward the camera in red shirts, their arms extended to span the frame. In light of red's familiar status as a "warm color" – reiterated by Kalmus and virtually every other color theorist then and since – the boost in redness suggests a spike in temperature. This warming effect is prominent in sequences in which the elevation in redness coincides with a decrease in camera distance. The Rhythm Boys sequence, for instance, opens with a cyan silhouette of the three singers and ends with a two-dimensional composition much like the opening shot but now in magenta. The concluding image is also framed more tightly, as if to bring the viewer closer to the performers. The schema recurs in sequence 10, the comedy sketch featuring crazy comic Jack White. The sketch begins in a naturalistic mode with White entertaining the band members in what is presented as an impromptu performance. Then, around three-fourths of the way into the sequence, comedian Jack shouts out the non sequitur "and then the war broke out!" and the set instantly floods with red light, which lasts up through the sketch's end and the closest framing yet, a medium shot of White and a band member huddling on the imaginary battlefield and peering out toward the camera.

The "getting warmer" variant of the movement-to-red image schema structures numerous individual shots, as Anderson had promised: "You'll see colors changing – colors of costumes, of sets; colors on players' faces" (quoted in Lang 1930: 75). These changes typically involve an increase in redness. For instance, the shot in sequence 3 featuring the violin section begins with the six violinists in darkness and ends with the reddish pink lights turning on. Further examples occur in the notorious Walter Lantz cartoon about Paul Whiteman's role in the invention of jazz (sequence 2) as in the shot of the dancing dogs that ends with the dogs turning to face the camera and sticking out their red tongues, or the shots of the lion whose red mouth gapes open each time it lunges toward the camera to occupy momentarily the foreground of the shot. The image of the lion anticipates the cartoon's final image: the animated Whiteman character, wearing a reddish shirt, leans out from the frame in close-up, dazed from a blow to the head, his eyes rolling and red tongue hanging out. More red at the end than at the beginning, these shots suggest a recursive pattern whereby the principle behind the film's color design overall becomes manifest on the microscale of the single shot.

King of Jazz is an unusual film in important respects. But its movement toward red-dominant images is evident throughout the history of motion picture color. Many of the films discussed at the Bristol conference count as examples: from *The Mills of Joy and Sorrow* (1912) through *O Brother, Where Art Thou?* (2000). The concept of the image-schema, which Johnson stresses includes hearing and other sensory modes besides vision (Johnson 2007: 42–45, 136–145), provides a way of illuminating the logic behind the close interaction of music and visual action in so many films. The question posed in this chapter has concerned how color might factor into the analysis, using as a case study *King of Jazz*, whose music, visual representation, vocals, and color – at key moments – come into formal alignment so that change in one parameter matches up to analogous change in the others, all working to simulate the viewer's own embodied movement into (or out of) the film's space.

notes

1. My sense of the prevalence in cinema of the movement-to-red motif or image schema derives mainly from my experience as a film viewer. The phenomenon has been noted by other critics, however. See, for instance Coates (2008: 2–23) and Brost (2007: 128).
2. The scene order presented here is that of the MCA Home Video VHS release of 1992. This video edition, Bob Britchard of the American Film Institute reports, derived from a print made for general release in Great Britain, and that the scene order for this print does not match that of the prints screened for the film's première showings in New York and London. For more on various versions of the film, including eight foreign-language versions, see Britchard's entry on *King of Jazz* in the 2011 edition of the American Film Institute's *Catalogue of Feature Films*.
3. The extent of the scene re-arrangement can be seen when MCA's video edition of the film is compared to the script for the 1933 re-release, available in the Margaret Herrick Library in Los Angeles.
4. *King of Jazz* is known today mainly by MCA's 1992 video release, which is rumored to have been "color corrected," with the cyan of two-color Technicolor changed into a peacock blue. Hoping to find a more authentic version, I obtained from eBay a DVD-r allegedly made from a 35 mm print. The blue on the DVD is closer to cyan than what appears in the Universal video, which has led me to rely upon the DVD for my analysis. Needless to say, a definitive analysis will require examination of a 35 mm print – preferably an original nitrate release print.
5. Anderson claimed that he insisted on colored lights against Technicolor's reliance on "regulation white arcs" (in Anon. 1930c: 122). See also the remark that Anderson's use of colored light allowed him to get "the effect of three tones where everyone else has been content with one" (in Bell 1930: 11).

references

Anderson, H. (1954) *Out without My Rubbers: The Memoires of John Murray Anderson*, New York: Library Publishers.

Anon. (1929a) "100 Features in Color," *New York Times* (29 Sept.), X6.

Anon. (1929b) "Universal Signs John Murray Anderson to Produce *King of Jazz*," *Universal Weekly* 30, no. 7 (21 September), 8, 20.

Anon. (1929c) "Wynn Holcomb, Cartoonist and Stage Designer Signed for Universal's King of Jazz Revue," *Universal Weekly* 30, no. 13 (2 November), 18.

Anon. (1930a) "Two Color Sequences Stand Out," *Los Angeles Times* (27 April), B.

Anon. (1930b) "Color and Sound on Film," *Fortune* vol. 11, no. 4 (October), 124.

Anon. (1930c) "A Director's Ambitions," *New York Times* (11 May), 122.

Anon. (1930d) "Warners to Feature Technicolor Program," *New York Times* (27 May), 38.

Anon. (1934) "What? Color in the Movies Again?" *Fortune* vol. 10, no. 4 (October), 94.

Babcock, M. (1929) "King of Jazz Lacks Throne," *Los Angeles Times* (18 August), 13, 24.

Bell, N. (1930) "Behind the Screens," *The Washington Post* (3 May), 11.

Berrett, J. (2004) *Louis Armstrong and Paul Whiteman, Two Kings of Jazz*, New Haven, CT, and London: Yale University Press.

Brost, L. (2007) "On Seeing Red: The Figurative Movement of Film Colour," in W. Everett (ed.), *Questions of Colour in Cinema: From Paintbrush to Pixel*, Bern, Switzerland: Peter Lang, 2007, 127–139.

Buhler, J., Neumeyer, D. and Deemer, R. (2010) *Hearing the Movies: Music and Sound in Film History*, Oxford and New York: Oxford University Press.

Coates, P. (2008) "On the Dialectic of Filmic Colors (in general) and Red (in particular): *Three Colors: Red, Red Desert, Cries and Whispers*, and *The Double Life of Véronique*," *Film Criticism* vol. 32, no. 3, 2–23.

G., R. (1930) "*The King of Jazz*," *Wall Street Journal* (5 May), 4.

Haines, W. (1993) *Technicolor Movies: the History of Dye-Transfer Printing*, Jefferson, NC: MacFarland.

Hall, M. (1929) "Dialogue and Color," *New York Times* (29 May), 30.

Herring, R. (1930) "The Whiteman Front," *Close Up* vol. 6, no. 1 (July), 60.

Higgins, S. (2007) *Harnessing the Technicolor Rainbow: Color Design in the 1930s*, Austin, TX: University of Texas Press.

Huron, D. (2006) *Sweet Anticipation: Music and the Psychology of Expectation*, Cambridge, MA, and London: MIT Press.

Johnson, M. (2007) *The Meaning of the Body: Aesthetics of Human Understanding*, Chicago and London: University of Chicago.

Kalmus, N. (1935) "Color Consciousness," *Journal of the Society of Motion Picture Engineers* vol. 25, no. 2, 145.

Lang, H. (1930) "He Didn't Know How," *Photoplay* vol. 38, no. 1 (1 June), 75.

Lusk, N. (1930) "Depression Felt in East," *Los Angeles Times* (11 May), B9.

Schallert, E. (1930a) "'Ghosting' Songs Now Favored," *Los Angeles Times* (19 January), B13.

Schallert, E. (1930b) "Revues Stir Controversy," *Los Angeles Times* (9 March), B11.

Scheurer, P. (1930) "Jazz Spectacle Sets Pace in Novelties," *Los Angeles Times* (13 April), 19.

Sime (1930) "*King of Jazz*," *Variety* (7 May).

Yumibe, J. (2009) "'Harmonious Sensations of Sound by Means of Colors': Vernacular Colour Abstractions in Silent Cinema," *Film History* vol. 21, no. 2, 164–176.

glorious agfacolor,

breathtaking totalvision

and monophonic sound

f o u r

colour and "scope" in czechoslovakia

a n n a   b a t i s t o v á

The cinema industry was one of the first industries to become state-owned in post-war Czechoslovakia.[1] Although state interference in film production, distribution and exhibition grew as the political climate of the cold war became increasingly tense, it did not stop Czechoslovak cinema from following technological changes which were happening abroad. However, isolation from the western world and political and economical dependence on the centre of socialist power in Soviet Russia caused considerable problems. Efforts to evolve independently inside the socialist block were affected by the growing internationalization, standardization and globalization of the cinema industry.

In this chapter I will examine how this tension between Soviet self-sufficiency and a global cinema market affected the adoption of colour in Czechoslovakian cinema in particular in relation to the change of colour process required by the adoption of widescreen. While the Czechoslovak film industry was content to use low-quality East-German colour film stock in the late 1940s, owing to the international adoption of widescreen it was forced to exchange it for Eastmancolor during the following decade. In this period therefore the necessity for technological change powered by the global industry overwhelmed the political realities of the Soviet system.

The first mainstream natural colour films were screened in Czechoslovakia well before 1945, including films utilizing various two-colour systems in the 1920s, American Technicolor productions in the 1930s and German Agfacolor films in the 1940s.[2] Although there were minor independent experiments with colour in the period, and Czech workers helped during production of Agfacolor features at Barrandov studios in Prague during the war, regular colour production would start only after 1945.[3]

The particular character of the Czech film industry between the wars did not allow for the earlier proliferation of colour films. Since the mid 1920s the state would only licence charitable organizations to run cinemas, which discouraged entrepreneurship and meant that film production was not seen as a profitable enterprise and thus was never supported by banks or other private investors. In addition so many distribution companies were set up in the post-First-World-War period, flooding the market with hundreds of films from all over Europe and the U.S. every year, that they did not leave much space for domestic releases, nor did they enjoy long lives in this highly competitive atmosphere themselves (Heiss and Klimeš 2003: 303–320).

After 1945 on the other hand, the state-owned industry was provided financial protection by vertical integration and, on account of the German occupation of the Barrandov studios during the war, not only were experienced workers and fully equipped laboratories available, but also a limited supply of colour film stock. However, before Czechoslovak cinema ventured into its own colour production, it needed more experience, hosting Soviet colour production in the first few post-war years.[4] But they could not wait long. Colour production was supposed to prove both the technological and the artistic maturity of the industry. As in other countries, the first attempts at colour cinema were made with short and non-fiction films, and from the latter half of 1945 colour stock was used prominently for both short and feature-length animation. While the focus on short films is understandable due to initial experimenting and high costs of colour stock, the choice of the animation genre not only copied foreign patterns, but also drew on the international reputation of Czechoslovak animation at the time, such as Jiří Trnka's *Animals and Bandits* (*Zvířátka a Petrovští*, 1946) or *The Christmas Dream* (*Vánoční sen*, 1945), collaboration of Karel Zeman, Bořivoj Zeman and Hermína Týrlová, both in Festival de Cannes competition in 1946. The young state-owned industry was in need of reorganization and lacked modern equipment in both production and cinemas, as well as the support of domestic manufacturers of technology and film stock.

In such a situation, colour animated films seemed an ideal product to be exchanged for much needed foreign currency.[5] For example, in 1947, thirteen out of seventeen short animated films were in colour, as was the only feature-length animated film produced that year, while only one feature out of eighteen and two out of fifty-three non-animated shorts were in colour. At the same time, only some of the films shot in colour were distributed as such at home, the colour copies being reserved for international festivals and the foreign market. The first live action feature film in colour, *Jan Roháč of Dubá* (*Jan Roháč z Dubé*, 1947), was made in 1947 and the production of colour films increased steadily every year until the mid-1950s. Even in the critical year of 1951, when only seven feature films were made in total, two of them were in colour.[6] The 1950s were also marked by an interesting (but quite understandable) inclination of colour productions towards popular films in general and children's movies in particular. Children's and animated films were successful at international festivals and often sold abroad. They constituted prestige product, not only securing the foreign currency, but also showing both possibilities and abilities of the newly nationalized cinema industry, advertising the idea of socialism.

Before 1945, domestic manufacture of film stock was virtually non-existent, and even in later years only a small amount of black-and-white positive material could be secured internally.[7] Czechoslovakia thus depended on foreign supply. The negative colour film stock used well into the 1960s was East German Agfacolor, initially bought through the Soviet Union administration after 1945, and later directly from the Agfa factory in Wolfen (from the mid-sixties, the same stock was called Orwocolor). However, since the mid-1950s, the industry had been experimenting with stock by other European manufacturers and with Kodak products, looking for new and better colour material.

It is important to consider at this point how similar the background for decision-making mechanisms are when it comes to comparison of technological change in the nationalized cinema of a socialist country such as Czechoslovakia, and other cinemas governed by the free market. This is largely due to the nature of cinema as an industry. While in the late 1940s and early 1950s the cinemas of the East-European countries tended towards separatism, as did other industries, quite soon the need of at least partial success in the international market became obvious. Also, while Soviet and other socialist countries' films were preferred by individual governments, tastes of the audiences in these countries did not differ much from those in the western world (Skopal 2009). Finally, although the main goal of the cinema was to educate the people in the ways of the new and future socialist world, economics constituted an inseparable force behind the control of the industry.

While shooting in colour was not without issues, screening colour films proved to be equally problematic. Firstly, the quality of the eastern Agfa stock was low. In various tests conducted in the period, Czechoslovak technicians found the definition of Agfacolor positive materials 50 per cent lower than that of Eastmancolor, while the sensitivity of the emulsion was uneven, sometimes in the same reel. Up to 10 per cent of the Agfacolor material was sent back to Wolfen as faulty every year. Reports from the period comment on the low quality of the colour stock causing problems during shooting and processing (Anon. 1955). Proof of this is evident in the poor colour saturation in scenes with lower intensity of light (for example night scenes) and changes of colour during dissolves which are visible on the surviving prints and recently released digital copies of some films. Second, domestic cinemas were very poorly equipped for the projection of colour films. Nation-wide surveys showed that some cinemas only had one projector and most of them had machines that were more than twelve years old. Even silent-era equipment, only later adjusted for sound screening, was not unusual. Old projectors were feared to be more likely to damage expensive colour copies during screenings. Furthermore, these projectors had very poor lighting properties. Not only did their optics absorb most of the light before casting it on a screen, but also the light sources were insufficient themselves, as were the reflective qualities of materials used to make screens. Before colour, even a dim projector light was enough: black-and-white films required less light to be sufficiently luminous and cinemas in Czechoslovakia were mostly small, with short distances between projector and screen.[8] Screenings in larger venues, however, revealed the inadequacy of the machines.[9] Not surprisingly, when reviewing projectors manufactured domestically after 1945, cinema representatives usually complained, about lamp houses and optical arrangement, which had the biggest effect on the light efficiency of the projector.

The survival of Czechoslovak cinema depended on foreign product and the ability to screen films produced abroad.[10] As coordination and division of labour and flow of product inside the Council for Mutual Economic Assistance (COMECON) was still poor, Czechoslovakia could not close itself inside the Eastern bloc, at least from the point of view of the cinema market. Being able to screen foreign films and occasionally sell some domestic product abroad was necessary, and therefore if the foreign product was in widescreen, Czechoslovakia needed to be able to adapt to new formats.

The widescreen revolution brought a new set of concerns for Czechoslovak cinema and they were to test the new organization of the industry after little more than a decade of its existence. Firstly, the administration of the centralized cinema industry had to decide which of the emerging new formats to adopt. Having more than one new format alongside academy ratio was impossible for economic and organizational reasons.[11] In the initial anarchy of emerging new formats, Czechoslovak cinema technicians had to decide, or rather guess, which of the formats would get the major share of the cinema screens in the world. As they started to consider a new format quite late, around the end of 1954 or the beginning of 1955 (and in these years only preliminary research was made, while the actual adoption was planned for 1956), the chosen format was CinemaScope, which was at that point the dominant widescreen format and had a number of fully compatible competitors. While the word CinemaScope appears (in various distortions of the original spelling) in cinema journals and archival documents of the period, this actual brand never made it to Czechoslovakia, and was substituted by compatible European technology for shooting (for instance French Totalvision), and by domestic equipment for screening.

Now that the decision was made, the next step was to prepare the industry for the transition as quickly as possible. A five-year plan was prepared for the period 1956–1960, during which ten features were supposed to be made, and forty cinemas adapted for the new technology. While the number of films actually made corresponded with the initial plan, over 250 cinemas were adapted during the period. Of these, however, only approximately forty had stereophonic sound reproduction alongside the wider image.

While Agfacolor negative stock was barely sufficient for academy ratio shooting and screening, it was even more inadequate for "scope" or even masked formats.[12] As a result, from 1957 the situation became more complicated. For "scope" films, Eastmancolor became the standard, while academy ratio productions continued to use eastern Agfacolor/Orwocolor. We can see this distinction in the film *Death in the Saddle* (*Smrt v sedle*, 1958). The film was shot in two formats, academy on Agfacolor and "scope" on Eastmancolor stock.[13] A similar situation arose with *Provisional Liberty* (*La Liberté surveillé /V proudech*, 1957), the first "scope" feature finished in Czechoslovakia, which was a co-production with the French Trident company. According to negotiations, the French co-producer was supposed to supply the Eastmancolor stock, although in fact what they provided was western Agfacolor. Czech cameramen working on the film found the quality sufficient, although the material needed some changes in lighting and laboratory processing. The release copies were printed on Italian Ferraniacolor.[14] *A Midsummer Night's Dream* (*Sen noci svatojánské*, 1959), a "scope" animated feature by Jiří Trnka that went into production in 1956 and was released in 1959, was shot entirely in Eastmancolor. However, in 1956 there was no laboratory to process Eastmancolor in Czechoslovakia, so the rushes were sent to Paris, while Trnka used black-and-white academy materials shot simultaneously to check the movements of his puppets. Also, he was forced to make alterations to his usual methods of puppet-making, due to the differences in colour rendering with Agfacolor and Eastmancolor.[15]

While the first colour widescreen films were being made, research groups were formed to compare the qualities of Agfacolor and Eastmancolor and to investigate possibilities of introduction of the latter into laboratory practice. The main problems were connected with old and insufficient machinery and inaccurate measuring instruments. However, unlike the Agfa/Wolfen factory, Kodak provided technical support during the introduction of the new laboratory equipment and processes, and remained in contact with the Prague laboratories. While preparing for Eastmancolor as a new negative material, Czechoslovak researchers continued to review other colour stocks produced in Europe. Small groups of technicians (usually two or three) were sent to the Soviet Union, as well as the DEFA studios in Germany, the Gevaert factory in Belgium and the Ferrania factory in Italy. During the 1960s and 1970s, Eastmancolor became and remained the main colour stock for negatives and intermediate materials, while cheaper colour processes (most often eastern Agfacolor, later Orwocolor) were used for distribution copies. There were however a few scope films using Agfacolor or Orwocolor negative film stock, especially in the late 1960s.

As in other countries, post-war cinema in Czechoslovakia was threatened by the growing popularity of television, but aspired to coordinate the media to the advantage of both, and the needs of the governing party. In 1972 almost half of the approximately 2,000 cinemas (or 3,400, if we count 16 mm, non-regular and various club, factory or union screening facilities as well) were equipped for "scope". At the same time, these cinemas collected more than 60 per cent of the overall income of the industry. Because of the limited use of widescreen films in television, and television's growing proliferation, 1972 was marked by a decision to save "scope" for productions described as "popular", supposedly attracting larger audiences to cinemas, while "politically important" films were to be shot at academy format, and as such to be more suitable for the new medium. While musicals, comedies or films for young people attracted large audiences during their first few weeks of release, and sometimes during the summer rereleases in open-air cinemas, political dramas and similar were supposed to find their viewers in private homes, repeatedly, for years after their original release (Pilát 1972: unpaged).

Although the widescreen revolution did not take a direct course and was held back, in Czechoslovakia probably more than elsewhere, it did significantly influence the transition from black-and-white to colour. While eastern Agfacolor was perceived as problematic and inferior from the very beginning, the major impulse for a change of colour system came with the introduction of widescreen in Czechoslovakia, as anamorphic processes tested the limits of the film stock, and made all the known issues even more visible. Czechoslovak studios never saw the real CinemaScope and worked with compatible European "scopes", as the cinemas had to use domestic technology, however clumsy it might be. It was therefore not glorious Technicolor, breathtaking CinemaScope and stereophonic sound at first in Czechoslovakia.

Furthermore, initially Czechoslovak encounters with colour were determined by the character of the cinema industry – low domestic production, small number of cinemas and dependence on international cooperation – rather than by the political situation. Yet after 1945 colour production gained an increasingly prestigious standing from both a political and economic point of view. Politically, colour films were meant to show the accomplishments of the state-owned industry, while economically they constituted a unique source of foreign currency. Ultimately the latter half of the 1950s and the 1960s saw a period of development and expansion in the Czechoslovak industry and liberation in politics and society, which encouraged and enabled the government to spend more on the superior Eastmancolor stock. Where colour film stock was concerned, political issues ceased to be important, and once it became economically possible, the cinema technicians and engineers went for the quality first. Eastmancolor was adopted as the standard negative stock material in the following decades, which in turn saw a significant increase in the number of films made in colour, leaving the use of black-and-white marginal by the end of the communist era in 1989.

notes

1. By the government decree no. 50/1945 on arrangements in the cinema sphere of business, the Czechoslovak state gained a monopoly on cinema production, laboratory processing, distribution, public screenings and international trade.
2. Short Prizmacolor films were distributed in 1921–1922. In December 1923 *The Glorious Adventure* (UK, 1922) premièred and *The Toll of the Sea* (US, 1922) in two-colour Technicolor was released in December 1924 (Štábla 1982: 355–357).
3. For example IRE-film, a Prague studio owned by Irena and Karel Dodal, made several animation shorts in colour between 1933 and 1938 (Strusková 2006: 99).
4. For example, the shooting of Alexander Ptuschko's colour film *The Stone Flower* (Kamennyy tsvetok, USSR 1946) began in August 1945, and the film was the first to be finished in the Barrandov studios after the war.
5. While the studios did not suffer much damage during the war (at least in comparison with other Central and East-European countries), the cinemas were in desperate need of new equipment. According to a post-war survey, up to 85 per cent of them were "insufficient for orderly operation", not only in terms of equipment, but also in issues of hygiene and safety (Bystřický 1947: unpaged).
6. In 1950, several films were reprimanded by communist party officials and a list of preferred topics was issued. This interference led to a production crisis in 1951, when only a fraction of the originally scheduled 52 films for that year were actually produced.
7. On the other hand, film for still photography had been domestically produced since 1914 by Neobrom, and from 1921 by Fotochema (now Foma), alongside other smaller companies.

8. According to the data collected in 1947, only 110 cinemas had an auditorium longer than 30 metres, and the maximum length was 42 metres (Anon. 1950a: unpaged). In 1950, only nine cinemas had a capacity of more than 1,000, while almost 85 per cent of all cinemas could seat less than 500 (Černík 1954: 89, 198). In later decades, the national cinema network was being improved, also by building new cinemas in previously neglected regions. Of these cinemas, some were constructed especially for widescreen or 70 mm, and as such, they tended to be larger. Also, open-air cinemas, with programming concentrated to summer months, had longer distances between the screen and the projector booth, and could have up to several thousands of spectators. For example, the first "scope" screening in Czechoslovakia during the International Film Festival in Karlovy Vary in summer 1956 took place in a newly constructed open air cinema, which would seat up to 3,500 spectators (Anon. 1956: 9).

9. As the report by a member of Cinema Technology Committee (FITES) states, during the screening at the Fair palace in Prague held in 1950 for the anniversary of the Soviet October Revolution, the visibility of the image was so reduced that a viewer could hardly have recognized that the film was in colour. In conclusion, the report suggested that if the minimum luminance required for colour screening is not achieved, colour films should not be shown at all, as that would ruin their political mission (Anon. 1950b: unpaged).

10. Because of the small number of cinemas, low ticket prices and high costs of production, an average Czechoslovak film would theoretically take thirty-six months to break even, during which time demand would fall dramatically. Thus only extremely popular Czechoslovak films or foreign films turned a profit (Bláha 1955: 12).

11. Although since 1964 some new large cinemas were built for 70 mm projection, Czechoslovak cinema never produced a film on 65 mm negative, except for a handful of co-productions with the USSR. A few other Czechoslovak films were released in 70 mm blown-ups from original 35 mm negatives. It should also be noted that masked formats (1:1,66 and 1:1,85), which could be screened with just small alterations to current projectors, were quite common in Czechoslovakia, but there is no data on their actual proliferation.

12. Only during the 1970s did colour become standard in Czechoslovakia. Until then the majority of both academy and "scope" films were shot in black-and-white.

13. This practice was used for a few early widescreen films, as the Prague laboratories did not have a way to make academy copies from the "scope" originals yet, and at the same time, only a few cinemas were scope-friendly. Having a film on widescreen only would substantially limit its use in distribution.

54

14. In general, co-production became the way of obtaining quality colour stock and better shooting technology in the late 1950s and during the 1960s (see Skopal 2009).

15. In a monograph on Trnka, the reason offered for switching from Agfacolor to Eastmancolor is the blurriness of the wider image towards the left and right extremes. Also, Eastmancolor is described as more "naturalistic", showing the materials used to manufacture the puppets for what they really are (Boček 1963: 247−248).

references

Anon. (1950a) *Zápis 60. schůze komise promítací FITES dne 19. 6. 1950* [manuscript], Filmový technický sbor, FITES 1950, Praha: Národní filmový archiv.

Anon. (1950b) *Zápis 65. řádné schůze promítací komise 14. listopadu 1950* [manuscript], Filmový technický sbor, FITES 1950–1951, Praha: Národní filmový archiv.

Anon. (1955) *Zápis plenární schůze Filmového technického sboru ze dne 28. září 1955. Zavádění nových technologií.* Filmový technický sbor, FITES 1951–1959, Praha: Národní filmový archiv.

Anon. (1956) "Preparations for the IXth International Film Festival at Karlovy Vary in Full Swing", *The Czechoslovak Film*, 4: 9.

Bláha, R. (1955) *Ekonomika čs. kinematografie. Učebnice pro III. a IV. ročník Průmyslové školy v Čimelicích a příručka pro filmové pracovníky*, Praha: Československý státní film.

Boček, J. (1963) *Jiří Trnka. Historie díla a jeho tvůrce*, Praha: Státní nakladatelství krásné literatury a umění.

Bystřický, J. (1947) *Zřizování kin a užití substandardních formátů pro veřejný provoz* [manuscript], Filmový technický sbor, FITES 1947, Praha: Národní filmový archiv.

Černík, A. (1954) *Výroční zpráva o čs. filmovnictví. Rok 1950*, Praha: Československý státní film.

Heiss, G. and Klimeš, I. (2003) *Obrazy času / Bilder der Zeit. Český a rakouský film 30. let/ Tschechischer und österreichischer Film der 30er Jahre*, Praha: Národní filmový archiv.

Pilát, F. (1972) *Studie dlouhodobého rozvoje filmové techniky*, Praha: Ústřední ředitelství Československého filmu.

Skopal, P. (2009) "The 'Provisional Liberty' of Colour and Widescreen: The Czech Co-Productions with the 'West', 1959–1969", paper presented at NECS conference at Lund, 2009. Also online. Available at http://www.phil.muni.cz/dedur/?lang=1&id=21534 (accessed 30 April 2011).

Strusková, E. (2006) "Iréna & Karel Dodal. Průkopníci českého animovaného filmu", *Iluminace*, 63: 99–146.

Štábla, Z. (1982) *Rozšířené teze k dějinám československé kinematografie*, vol. 2, Praha: Filmový ústav.

glorious and other

adventures with

prizma

f i v e

s a r a h   s t r e e t

Prizmacolor was an important marker of early two-color, subtractive pro-cess experimentation, contributing to the subsequent development of later commercially exploited processes including Vitacolor, Magnacolor, Multicolor and Cinecolor. Prizma underwent several experimental phases before being used for *The Glorious Adventure* (1922), a British film that was the first full-length feature shot using a subtractive color process. This chapter will demonstrate how Prizma and *The Glorious Adventure* are more than foot-notes in the history of color cinematography on the road to Technicolor's domination. *The Glorious Adventure* relates to trans-national experimentation with early color systems, as well as to specific aesthetic and technical con-cerns which in retrospect had a broad significance. The film has tended to be written-off by critics who failed to appreciate its multifarious approach to color (Low 1971: 126). Yet the aesthetic choices demonstrated a practical awareness of how to work creatively within the constraints of prevailing systems and critical assumptions about what constituted "good" color in the early 1920s.

Prizma's roots go back to the vision of inventor William Van Doren Kelley who had experience working with the additive process Kinemacolor. In 1913 he developed a four-color additive process called Panchromotion which used a rotating disc divided into sections of red-orange, blue-green, blue-violet and yellow, with each separated by a small transparent segment. Projection required a similar colored filter disc and a fast speed. This process was subsequently adapted and re-named Prizma, again using four filters but replacing the clear filter with a wheel that reduced the saturation level of the colors from the centre outwards. In projection red-orange and blue-green filters were used, and the film was shown at twice the normal speed (Nowotny 1983: 155–158). When this proved unsuccessful a three-color disc was developed, and Prizma was first demonstrated with *Our Navy* in February 1917 at the American Museum of Natural History in New York before being commercially released. The link with later incarnations of Prizma was an "ingenious" double-sided stock whereby one side of the film is dyed a combination of colors that seem to include and blend the red half of the spectrum; the other side is admixture of the green complements. Thus *all* the colors of the spectrum are filtered in each frame, for the frame is transparent and the light passing thru it catches the combination by projecting what it finds on both sides of the strip of film (Phillips 1923: 95).[1] The significance of this was that bi-pack color became the most economical means of achieving natural two-color moving pictures until the introduction of monopack stocks in the 1940s. Experimentation with this approach took place over several years via analogous processes, most notably Kodachrome, Brewstercolor and Kesdacolor (Cornwell-Clyne 1951: 11).

Kelley developed Kesdacolor in New York in partnership with Carroll H. Dunning and Wilson Salisbury. It was a subtractive process that used a camera with two lenses. The technical details were as follows:

> Between both lenses and the camera negative Kelley had positioned a vertically banded two-color line screen. These minute bands of red and green, running parallel with the film, thus gave a latent color record to the black-and-white image produced by the primary, or picture-forming lens. Directly above the primary lens was a secondary lens. In addition to being fitted with the vertically banded line screen, this secondary lens possessed either a right angle mirror or prism. Rather than receiving its light from the scene, the upper right lens collected ambient light from above. So that no distinct outlines or images would be transmitted to the film, this ambient light first travelled through a diffusing surface located above the prism. The film was advanced two frames at a time, thus producing a

pair of exposed frames simultaneously. The lower frame of the pair contained a black-and-white image of the scene as well as latent color values due to the presence of the line screen. The upper frame (exposed by diffused sunlight) merely contained latent red and green color records from the line screen itself. During the printing stage each pair of simultaneously exposed frames was combined and superimposed on duplitized positive film. (Nowotny 1983: 163–164)

No standard attachments were required for projection and the film could be run at the normal speed of 16 frames per second. The process was first publicly demonstrated in September 1918 with the one-minute film *Our American Flag*.

The experiments with Kesdacolor enabled further development of Prizma as a subtractive process whereby alternate positive frames were stained red and green and the film projected on standard apparatus (Cherchi Usai 2000: 35). The film was taken through a color filter disc before the camera lens in traditional fashion, the camera recording successive red and blue-green records of the original scene at 32 frames per second. Unfortunately, the successive nature of the device produced "fringing" (colors appearing to "bleed" with movement), a technical problem that was never solved. These records were printed onto a double-sided positive film which had two emulsions separated by a base which was dyed so that no light would pass through from one side to the other, the dye being dissolved during processing. A special printer moved the negative forward two frames and the positive only one, so every other one of the alternate red and green frames was printed onto one positive, making individual red and green positive records. The side with the blue-green record was dyed red-orange and the other, the red record, was dyed blue-green (Nowotny 1983: 167–169). On a technical level, Prizma is significant for its anticipation of bi-pack color systems, and for offering an ingenious printing method with its double-sided film, one side toned blue-green by an iron solution, and the opposite side toned red-orange with uranium. It also had the advantage of not needing a special projector (Cornwell-Clyne 1951: 335). Even so, it was more expensive than black-and-white film, estimated at eight times as much per linear foot for prints (*Exhibitors Herald* 1922: 44).

A Prizma Color Visit to Catalina was shown in New York's Rivoli Theatre in January 1919, followed by *Everywhere with Prizma*, a one-reel travelogue. *Bali the Unknown*, a four-reeler, was premièred in New York in February 1921. The first screening of Prizma in Britain was in 1921, at a private event for exhibitors at the Alhambra in London. The programme included films of Niagara Falls, a volcano in Hawaii, a film about fashion and studies of fruit and flowers, first seen in monochrome and then in color to demonstrate

Prizma's qualities. While enthusiastic about Prizma's potential, a reporter noted that it probably was not ready yet to record fictional subjects, since "fringing" presented a problem with figure movement (*British Journal of Photography*, 6 May 1921: 18–19). Another however recorded that "in all of them [the pictures] the color reproduction was wonderfully good" (*The Times*, 9 Apr 1921: 6).

The Glorious Adventure was directed by James Stuart Blackton. He was born in Sheffield, but his film career was forged with Vitagraph in the USA before he returned briefly to Britain to make films in the early 1920s. Blackton was impressed after seeing *Everywhere with Prizma* in 1919, and became convinced that color and Prizma were the way forward for cinematographic art (Cornwell-Clyne 1951: 18). The cinematographer was William T. Crespinel who had worked with Kinemacolor in Britain and America. He was employed by Blackton in 1915, worked with Kelley on Prizma from 1917 and founded Cinecolor in 1932. *The Glorious Adventure* was filmed by Crespinel at Stoll's Cricklewood Studios, near London. He later recalled his experiences on shooting the first full-length film using a subtractive process. Experimentation with Prizma clearly took place during the production, namely the negatives used for photographing interiors were super-sensitized, adding 30 per cent to the film speed (Crespinel 2000: 64). In addition, a report on the latest Prizma patent in 1920 demonstrated that work had progressed on developing a camera (*British Journal of Photography*, 5 Aug 1921: 32). In addition, costly experimentation continued with building accurate double printing machines, as well as machines for the continuous automatic tone-dyeing of both sides of the film (Raleigh 1922: 37). In this sense, *The Glorious Adventure* represented a high-point of maturity for Prizma's development.

Reviews in Britain of *The Glorious Adventure* were quite favorable, for example, observations that Prizma achieved in particular "exquisitely beautiful reproductions of natural scenes, and gorgeously colored Court dresses" (*Daily Film Renter and Moving Picture News*, 28 Jan 1922: 10). The scenes of the Great Fire of London, commented on by the majority of reviewers as genuinely spectacular, were much appreciated, as well as shots which picked-out detail such as fruit on the court banqueting table. But in spite of these accolades problems with "fringing" were confirmed by the observation that whenever characters moved quickly, "detail becomes lost, and color merges and becomes blurred and indistinct" (ibid.). *The Glorious Adventure* was publicized as a "high class," quality product, emphasizing the cast's aristocratic connections and generating "enormous interest" at the première at the Royal Opera House, Covent Garden on 18 January 1922 (*Illustrated London News* 1922: 88–89).

Viewing the British Film Institute's restored version of *The Glorious Adventure* allows some of these comments to be considered from the perspective of how Prizma was demonstrated in the context of historical melodrama.[2]

The film begins in the Cromwellian period, introducing Hugh Argyle and Lady Beatrice, a young couple who are separated when Hugh goes away to sea. The Restoration of the Stuarts occurs and Lady Beatrice, played by society beauty Lady Diana Manners, waits for Hugh's return. The castle where she lives is temporarily occupied by Charles II and his court which provides the occasion for outdoor scenes of pageantry and revelry. A parallel narrative strand shows Hugh at sea being tricked by rogues who steal his inheritance papers and throw him overboard. One of the rogues, Roderick, double-crosses another called Bullfinch, so that Bullfinch alone is blamed for murdering Hugh. On arrival in London Bullfinch is put in prison and Roderick pretends to be Hugh in order to claim the inheritance and marry Beatrice. Since a long time has passed since she previously knew him, Roderick's pretence is just about plausible although Beatrice looks a little puzzled when she sees him again. Meanwhile, Beatrice's financial difficulties force her to marry a condemned criminal (Bullfinch) so that he can assume her debts. Having escaped drowning, Hugh also appears in London and attempts to recover his inheritance claim from the scheming Roderick. The film climaxes with the Great Fire of London and after the resolution of several interlinking plot twists, Hugh and Beatrice are finally united.

The film raises several key issues which are important in considering color during this period. The first is that with many processes a single, identifiable aesthetic signature was not always evident. What we get is a mediated, multiple application of color which imported conventions already in current use. Although Prizma was marketed as a subtractive process, on occasion the film demonstrates approaches to color associated with tinting and toning. For example, when Bullfinch escapes from prison and searches for Lady Beatrice in the moonlight, the use of blue to indicate night time is highly reminiscent of the blue tinting for night which was common in silent cinema. So, while Prizma is the "star" of the film, aesthetic approaches from applied color persist with the bathing of frames with a single color. Similarly, but adding color contrast, the scene just before Hugh departs to go to sea presents an opportunity for color spectacle with a shot of him in the dark, bathed in blue light, as Beatrice runs to wave him goodbye wearing a cloak in shades of red. The set of the "Golden Swan" ship provides another occasion for an emblematic shot (a visually arresting shot of relatively long duration, common in silent cinema for encapsulating the essence and mood of a sequence or entire film) with the ship on the horizon framed with deep blue sea and red clouds. (**See Plate 2.**) The almost translucent qualities of this shot are an example of the lantern-like, "stained-glass color effect" criticized by art supervisor Walter Murton for being "unnatural", but which stand out as visually striking (Murton quoted by Phillips 1923: 95). Also, the inter-titles are color-coded as in tinted films, so that this scene is announced with a blue title card, and the next with a yellow one, as we learn that the

Restoration of the Stuarts has occurred while Beatrice grows up. In this way color guides the film's episodic structure as the more up-beat "tone" of the next scene is declared.

As with most color processes, Prizma was subject to close analysis, and one of the "litmus tests" for color was how it reproduced flesh, particularly with stars normally seen in monochrome. Lady Diana Manners was the youngest daughter of the Duke of Rutland. She married Duff Cooper, a future Member of Parliament in 1919, and gained a reputation for being a fast-living society beauty who acted on the stage and in films. Quite apart from the color, her presentation in *The Glorious Adventure* was a spectacle in itself. The revelation of the young "Lady Beatrice Fair", as the title describes her (played by Violet Virginia Blackton), is accentuated by a close-up of her face against a blue background which demonstrates Prizma's ability to render skin tones in the context of an English drama. (**See Plate 3.**)

The narrative features color at several key points but in a complex rather than a straightforwardly symbolic manner. At first Beatrice does not recognize Hugh when he returns to London. The villain Roderick pursues her and tries to break into her bedroom. Hugh comes to her rescue and after gaining her trust as a gallant stranger, he tells Beatrice that if any more trouble occurs she should send a white rose to the landlord at the inn where he is staying. A color motif is therefore introduced to assist the plot and in contrast to the deep red clothes worn by the villain Roderick when we first see him in London. Beatrice falls in love with her protector (she is unaware that he is Hugh), who offers to marry her when he learns of her financial difficulties and in view of his imminent inheritance. She waits for him in the garden, clutching a red flower and smelling it, creating a sensual link between color and fragrance and apparently changing the association of red with Roderick and, by extension, danger. But this is not entirely the case since danger is still present because Roderick's gang of thieves overhear this plan and capture Hugh. It is also the case that a white rose has earlier been suggested as the way to alert Hugh when Beatrice is in danger. Making conclusions about consistency in color symbolism in the film is therefore problematic. This instability around meaning is further demonstrated when in a later twist the thieves send Beatrice a box with a white rose and a threatening message. Such play with color, symbolism and narrative can be related to Eisenstein's observations that interpretations of color must always be related to context which means that meaning will inevitably shift: "The problem is not, nor ever will be, solved by a fixed catalogue of color-symbols, but *the emotional intelligibility and function of color will rise from the natural order of establishing the color imagery of the work, coincidental with the process of shaping the living movement of the whole work*" (Eisenstein [1942] 1968: 120–121). Blackton anticipated this view, clearly exploiting the opportunities offered by color for experimenting with symbolism.

Play with color − particularly red − also occurs in the lead up to the climactic scenes of the Great Fire of London. Beatrice marries the prisoner Bullfinch who awaits his fate in jail. The marriage scene uses close-ups very effectively, as the menacing Bullfinch contemplates his bride. Although separated from him by a door, she can see his face through the bars and vice-versa. Suspense is created as physical contact occurs when he puts the wedding ring on her finger but instead of letting go of her hand he pulls it through the bars towards him. To distract him, the character Stephanie taunts Bullfinch by waving her red cloak, using color to both assist the plot and also to create a visually arresting display as he tries to grab hold of it and releases Beatrice's hand. The color red and fire are used at other key points in the film, as an earlier title, "Playing with Fire" announces, followed by shots of Soloman Eagle (Tom Heselwood), a fanatic who we later see start the Great Fire of London. Indeed, the various threads of the narrative are brought together when the Great Fire breaks out, producing scenes which for many distinguished the film and its color. The flames and light are particularly effective when they appear as dynamic, flickering shades of orange and red, often shown through doorways and windows. **(See Plate 4.)** In this respect, any indication of "fringing" does not matter, since the vitality of the flames and their changing hues are enhanced by the sensation and sight of movement.

The debate on "fringing" was not a new one, dating from the early history of additive color processes when "fixing" color during movement became the most difficult challenge for achieving what was perceived as successful, "natural" color. Judgements of Prizma similarly focussed on whether "fringing" was evident and even though the fire was praised for its dramatic force, the shots of static, brightly-colored objects were considered to be one of the film's best features. Once color became the focus of discussion the standard ways of assessing its merits persisted, as reviewers drew on established terms of discourse.

In the film's publicity much was made of period authenticity, the beauty and colors of the costumes and the extent to which designs from the period were well-researched. Blackton liked to quote from *Conquest*, a popular science magazine which praised *The Glorious Adventure* for "every dress, every piece of tapestry and every color in the gorgeous sets", and how "the reproduction of nature's own colors on the screen has given to the film a resemblance to stereoscopic depth entirely lacking in the old black and white pictures" (Blackton 1921b: 14). Such reportage tended to shift the focus away from questions of narrative to observations about costumes and sets which required the eye to appreciate them as static objects rather than as narrative/plot elements. In view of the problems most processes experienced at the time with "fringing" such commentary made sense, to draw the viewer's attention to an appreciation of color as an enhancement of the presentation of static objects. This required that for some parts of a film principles of continuity were sacrificed to ponderous shots which enticed the eye with the spectacle of color. The ostentatious display of color associated with scenes featuring King Charles, for example, provide opportunities to use relatively static objects to show off color effects. Likewise, the scenes in Whitehall provide scope to demonstrate color contrasts in Prizma, particularly in shots where there is little or no movement, such as the close-ups of grapes, oranges and wine on the banqueting table.

Blackton's daughter recalled that while in London audiences were impressed by Lady Diana Manners' aristocratic connections, her social magnetism held less sway elsewhere. The "restrained" approach to exteriors, sets and performance style went with a narrative which veered from being ponderous to full of suspense. When she observed a young couple watching the film at a Leeds cinema she noted how they responded to the film's various shifts in pace: "They were silently attentive through the early part of the picture, but grew restless as Lady Di and her lover moved ever so politely through a series of mishaps that were to lead them finally to near-cremation in the crypt of St Paul's Cathedral, while all London blazed around them, and the molten metal from the fabulous dome oozed down to form a sizzling, engulfing, lethal lake at their very feet". (Blackton Trimble 1985: 108)

This was a preferable way however to show off a process rather than to draw attention to how color appeared to shift with movement. Indeed, the acting style adopted by Diana Manners was suited to the repression of movement and gesture. While this can be linked to her theatrical affiliations and aristocratic demeanour, it is also indicative of prevailing film performance styles of "restraint" with "passion", which Christine Gledhill has argued typified British cinema of the 1920s (Gledhill 2003: 62–89). When Lady Diana was interviewed by *Picturegoer* during training for her role in *The Glorious Adventure*, she confirmed that this was her favoured method, arguing that: "Repression in one's movements without exaggerated gestures I feel represents the highest plane of screen art." The report went on to note that

> Blackton worked on the vivid personality of Lady Di, and taught her the art of registering the emotions of horror, surprise, and sorrow. Always she was the confident, self-possessed aristocrat. There was no temperament here. She clenched her slender bejewelled hands and mirrored fear in depths of her expressive blue eyes with an assurance which told of her descent from a line of fighting ancestors who for centuries faced the world with courage and self-reliance. (*Picturegoer*, July 1921: 20, quoted in Gledhill 2003: 63)

That this performance style suited color made both the actress and the scenario appropriate for Prizma since it detracted from exaggerated

63

movement and gesture which would have drawn further attention to "fringing".

Blackton's claim to have achieved "stereoscopic values" through color with Prizmacolor in *The Glorious Adventure* revives an area of debate which by then had a long association with color film (Blackton 1921b: 14). Kinemacolor films such as *Pleasure Seekers at Manly, New South Wales, Australia* (1912), for example, featured a diving exhibition which was noted for its "stereoscopic quality" (*Kinematograph Monthly Film Record* Nov 1912: 25). The impression is that color would emphasize planes of depth in much the way that deep-focus photography allows the detail of a shot to be appreciated from the foreground into the background. Joshua Yumibe notes how stencilling color processes, most famously the one developed by Pathé in 1905, created the impression of three-dimensionality, and how the marketing of color often commented on a resulting stereoscopic effect. In some cases this produced "a projective dimensionality that proceeds from the background into the foreground of the image, out toward the viewer" (Yumibe 2007: 168). Color thus "leaps from the screen" as a sensational effect which is similarly evident in *The Glorious Adventure* with shots designed for color spectacle, such as the ship on the horizon with blue sea and red clouds, and even more obtrusively when the flames of the fire are seen through doorways and windows, appearing to come towards the viewer as the fire gets out of control. In this way the apparent shortcomings of the Prizma process unwittingly assisted in making sure that a display of color was necessary, and that apparent "imperfections" such as fringing did not matter in shots which depended on flickering, unstable color in projective scenes which gave the illusion of being "stereoscopic".[3]

As the above analysis has demonstrated, a film showcasing a relatively new process demonstrated a multifarious approach to color that connected with past endeavours and current practices. Presenting a pragmatic but creative response to Prizma's technical deficiencies produced interesting aesthetic results that made the most of what Prizma had to offer. At the same time color was actively deployed in the narrative to both support and play with symbolic meaning. As such the film remains as a fascinating document of color experimentation in the 1920s, a period normally overshadowed by the early development of Technicolor.

Blackton directed Lady Diana Manners again in *The Virgin Queen* (1923), but this was only partly shot in Prizmacolor. Compared to *The Glorious Adventure*, the film was not considered to demonstrate a move forward for Prizma. Interestingly, the Prizma scenes were similar to those considered to be most successful in *The Glorious Adventure*, static shots of food and the drama of flickering flames (*British Journal of Photography*, 2 Feb 1923: 8). Towards the end of 1922 Crespinel went to Italy to shoot carnival sequences in Prizma for *Pagliacci*, a British film of the opera. Blackton returned to the

USA in 1923 and a few more short films were shot in Prizma. Complaints about "fringing" persisted, and the company got into financial difficulty. According to Crespinel, keeping the laboratories in Jersey was a mistake when most film production had gravitated to Hollywood (Crespinel 2000: 64). Kelley started work on a new imbibition process called Kelleycolor and in 1928 the Prizma patents were acquired by Consolidated Film Industries, part of Republic Pictures, and the name was changed to Magnacolor. Crespinel also used the Prizma patents for Cinecolor, a process developed from 1932 and which went on to gain some success after the Second World War (Belton 2000: 344–357). Color continued to be a "glorious adventure" for many in Britain during the 1920s and 1930s. As elsewhere, Britain's color adventure demonstrated a *longue durée* in which experimentation was accompanied by protracted discussion, often masking nationalist discourses and repeating earlier rhetorical positions. Like Blackton and the characters in *The Glorious Adventure*, many got burned, while others persisted in grappling with the aesthetic and technical challenges posed by capturing elusive, yet "glorious" color on screen.

notes

1. Phillips refers to "all the colors", but as a two-color process this would not have been possible with Prizma.
2. It is important to note that a modern copy of an obsolete color process will often only approximate the experience of seeing the original. The viewing copy in the BFI National Archive was printed on modern color stock via an internegative from an original Prizmacolor print, and the result has more contrast than the original would have had.
3. The separation of colors results in an illusion of color planes. Also, in terms of the retina, red colors advance and blue colors recede, providing an illusion of depth.

references

Belton, J. (2000) "Cinecolor", *Film History*, vol. 12, no. 4: 344–357.

Blackton, J. S. (1921a) *British Journal of Photography*, color supplement, 1 July: 28.

Blackton, J. S. (1921b) "A Milestone Passed", *The Motion Picture Studio*, vol. 1, no. 25, 26 Nov: 14.

Blackton, J. S. (1922) "A Future for British Films", *The Motion Picture Studio*, vol. 1, no. 2, 19 Aug: 21.

Blackton Trimble, M. (1985) *J. Stuart Blackton. A Personal Biography by his Daughter*, Metuchen, NJ, and London: Scarecrow Press.

British Journal of Photography (1921) color supplement, 6 May: 18–19.

British Journal of Photography (1921) 5 Aug: 32.

British Journal of Photography (1923) 2 Feb: 8.

Burrows, J. (2003) *Legitimate Cinema: Theatre Stars in Silent British Films, 1908–18*, Exeter: University of Exeter Press.

Cornwell-Clyne, A. (1951) *Color Cinematography,* London: Chapman & Hall, 3rd edition.

Cherchi Usai, P. (2000) *Silent Cinema: An Introduction,* London: British Film Institute.

Crespinel, W. A. (2000) "Pioneer Days in Color Motion Pictures with William T. Crespinel", *Film History,* vol. 12, no. 1: 57–71.

Daily Film Renter and Moving Picture News (1922) "The Progress of Color Kinematography", 28 Jan: 10.

Eisenstein, S. (1942, trans. Jay Leyda, 1968) *The Film Sense,* London: Faber and Faber.

Exhibitors Herald (1922) 15 April: 44.

Gledhill, C. (2003) *Reframing British Cinema, 1918–29: Between Restraint and Passion,* London: British Film Institute.

Illustrated London News (1922) "With a Duke's Daughter as the Leading Lady – *The Glorious Adventure* – The First Natural-Colour Film Play", 21 Jan: 88–89.

Kinematograph Monthly Film Record (1912) Nov: 25.

Low, R. (1971) *The History of the British Film, 1918–29,* London: Allen & Unwin.

Motion Picture Studio (1921) "Tinting Troubles", vol. 1, no. 30, 31 Dec: 15.

Nowotny, R. A. (1983) *The Way of All Flesh Tones: A History of Color Motion Picture Processes, 1895–1929,* New York and London: Garland.

Phillips, H. A. (1923) "Pictures in Natural Colors", *Motion Picture Magazine,* Nov: 95.

Raleigh, C. (1922) "Reminisces of Commercial Color Cinematography – Its Possibilities", *British Journal of Photography,* color supplement, 5 Oct: 37.

The Times (1921) 9 Apr: 6, issue 42690.

Yumibe, J. (2007) "Moving Color: An Aesthetic History of Applied Color Technologies in Silent Cinema", unpublished PhD thesis, University of Chicago.

the color of

prometheus

thomas wilfred's lumia and the

projection of transcendence

s i x

a n d r e w   r o b e r t   j o h n s t o n

> *Our normal waking consciousness, rational consciousness as we*
> *call it, is but one special type of consciousness, whilst all about*
> *it, parted from it by the filmiest of screens, there lie potential*
> *forms of consciousness entirely different.*
>
> (James 1982: 388)

In September 1919 Van Dearing Perrine, Claude Bragdon and Thomas
Wilfred formed a communal artists' society called the Prometheans that
was dedicated to exploring patterns of abstract light as a "medium of emotional expression" (Bragdon 2006: 102). Soon after setting up a laboratory
on the Huntington, Long Island estate of a mutual friend of the group,
William Kirkpatrick Brice, Wilfred was given financial support by Brice so
that he could dedicate all of his time and energy to producing a keyboard
instrument for light projection performances. Wilfred soon dominated
the group, to the point of denying the admission of others who were nominated for membership by Bragdon and Perrine, and precipitated its pre-
mature end through the influence of his clear and singular vision. In his

memoir, Bragdon explains how he and Perrine were rendered as spectators to the speed and technical facility Wilfred displayed in constructing devices that realized the aesthetic ambitions they had earlier conjured. The success of Wilfred's first public performance of one of these devices, which he called a clavilux, on January 10, 1922, at New York's Neighborhood Playhouse, opened up other performance opportunities and indicated that he was free to examine his "fourteen-year-old dream: a silent and independent art of light," which he later called lumia (Wilfred 1947: 250). **(See Plate 5.)**

The allusion to a long-held fantasy that Wilfred includes in his description of lumia is a reference to his precocious childhood studies of color music and the works of prominent color organists and theorists of the eighteenth and nineteenth centuries, such as Father Louis Bertrand Castel, Bainbridge Bishop and Alexander Wallace Rimington. Although fascinated with synaesthesia and the possibility of translating music into light and color, Wilfred rejected these ideas at a young age in 1905, and later summarized their histories to explain how color organs and "the repeated failures of 'color music' demonstrations" obscured the possibility of cultivating the use of light as an independent medium (Wilfred 1947: 250). He says that "lumia may never be played in the manner of music [...] and I see no reason at all for striving toward this goal" (Wilfred 1948: 89). Nonetheless, the devices that Wilfred dismisses greatly influenced his work and he repeatedly positions himself as a figure who realizes what he sees as the obscured aesthetic goal buried in color music. This lost focus is motion, which, when combined with color, has the power to open spectators to new realms of perceptual experience.

The Prometheans were short-lived, but the influence of Bragdon and his ideas of the fourth dimension, along with other mystical and Romantic thinkers, are vital to understanding lumia's aesthetic forms and relationships with other media. Lumia developed out of an aesthetic and philosophical idealism as well as a technological amalgamation of film projectors and color organs. What resulted initially appears as a detour in cinema's history, but the impact and legacy of Wilfred's lumia can be directly tied to abstract animators such as Jordan Belson, Mary Ellen Bute and Oskar Fischinger, as well as numerous kinetic and light artists.[1] Throughout this essay I argue that this enduring, though many times obscured, influence stems from Wilfred's coupling of the color organ tradition with cinema's ability to project movement and color. Wilfred viewed these as the medium's most basic and important elements, but ones that were technologically imperfect at the time. Because of these perceived deficiencies, lumia does not use celluloid filmstrips to create motion through the succession of frames, but instead a number of different techniques and mechanisms, such as rotational discs, filters and moving light filaments. Wilfred argues that this produces a clarity and fluidity of motion that cinema in the 1910s, known for its flicker and unstable celluloid base, could not match. However, his proposed technological improvement was not only developed out of a desire for greater visual fidelity. Lumia emerged out of a framework and idea of cinema, but was also shaped by the legacy of a constellation of aesthetic discourses that were circulating among artists examining and experimenting with abstraction in the early twentieth century.

Wilfred's interest in abstraction developed out of a desire to achieve an aesthetic experience that was mystical in orientation, where viewers could commune with the hidden spiritual force surrounding and inside objects in the world. While the existence and legacy of beliefs in the occult has been recognized in other artistic forms, such as abstract painting and photography, its extensive presence in pre-World War II abstract film has tended to escape attention. In short, the gnostic operation of these works provided meaning to the abstractions in them and functioned as the driving force behind their creation. Though aesthetic pleasure and perceptual reverie were also explored, formal elements such as line, color, motion and luminosity became symbolic in orientation, containing either direct or indirect correspondences with a spiritual realm. Léopold Survage, whose dream of producing colored abstract animations failed to develop because of material constraints, explained that abstractions which lack spiritual character are nothing but "a simple graphic notation" and that formal elements such as color are "at one and the same time, the cosmos, the material world, and the energy-field of our light-sensitive apparatus – the eye" (Survage 1988: 91). But how did one make such connections between spiritual and material realities apparent? What aesthetic practices could avoid the production of what Survage warned of as "confused sensation" at the sight of abstraction and instead project viewers into a state of transcendence?

Wilfred continually wrestled with these questions, as did other artists like Wassily Kandinsky whose responses are the best known and the most influential. In his essays Kandinsky repeatedly describes the cosmic or spiritual reality that lay buried in forms and explains that we constantly perceive this non-material state of things through sensation, which is composed of vibrations of energy. Other writers, like Theosophists Annie Besant and C. W. Leadbeater, turned to particular graphic elements, such as rings of concentric circles or mandalas, and argued that these structures were not only more directly linked to the spiritual world, but that each of them also had a particular symbolic correspondence that viewers could deduce (Besant and Leadbeater 1905). Although Wilfred rarely employed such "sacred geometry" in his lumia, he did study n-dimensional geometric theory and believed that the spiritual realm existed on a fourth-dimensional plane that is normally imperceptible. Through the nineteenth century n-dimensional and especially fourth-dimensional geometry had been a topic of research in mathematics and physics, later growing in the popular imagination around the turn of the century. Though it shed many of its scientific roots, it became increasingly associated with idealist philosophy and a realm of existence beyond three dimensions. This shift prompted an analogous explanation of the existence of dimensions beyond those perceived in Edwin A. Abbott's popular *Flatland: A Romance of Many Dimensions* (1884), which is written from the perspective of a square in the second dimension who briefly visits the third. Although there were divergent theories addressing the aesthetic means necessary to access the fourth dimension, most agreed on its spiritual qualities. As P. D. Ouspensky explains in one of the first descriptions of the fourth dimension, it was perceived as a "sensation of infinity" that could not be rationally understood but only accessed in ecstasy through "the liberation of your mind from its finite consciousness" (Ouspensky 1922: 242). Linda Dalrymple Henderson shows how Ouspensky's writings on the fourth dimension, along with those of Bragdon, Max Weber and Guillaume Apollinaire, couple it with a type of cosmic consciousness that is experienced in moments of ecstatic liberation that usually stem from aesthetic experience or contemplation (Henderson 1986).[2]

Wilfred had been exposed to these ideas through his close friendship with Bragdon and Alfred Stieglitz, whose journal *Camera Work* published Weber's article "The Fourth Dimension from a Plastic Point of View" (1910).[3] While still drawing from Kandinsky and Theosophical writings, Wilfred eventually argued that direct symbolic correspondences with the cosmic realm were unreliable and that it was nearly impossible to access this sphere through two-dimensional compositions. Only through a coordination of movement, color and form could the hidden spirit of matter be revealed while simultaneously having the power to project viewers into a cosmic dimension. Lumia were not simply projections of how the cosmic realm might seem, but were visualizations of forces or intensities that serve as the basis for sensations in and around the body. Wilfred believed that a projection of the quintessence of experience could lead to something beyond it. He argued that his abstractions served as gateways of sorts, perceptual phenomena that began in one world, but launched spectators into another. His attraction to cinema developed out of its ability to put images and color in motion and thus create a magical aesthetic experience where perceptual registers were stretched or even transcended. This generated a technological fanaticism in Wilfred who wished to better its aesthetic and mechanical articulations by borrowing from a variety of sources in the media landscape of the 1920s and 1930s. The clavilux emerges out of elements taken not only of film, but color organs and television as well.

While developing the clavilux, Wilfred initially drew from the color organ tradition he was familiar with, as well as the patents of other artists like Mary Hollock Greenewalt. However, he quickly began to emphasize projected light's immersive qualities and its ability to show continual metamorphoses of color. These were aspects that had been neglected by

previous color organists like Rimington, whose strict color-music correspondences produced, according to Wilfred, "no form, only restless flicker,
hue after hue, one for each musical note sounded" (Wilfred 1947: 249).
For Wilfred, such problems exemplify Johann Wolfgang von Goethe's
discussion of how color and music are related to one another in a "higher
formula," through the analogy of two rivers that have one mountain as a
source, but that then "pursue their way under totally different conditions
in two totally different regions" (Goethe 1970: 299). In this sense, color
and music act "in wholly different provinces, in different modes, on different elementary mediums, for different senses" (ibid.). Wilfred wrote this
passage from Goethe down in a notebook along with other theories of
color as he tried to understand the aesthetic effects of light. While Wilfred
believed that color could be projected rhythmically in a durational
form like music, he suggested that the visual rhythm of the moving
forms of his lumia dictated how they were thematically characterized
more than the selection of colors used. In contrast to some Romantic theorists who believed that states of being are associated with certain colors,
Wilfred argued for a more intuitive and dynamic model that took into
account form and motion. Combinations of these elements could produce
certain moods, but with so many variables a strict correspondence was difficult to deduce.

Engineering such an aesthetic that balanced all these features required
extensive effort and was worked out by Wilfred through a process of trial
and error. He produced eight different clavilux for public lumia performances in addition to several smaller home units called Clavilux, Jr., as
well as internally programmed machines for mural-sized compositions.
All the instruments operate through the same basic principles and employ
high wattage light bulbs, many of whose filaments were custom designed
to produce different projected shapes. These could then be rotated within
the clavilux to create abstract patterns in addition to the moving mirrors
and lenses that reflected and passed light through the machine. Color
gels and filters, as well as three-dimensional form elements and rolls of
modifiers, added more options for the manipulation of shapes in lumia
compositions. As Wilfred progressed from his original Model A to Model
H, the compositional possibilities of each clavilux also expanded, as did the
large keyboards that controlled all these features with sliding keys assigned
to individual elements. (**See Figure 6.1.**) The pacing of a composition's
performance was determined by the operator who worked from a nota-
tional system that Wilfred developed for guiding the texture, shape and
color of a form within different cycles of motion.

Importantly, the abstractions are always moving and changing across
time. It is the shape and fluidity that this modulation takes rather than
its speed that Wilfred is most interested in. As Sheldon Cheney describes
in 1924, time in lumia grows evasive as metamorphoses and colors develop

Figure 6.1
Photograph of the internals of Clavilux Model C (Thomas Wilfred Papers, Manuscripts and Archives, Yale University Library).

distinctive qualities and themes to produce "that feeling of detachment, of ecstasy, which is a response only to the most solemn religious or aesthetic experience" (Cheney 1966: 180). Cheney recounts what can be best described as a sublime experience, which, as Henderson points out, was synonymous with the fourth dimension in the early twentieth century through their shared interest in an experience of infinity (Henderson 1986: 221). Wilfred, however, intended to reproduce the pleasure of the sublime without its terror. The fluid transformation of color was key to this project in contrast to the assaultive power he saw in static color. In a lecture at the Art Institute of Light in New York that Wilfred founded, he explains that

> Form and motion are the two most important factors and
> they determine to a great extent the effect a given color
> has on us. Red, for instance, the color of fire and blood is
> basically exciting if it flashes before the vision in flamelike
> waves [...] But if we stop all motion and show a large even
> area of plain red the effect is provocation and irritation and

the subconscious reason is: Flames always flicker, rise and
fall, this red does not move, it is unusual. (Wilfred n.d.a)

The influence of Bragdon in this statement is clearly apparent, especially
his conceptualization of how colored light takes on a paradoxical immaterial body in the articulation of four-dimensional space, which can be sensed
but not through the apprehension of a static object in space and only in
co-ordination with imaginative faculties (Bragdon 1918). In an effort to
create an environment for this activity Wilfred painstakingly manipulated
his performance venues, covering windows with cloth and painting walls
black so that the phenomenal world would seem to melt away in the absolute darkness before lumia performances, representing "a transition [...]
the dark before the dawn" (Wilfred 1948: 90). Wilfred also explained how
the new intervening light can transfix materialized vision into believing
that it witnesses "a large window opening on infinity [...] a radiant drama
in deep space" (Wilfred 1947: 252) to enact a breakthrough of sensual or
physical vision into imaginative seeing, a movement from material embodiment to transcendent illumination that also produces "a balance between
the human entity and the great common denominator, the universal
rhythmic flow" (Wilfred 1948: 90). (**See Figure 6.2.**)

Wilfred's use of fire as a metaphor for describing his lumia in the above
passage was not original. In 1922 Stark Young used this image as a way to
characterize lumia as an aesthetic that mechanically replicates the sensual
reverie natural abstract forms produce. Quoting Coleridge on the wonder
of science, Young emphasizes the perceptual effects of lumia and its shared
spectacular logic with fire (Young 1922: 20–21). Sergei Eisenstein more fully
explains this attraction of fire and also identifies its affinities with animation. Through their shared variability of form in time, fire and animation
show "an image of coming into being, revealed in a process," an aesthetic
whose constant changes perceptually grip and fascinate viewers (Eisenstein
1988: 47). Wilfred recognized these affinities, working not only from cinematic technology to develop his lumia, but also the aesthetics of the projected film image and especially abstract animation. He kept articles and
advertisements on abstract animation and was particularly interested in
Walter Ruttmann's work as well as John and James Whitney's *Five Film
Exercises* (1943–44). In a personal volume that contained press articles on his
lumia, one of the rare pieces not about Wilfred is from *Shadowland* and
explains how Ruttmann uses moving color to produce transcendent forms
that function like a visual music. The influence of avant-garde animations
from the 1920s like Ruttmann's is clear in much of Wilfred's aesthetic,
especially the inclusion of plastic rolls of modifiers that project different
abstract shapes in succession and that look like the scroll paintings
that artists like Hans Richter and Viking Eggeling created. But for Wilfred,
the key distinction between film and lumia lay in the question of how a

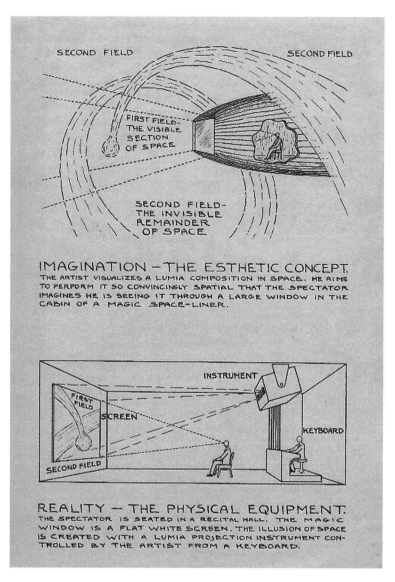

Figure 6.2
Wilfred's depiction of the ideal spectator's engagement with lumia (Thomas
Wilfred Papers, Manuscripts and Archives, Yale University Library).

continuity of motion was generated on their respective screens. Much of
the projection equipment itself was the same; Wilfred even worked from a
patent of D. W. Griffith's for a film projector with color effects when designing one of his clavilux (Griffith 1920). But Wilfred argued that lumia presented an absolute continuity of motion which could be manipulated
without creating any flicker that would otherwise call attention to the

apparatus through which the spectacle was generated, and thus ruin the intended transcendence of sensation. Though speed was not proscribed in lumia, the freedom to create an "even flow of motion at *any* velocity" distinguishes lumia for Wilfred as a superior form to its closely related medium, film, since 24 frames per second was simply "not nearly fast enough" (Blake and Wilfred 1948: 266, 272).

While Wilfred had evaluated lumia's relationship with film when constructing some of the first clavilux machines, this issue became publicly debated in a 1948 issue of *The Journal of Aesthetics and Art Criticism* when a mathematician and fan of Wilfred's lumia, Edwin Blake, wrote to the editor of the journal questioning why Wilfred did not produce abstract films that play with color, form and rhythm in the same way a lumia does, but that could also create a permanent record suited to wider circulation and exhibition. Wilfred's response reveals that he is less dogmatic about recording and distributing lumia since he began such a practice in 1930 through colored discs for his Clavilux, Jr. and lumia installations, but is more attendant to the phenomenological distinctions generated through different projection apparatuses (Blake and Wilfred 1948).

This is evident in his work with television in the late 1930s. NBC and CBS contacted Wilfred with, as Gilbert Seldes of CBS says in a 1939 letter to him, hopes of finding a way to directly transmit lumia to television rather than simply recording the compositions for possible use between features (Seldes 1939). Wilfred stayed true to his prior agreement with NBC and turned this offer down. In 1938 Wilfred had begun construction of a clavilux made especially for television, which he saw as *the* future exhibition venue for lumia, citing its scanning technology as more suited to representing motion than film. His device was completed and used for a 1939 broadcast, but this one-time venture was unfortunately not repeated, since the NBC executive Clarence Farrier failed to hold up his end of the contract. Farrier not only forgot to contact Wilfred about future work with the studio, but also forgot to pay him for that first exhibition. When Farrier was fired in 1941 NBC pursued other interests and Wilfred's new dream of reaching a more mass audience ended. He was not too disappointed, since this experiment proved that motion was not rendered as properly as he had hoped and the light of lumia was distorted. Most importantly, as he states in his book-length manuscript on lumia, early television did not have color (Wilfred n.d.a).

Wilfred nonetheless believed that television would eventually be technologically capable of at least adequately presenting lumia and he desired a larger audience than he was garnering through public exhibitions at various venues, including film theaters. The Clavilux, Jr. was one attempt to bring his aesthetic a larger mass appeal, which, based on the articles and research he gathered, was modeled off technology that could project different patterns of colored light based on the interpretation of sound waves, specifically

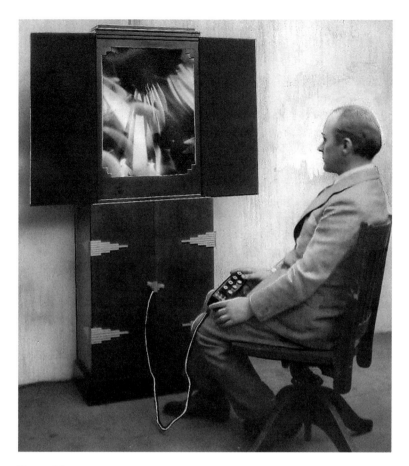

Figure 6.3
Wilfred with a Clavilux, Jr. (Thomas Wilfred Papers, Manuscripts and Archives, Yale University Library).

the Luxatone first demonstrated in 1916 and the Telecolor from 1931. Wilfred's Clavilux, Jr. was of a similar size to these machines and was intended for the home market, with models that allowed for input through a remote control, similar in orientation to a regular clavilux. (**See Figure 6.3.**) Other Clavilux, Jr. models had automated projection technology that read data from recorded compositions on light discs. After World War II, Wilfred also began accepting commissions to do mural-sized installations of programmed lumia, constructing at one point a clavilux for the lobby of Clairol's New York business offices. Regardless of the venue or type of mechanism, technology for Wilfred served as a means of achieving mystical illuminations in moments of ecstasy. The fluid rhythms of color in lumia were not an end unto themselves, but were a play with sensation that did not translate different stimuli across perceptual registers, but rather went beyond perception, beyond the body, out into an infinite fourth dimension.

notes

1. Upon seeing a Wilfred clavilux and lumia projection in the 1950s, Jordan Belson explains that he dramatically changed his aesthetic and technological practices of animation and continued to distance himself from his earlier works throughout his career (Moritz 1995, 2001). Mary Ellen Bute knew Wilfred in the late 1920s while an undergraduate at Yale University. She was interested in both stage lighting and colored music and assisted Wilfred when he installed a clavilux at St. Mark's-in-the-Bouwerie (Bute 1995; Starr 1988). Oskar Fischinger also developed a colored light projection apparatus akin to the clavilux called the lumigraph, which produced a similar aesthetic effect as well (Brougher 2005: 89; Moritz 2004: 137–138).
2. Richard Maurice Bucke popularized the term "cosmic consciousness" (1901) in his 1901 book, *Cosmic Consciousness: A Study in the Evolution of the Human Mind*, a work Wilfred was very familiar with and drew from for his writings on lumia.
3. Wilfred was also introduced to Henri Bergson's writings through Bragdon and Stieglitz in the late 1910s. Bragdon's ideas of the fourth dimension as being accessed through a form of intuition were greatly influenced by Bergson and Alfred Stieglitz's *Camera Work* which published a translated excerpt of *Creative Evolution* (Bergson 1907) about aesthetic intuition in relation to forms of perception in its October 1911 edition. According to his papers, Wilfred had carefully read *Creative Evolution*. I trace the influence of Bergson on Wilfred, as well as specific texts on the fourth dimension by Bragdon and Max Weber, at length in my dissertation (Johnston 2011: 33–77).

references

Abbott, E. A. (1884) *Flatland: A Romance of Many Dimensions*, London: Seeley & Co.

Bergson, H. (1907/1988) *Creative Evolution*, trans. Arthur Mitchell, Mineola, NY: Dover.

Bergson, H. (1911) "An Extract from Bergson", *Camera Work*, 36: 20–21.

Besant, A. and C. W. Leadbeater (1905) *Thought-Forms*, London and Benares: The Theosophical Publishing Society.

Blake, E. M. and T. Wilfred (1948) "Letters Pro and Con", *The Journal of Aesthetics and Art Criticism*, 6.3: 265–276.

Bragdon, C. (1918) *Architecture and Democracy*, New York: Knopf.

Bragdon, C. (2006) *More Lives Than One*, New York: Cosimo.

Brougher, K. (2005) "Visual-Music Culture", in K. Brougher, J. Strick, A.Wiseman, J. Zilczer (eds), *Visual Music: Synaesthesia in Art and Music since 1900*, London: Thames and Hudson: 88–179.

Bucke, R. M. (1901) *Cosmic Consciousness: A Study in the Evolution of the Human Mind*, Philadelphia: Innes & Sons.

Bute, M. E. (1995) "Statement I", *Articulated Light: The Emergence of Abstract Film in America*, Harvard Film Archive & Anthology Film Archive: 8.

Cheney, S. (1966) *A Primer of Modern Art*, New York: Liveright.

Eisenstein, S. (1988) *Eisenstein on Disney*, ed. J. Leyda, trans. A. Upchurch, London: Methuen.

Goethe, J. W. (1970) *Theory of Colors*, trans. C. L. Eastlake, Cambridge, MA: MIT Press.

Griffith, D. W. (1920) *Method and Apparatus for Projecting Moving and other Pictures with Color Effects*, U.S. Pat. 1,334,853.

Henderson, L. D. (1986) "Mysticism, Romanticism, and the Fourth Dimension", in M. Tuchman (ed.), *The Spiritual in Art: Abstract Painting, 1890–1985*, New York: Abbeville: 219–237.

James, W. (1982) *The Varieties of Religious Experience: A Study in Human Nature*, ed. M. E. Marty, New York: Penguin.

Johnston, A. R. (2011) *Pulses of Abstraction: Episodes from a History of Animation*, Ph.D. University of Chicago.

Moritz, W. (1995) "Jordan Belson", *Articulated Light: The Emergence of Abstract Film in America*, Harvard Film Archive & Anthology Film Archive: 12.

Moritz, W. (2001) "Jordan Belson", *KINETICA 3 Catalog*, Los Angeles: iota Center: 20.

Moritz, W. (2004) *Optical Poetry: The Life and Work of Oskar Fischinger*, Bloomington, IN: Indiana University Press.

Ouspensky, P. D. (1922) *Tertium Organum, the Third Canon of Thought: A Key to the Enigmas of the World*, trans. N. Bessaraboff and C. Bragdon, New York: Knopf.

Seldes, G. (1939) "Letter to Thomas Wilfred", Thomas Wilfred Papers, Manuscripts and Archives, Yale University.

Starr, C. (1988) "Mary Ellen Bute", in R. Russett and C. Starr (eds), *Experimental Animation: Origins of a New Art*, New York: De Capo: 102–104.

Survage, L. (1988) "Colored Rhythm", in R. Abel (ed.), *Film Theory and Criticism: A History/Anthology, Volume 1: 1907–1929*, Princeton, NJ: Princeton University Press: 90–92.

Weber, M. (1910) "The Fourth Dimension from a Plastic Point of View", *Camera Work*, 31: 25.

Wilfred, T. (n.d.a) "First Lecture", Thomas Wilfred Papers, Manuscripts and Archives, Yale University.

Wilfred, T. (n.d.b) "Lumia, the Art of Light", Thomas Wilfred Papers, Manuscripts and Archives, Yale University.

Wilfred, T. (1947) "Light and the Artist", *The Journal of Aesthetics & Art Criticism*, 5.4: 247–255.

Wilfred, T. (1948) "Composing in the Art of Lumia", *The Journal of Aesthetics & Art Criticism*, 7.2: 79–93.

Young, S. (1922) "The Color Organ", *Theatre Arts Magazine*, 6.1: 20–32.

theory

part two

where do colors

go at night?

t o m   g u n n i n g

suppression of color?

> [A]nd there she let make herself a nun, and ware white
> clothes and black. (Sir Thomas Malory, *Morte D'arthur*)

In spite of recent works of admirable scholarship, color has not been systematically pursued in film studies. One might even claim color in film
has been suppressed through not being readily available as material arti-
fact, or fully defined as a historiographic issue. This chapter raises two
issues that deal with the elusive and fragile nature of film color: problems
in the preservation of film color from the silent era; and an aesthetic consideration of the absence of color, both blackness and black-and-white,
during the sound era.

Two forms of film color existed during the silent era: color generated
through photographic processes (sometimes called natural color), and color
applied to film directly as pigment (Cherchi Usai 2000; Hanssen 2006; Yumibe
2007). Early photographic color was *additive*, projected and photographed

through color filters using black-and-white film, such as Kinemacolor and Gaumont's Chronochrome. These color processes remained limited in scope due to expense and difficulty in maintaining consistency, although results were sometimes impressive. From the second decade of the twentieth century on, experiments in photographic *subtractive* processes appeared that generated positive prints dyed with a range of hues that could be projected without filters, but these remained very rare during the silent era. The major form of color in silent cinema was *applied color*, colors not achieved by photographic processes, but applied to the positive print. In the most common process, *tinting*, a black-and-white positive print was immersed in a translucent dye. Thus the lighter areas of the image were colored, while the darker, and especially the entirely black areas, remained unchanged. A tinted image could be described as black and red (or black and green, or blue, or yellow, etc.). Toning, less frequent but still common, involved a process of printing and processing in which the actual chemicals that created the range of grays and blacks in the image were colored. Thus instead of a black-and-white image toning produced a blue and white one (or orange and white, red and white, green and white, etc.). In the era of shorter films some filmmakers colored areas of the image with a variety of colors, either by hand or with the aid of stencils, often with a realistic effect such as green trees, blue water, red flames, golden armor, or blue dresses. Tinting or toning were common practices from the feature era, appearing in most films until at least the mid-1920s.

However, color prints from the silent era were rarely screened until recently, leading to the distorted view that color film emerged gradually during the sound era awaiting the technical perfection and industry adoption of color photography. This was mainly due to archival policy. Until a few decades ago, color film stock was vulnerable to decay and deterioration and less suitable as an archival preservation medium than more stable black-and-white stocks. Applied color appears only on positive projection prints, not on negatives, and not on all prints of a film. Silent films were primarily printed on nitrate stock, whose chemical instability demanded their transfer to more recent stocks for preservation. Should an archivist copy a colored nitrate print onto color stock in order to preserve its tints, knowing that the color stock would itself eventually fade, or should she transfer it onto more stable black-and-white stock? Official policy of film archives until recently recommended duplicating nitrate prints onto black-and-white stock, an entirely defensible decision given the necessary trade-off that all preservation involves.

Certain archives screened nitrate prints with original tints publicly. I remember the excitement when MoMA would screen their tinted prints of *Intolerance* (D. W. Griffiths, 1916) or *Broken Blossoms* (D. W. Griffiths, 1919). Scholars realized that color, especially tinting, formed part of the silent film aesthetic. But that color appeared in most silent films was not widely realized until the 1980s, when archivists' attitudes towards color changed, partly due to more stable color stocks. The decision not to preserve silent films in color came from practical preservation concerns, but it also reflected an attitude towards color that has cultural and aesthetic roots. Tints were considered secondary to the photographic aspects of the film. Color remained a supplement. Film scholars often viewed color as an add-on rather than an essential aspect: tints were applied after the production and directors may have had little or nothing to do with the process, instead leaving them in the hands of technicians. Some critics claimed that tinting was vulgar and obscured photographic qualities, a claim sometimes made by critics in the silent era as well. This viewpoint reflects a strain of chromophobia that runs through Western culture, often directed towards popular arts with their loud carnival colors. Philosophers held that color was not a primary, but, according to Descartes, a secondary accidental quality; certain forms of Puritanism claimed color was a sign of vanity and a cause of distraction; while some schools of painting suggested that color offered only a minor aesthetic quality compared to drawing which outlines essential forms (Batchelor 2000).

Awareness of color in silent film has come full circle with a new fascination in color processes and the effects (and affects) of color in cinema generally. But problems from the preservation side remain. Archivist Giovanna Fossati surveyed color prints made from nitrate originals in the collection of the Nederlands Filmmuseum (Fossati 2009: 83–89). Fossati found colors rarely strictly corresponded. The reasons were multiple. Photographic duplicates from applied color original prints involve a process of translation and unintended transformation. As anyone who has studied photographs of paintings knows, color photography is always selective and particularly responds differently to colors placed in close juxtaposition. But even if the photograph were strictly accurate in the reproduction of the original, neither color system is totally stable. The applied dyes in silent film are always in a process of fading or transforming. (**See Plate 6.**) Even an accurate photograph will only capture one moment in this process. Color in film remains transitory, subject not only to changes wrought by time, but changes as it migrates through different film stocks and modes of processing. Attempts to preserve colors produced by different processes means those changes can be immense. Video not only offers new tools for the control of color, with its millions of differentiated colors, but also new problems in reproducing them yielding the old joke about the meaning of the initials NTSC – the video standard set in the US by the National Television System Committee – that they actually indicate "never the same color," still applies (Fossati 2009: 45–49).

All of these aspects indicate the headache color presents to archivists and historians of film stylistics. While one inevitably regrets the loss of aspects of an artwork, some archivists have decided to acknowledge and even embrace the inevitable ephemerality of our medium. Paolo Cherchi Usai in his work as archivist, theorist and filmmaker has embraced this inevitable death of cinema and the role historians and filmmakers play in constructing requiems willing to acknowledge the mortality of film works (Cherchi Usai 2001). Such filmmakers include Pieter Delpeut in *Lyrical Nitrate* (1991) or Bill Morrison's *Decasia* (2002), and the filmmakers who have used colors obtained by unconventional chemical processes, such as David Gatten in *What the Water Said* (1998–2007) and Peggy Ahwesh in *The Color of Love* (1994).[1] Color belongs to the material side of film. While it may be stored as digital information, its dynamic unstable chemical nature balances the serendipity of alchemical transformation with the inevitability of decay. This inherently unfixed nature of color combines with its unique perceptual and emotional effects to create a power foreign to either Cartesian certitude or the Platonic ideal eternity.

From the perspective of archiving and preservation, film color remains uniquely vulnerable and its relative absence from earlier accounts of silent film history may derive less from suspicion or ideological suppression than from the nature of color itself, elusive and ungraspable, as eager to appear to us as to flee from us. But what I am calling the suppression of color refers also to our incomplete understanding of another aspect of the history of color in silent cinema: less the prevalence of color during most of the silent era, now widely acknowledged, but the near total disappearance of applied color by the 1930s, which has rarely been remarked upon – even though everyone recognises it! The true mystery of color in film may lie in the emergence of black-and-white in the 1930s through the 1950s as the standard of cinema. Because the preservation of applied color in silent prints remains spotty, the nature of this transformation remains unclear. Was it abrupt, and did it basically coincide, as has often been supposed, with the coming of sound or did it occur gradually, as some preliminary evidence seems to indicate, with a reduction in colored prints during the late 1920s? It has often been claimed that the disappearance of tinting had a technological basis since the dyeing process interfered with the soundtrack. While this sounds plausible, given that some early sound films were tinted, it needs to be questioned and subjected to further investigation. Could the addition of a soundtrack offer a different sort of explanation, more aesthetic and stylistic, as synchronized sound and dialogue clashed with, or somehow rendered redundant, the addition of color? For example, it is useful to recall that early talkies often eliminated the continuous musical accompaniment that had defined silent film, or restricted it to opening and closing credits. It is most likely that streamlining the production of projection prints with sound played a major role, since applied color processes added a complicated stage in the preparation of prints. But why did the aesthetic addition of color at this point seem no longer worth the effort? Histories of laboratory and print preparation may well hold the answer to our question, although aesthetic effects must also have been a consideration. Whatever the explanation may be, this literal suppression of color in the 1930s or late 1920s remains a stylistic change that has basically been taken for granted.

How was black-and-white film viewed during the silent era? Was it a stylistic alternative to color, a seemingly random variation, or was it rarely seen at all? Undoubtedly this question needs to be asked in terms of specific periods (e.g. pre-1907; 1908–1913; 1914; 1919; 1920–1924; 1924–1929); for different national cinemas; and for genres (was tinting and coloring more common in dramas than in slapstick, in fiction than in newsreels?). In how many films did tinting appear only in a few sequences and what sort of scenes were these (to what extent was tinting limited to blue night scenes, red fires, or did it operate as stylistic markers within otherwise black-and-white films)? The *lack* of tinting was remarked upon in the admittedly limited showings of the Expressionist film *Von Morgens bis Mitternacht*, Karl Heinz Martin's 1920 adaptation of George Kaiser's expressionist play. Recent restorations of classic Weimar films reveal the expressive possibilities of tinting in such films as *The Cabinet of Doctor Caligari* (Robert Wiene, 1919), *Nosferatu* (F. W. Murnau, 1922) and *Orlacs Hande* (Robert Weine, 1924).[2] But if *Von Morgens bis Mitternacht* avoided tints, was this for expressive motives? Did stark black-and-white make the film seem closer to the severe woodcuts of the early German Expressionist group of artists, Die Brücke? (**See Figure** 7.1.)

Issues of archival restoration of color also raise stylistic considerations. However, when a modern photographic color print is made of prints

Figure 7.1
The black-and-white of the German film *From Morning to Midnight* evoked German Expressionist woodcuts.

originally using these processes, these distinctions tend to blur. The blacks of a tinted print lose their integrity, while the whites in a toned print tend to merge with the dominant color. To address this problem The Royale Cinémathèque of Belgium introduced an alternative called the Desmet process (Fossati 2009: 89–90). Instead of simply photographing the original colored print onto color stock, a black-and-white print is flashed into color in order to preserve the original dark blacks, preserving the original tonal contrast.

the color that is not one

> I am the darkness that drinks the light,
> That through its unquenchable thirst for light gives birth
> to all life.
> I am the dark star. (Par Lagerkvist 1975: 159)

Is black a color? I recall my confusion as a child when my older sister told me that neither black nor white were colors, information she had gleaned from her science classes. Didn't my box of 64 Crayola crayons, the embodiment of color and its possibilities, include both black-and-white, and weren't they among my favorite colors to draw with? But my sister pronounced with authority that white was actually the mixture of all colors, while black was the absence of any color. A paradox threatened my visual imagination: imagining a composite of all my crayons yielded a thick mass of blackness rather than white, which seemed to merge with the blank page. Eventually this confusion helped me understand the difference between subtractive color that applies to pigments as opposed to the additive colors of light. Each colored pigment subtracts the other hues; thus the combination of all subtractions yields black, while the union of all hues of light adds each wavelength and returns to the original white light.

As the conflict over the nature of the spectrum between Goethe and Newton demonstrates, rival color systems involve different frameworks of reference and associations: embodied color versus color as the analysis of light (Gage 1999; Kemp 1990). Goethe's investigations explored color as a subjective phenomenon, as well as the practical employment of color in crafts, from dyeing to metallurgy, and in natural phenomena, observing minutely color in the plumage of birds, the sap of plants and the scales of fish and insects (Goethe 1970). Goethe's thick descriptions of colored halos seen through the frosted window of a carriage or the mists of mountaintops contrast sharply with the geometrical diagrams of vectors of light rays and the angles of their refraction, or the mathematical tables that characterize the *Opticks* of Newton (Newton 2003). The gulf between Goethe and Newton does not lie simply in the contrast between material colors of pigments and the quantification of the spectrum produced by a prism, but in the aims of their respective systems. The limits of Goethe's speculations come from his inconsistent grasp of the methods of science and observation that had been evolving since Newton. Goethe wished to maintain a continuity between the methods of science and the realms of experience and culture, to place scientific observation under the guidance of natural curiosity and absorption, to discover less an invisible logic than a tangible and visible immersion in phenomenon. Goethe's investigations of color aspired to a phenomenology of experience that he could not theorize.

Their respective attitudes towards black reflect their purposes and assumptions. For Newton, black cannot be a color, since it does not appear in the analysis of the spectrum. (**See Figure 7.2.**) Black can only appear as shadow, the absence of light. For Goethe, black is the visible form of darkness, the absence of light, but also the generative source of color. Goethe's theory of color proceeds in the tradition of Aristotle from a primal experience of light and shade with the range of color actually expressing the growing darkness, from yellow, the closest to pure white light, to dark blue, the closest to black and darkness, with the red he called *pupur* and the noblest of all colors balancing the middle as the epitome of color and its power. Goethe proposed less a mathematically derived spectrum, than a mythology that binds everyday and cultural experience with the wonder of color in embodied forms and as the diurnal mystery of light and dark – a myth steeped in the polarity that Goethe believed ruled nature.

Cinema color in its subtractive forms, which was dominant during the last decades of the twentieth century, weds color as a dye on film with

Figure 7.2
Newton shows the spectrum produced by a prism to his daughters.

projected light as medium. Yet, film more frequently evokes an art of shadows than the projection of colors – one reason the restoration of photographic blacks by the Desmet process held stylistic importance. Black *is* a color in cinema: it is the color of darkness, of night, of shadow, of nothingness or invisibility. In cinema, the realm of color borders the regime of black-and-white – the alternatives of dazzlement and eclipse. White recalls (by conveying directly) the light of the projector, potentially sweeping the screen clear of images; black withholds both light and color and returns us to the darkness of the theater, the condition of film projection.

From the perspective of film aesthetics and stylistics (and possibly technology, archiving and even film theory), it seems a foolish consistency to exclude black or white from our consideration of color. Black as a hue creates the forms of objects that play important roles in the color systems of films, from the Batman's costume in *The Dark Knight* (Christopher Nolan, 2008) to the abstract figures in Brakhage's *Black Ice* (1994). In the stylistic system of individual films, black interacts with other colors. It marshals powerful cultural connotations (death, evil, mystery, nothingness), but all colors carry such baggage to some degree. Black, however, can swallow or overwhelm other colors in darkness, asserting control over visibility itself. Black's ability to obscure or eclipse the essential projected light of cinema allows intense thematic deployment – as in the gradual domination of the monks' black cloaks in the color sequence of *Ivan the Terrible II* (1944).[3] Although Eisenstein produced major works of color theory, his opportunity to work with color film remained limited. In spite of the crucial role applied color plays in his silent films, such as a tinted red flag marking the climax in *Battleship Potemkin* (1925), which has been restored in some recent prints, it is unclear if any tinted version of the cream separator sequence from *The Old and New* (1929) survives, in his "non-color" films Eisenstein used black-and-white to evoke both the condition of visibility and invisibility, as in the engulfing white ice and swallowing dark water that ends the battle in *Alexander Nevsky* (1938).

If black functions as a color within a color film, can it play the same role in a black-and-white film, or does it simply fade into the monochromatic gamut which composes the world of the film? *Nevsky* shows black in a monochromatic film overwhelming the image, taking on a dramatic role. Here we encounter another paradox. Although black frequently defines an object, such as the monks' black cloaks in *Ivan*, it can, however, also convey the insubstantial: in the shadow cast by unseen threat; the darkness that looms through an opened door; the undefined space of night. Black in film renders darkness visible, the non-shape of nothingness. Today, as black-and-white film no longer forms the default mode of cinema, we must speculate on its origins, and recognize its unique formal properties. What effects did this world composed of black-and-white images carry and how does it differ from the color cinema that eventually overwhelmed it?

Although black-and-white formed a pair in a number of contexts through cultural history, including the nun's habit assumed by Queen Guinevere in my opening quote, historian of color Michel Pastoreau claims an exclusively black-and-white-world first emerged with the printed book. "Ink became the black product *par excellence*" (Pastoreau 2009: 115). Black ink printed on white paper differed from the ink of earlier handwritten manuscripts which remained gray or brown, while parchment rarely achieved pure white; the printed book offered a self-contained world, composed of two polar, contrasting tones. Printing spawned illustrations, also in black-and-white, and created a new realm of images bereft of color.

For centuries black-and-white images evoked the printed book with its connotation of a self-contained realm. As the art of etching and photography developed, black-and-white images spawned a range of tones and values mediating between the extremes, without abolishing their polarity. The cinema may have inaugurated an ongoing struggle between moving images and the printed word. But films, perhaps defensively, have also asserted an affinity with the book and printed word, and not only through adaptation. Printed words punctuate films, from the inter-titles of silent cinema to the images of books that often open movies. With the coming of sound, the recurring printed words of intertitles disappeared, a transformation whose visual effect needs investigation. Was the triumph of black-and-white in the sound era partly due to the cultural bond it asserted with the world of the book? (**See Figure 7.3.**) While some animators, such as Disney, enthusiastically adopted color processes, other cartoons displayed cinema's affinity to black-and-white drawings, from Windsor McCay's *Little Nemo* through to the Fleischer brothers, often evoking the materiality of black ink and white paper to create a self-contained and even self-generating world.

In films black asserts its power among colors, not simply as their negation, but in the Goethean tradition, as their potential. A figure for darkness that evokes both the infinity of old night and the intimacy of surrounding theater space, black evokes the origin of color through its polar relation to the white of the illuminated screen. The blank and the dark screen alternate as images of nothingness and everything. In his "Lecture," Hollis Frampton described the screen, the material support on which all films are projected:

> Our white rectangle is not "nothing at all." In fact it is, in the end, all we have. This is one of the limits of the art of film. So if we want to see what we call *more*, which is actually *less*, we must devise ways of subtracting, of removing, one thing and another, more or less, from our white rectangle. (Frampton 2009: 108)

Color, as the term for the dominant mode of color reproduction indicates, offers one such subtraction. Quoting Frampton: "A red film would

Figure 7.3
Did the black-and-white of the sound era evoke the print medium? *Citizen Kane* (Orson Welles, 1941).

subtract green and blue from the white light of our rectangle" (Frampton 2009: 108). But total darkness, such as a hand blocking the lens, not only removes the white light, but the rectangle itself. It gives us nothingness. Or it gives us total possibility.

An extraordinary film by Patrick O'Neil, *Coreopsis* (1998) displays black as, not simply the negation, but the matrix, of all colors. O'Neil, one of the great masters of optical printing and special visual effects within the commercial industry, has made the luxurious sensuality of such devices available to the avant garde, allowing us to witness what can be done to transform vision with cutting edge technology and 35 mm film in such films as *The Decay of Fiction* (2003) and *Water and Power* (1989). In *Coreopsis* he combined optical printing with the hand-wrought tradition of inscribing directly on film. He described his process to me in an email:

> The film was made by scratching through the emulsion of exposed 35mm leader such as appears on the head and tail of daily rolls of work print. This was reproduced in the optical printer on camera negative. The recursive nature of the imagery is obtained by progressive repetition (for instance, shooting 5 frames, rewinding the projector 4,

shooting 5, rewinding 4, and so on, so that each repetition is 1 frame ahead of the last and a new frame appears). (O'Neil 2009)

The roll of film that O'Neil worked on was black, but as he scratched at its surface with sharp etching tools, color appears, especially a striking yellow which recalls the bright hue of the flower for which the film is named. O'Neil had discovered some coreopsis seeds in an envelope labeled "Helen's Coreopsis 1935" while going through his mother's effects after her death. He planted them and found that one of them actually bloomed, producing the vivid yellow daisy-like flower. The title evokes flowers blossoming from dark earth. Coreopsis, which means "resembling a bed bug" in reference to the plant's fruit, carries the term *opsis*, which means appearance, but more fundamentally sight itself, or, visual appearance. In Aristotle's *Poetics*, *opsis* denotes the spectacular aspect of theater and in the New Testament *opsis* refers to the countenance, the face, as in the description of Lazarus risen from the dead, or the angel of the Apocalypse whose face shone like the sun at its brightest. *Opsis* is the very condition of sight and appearing, which is what color is. O'Neil's film reminds us that color emerges from something, or perhaps from nothing, not simply from visible light, but from the invisible – which we figure through blackness.

notes

1. *What the Water Said* was a series of films made by David Gatten from 1998 to 2007.
2. Contemporary critics remarked on the lack of tinting in the Expressionist film *Von Morgens bis Mitternacht*, Karl Heinz Martin's 1920 adaptation of George Kaiser's Expressionist play (although the film had admittedly very few screenings).
3. Although produced in 1948 *Ivan the Terrible II* was not released until 1958.

references

Aumont, J. (1995) (ed.) *La Coleur en Cinema*, Paris: Cinémathèque Française.

Batchelor, D. (2000) *Chromophobia*, New York: Reaktion.

Bordwell, D. (1993) *The Cinema of Eisenstein*, Cambridge, MA: Harvard University Press.

Cherchi Usai, P. (2000) *Silent Cinema: An Introduction*, London: British Film Institute.

Cherchi Usai, P. (2001) *The Death of Cinema: History, Cultural Memory and the Digital Dark Age*, London: British Film Institute.

Eisenstein, S. (1975) "Color and Meaning", trans. Jay Leyda, *The Film Sense*, New York: Harcourt Brace, Jovanovich: 113–156.

Fossati, G. (1996) "Colored Images Today: How to Live with Simulated Colors (and be Happy)", in D. Hertogs, N. de Klerk (eds), *Disorderly Order: Colors in Silent Film*, Amsterdam: Stichting Nederlands Filmmuseum.

Fossati, G. (2009) *From Grain to Pixel: the Archival Life of Film in Transition*, Amsterdam: University of Amsterdam Press.

Frampton, H. (2009) *On the Camera Arts and Consecutive Matters: the Writings of Hollis Frampton*, B. Jenkins (ed.), Cambridge, MA: MIT Press.

Gage, J. (1999) *Color and Meaning: Art Science and Symbolism*, Berkeley, CA: University of California Press.

Goethe, J. W. ([1810]1970) *Theory of Colors*, trans. Charles Lock Eastlake, Cambridge, MA: MIT Press.

Hanssen, E. F. (2006) "Early Discourses on Color and Cinema", thesis, Stockholm University.

Higgins, S. (2007) *Harnessing the Technicolor Rainbow: Color Design in the 1930s*, Austin, TX: University of Texas Press.

Kemp, M. (1990) *The Science of Art: Optical Themes in Western Art from Brunelleschi to Seurat*, New Haven, CT: Yale University Press.

Lagerkvist, P. (1975) *Evening Land (Aftonland)*, trans. W. H. Auden and L. Sjöberg, Detroit: Wayne State Press.

Limbacher, J. L. (1969) *Four Aspects of the Film*, New York: Brussel and Brussel.

Malory, T. (1961) *Le Morte D'Arthur*, New Hyde Park: University Press: 494.

Newton, I. (2003) *Opticks*, Amherst, NY: Prometheus Books.

O'Neil, P. (2009) "Correspondence with Tom Gunning". E-mail (30 June).

Pastoureau, M. (2009) *Black: the History of a Color*, Princeton, NJ: Princeton University Press.

Yumibe, J. (2007) "Moving Color: Aesthetic History of Applied Color Technologies in Silent Cinema", thesis, University of Chicago, Cinema and Media Studies.

"brash ... indecent ...

libertine"

derek jarman's queer colors

r o s a l i n d   g a l t

Derek Jarman was well aware of the chromophobic histories of Western art. In his study of color, *Chroma*, he writes, "As the Roman Empire collapsed, iconoclasts waged war against the graven image. Color became the fount of impurity. A chasm opened up between the terrestrial and celestial world. The dog chased its own tail to bite it off" (Jarman 1995: 45). He also made a direct connection between color and queerness, writing that "Leonardo took the first step into light, and Newton, a notorious bachelor, followed him with Opticks. In this century Ludwig Wittgenstein wrote his *Remarks on Color*. Color seems to have a Queer bent!" (58). Jarman was a radical, even iconoclastic, figure in 1980s British art cinema, and scholarship has considered both the queer politics of his feature films and the use of color in his final film *Blue* (1993). However, his experimental films were for a long time unavailable, and perhaps for this reason have not been widely analyzed. Ranging from diaristic home-movies to theatrically staged scenes, these films demonstrate the importance of rich, monochromatic color schemes, image layering and surface effects to Jarman's aesthetics.

Significantly, the films bring together color and queer politics as questions not only of representation but of form. Here, I will examine iconoclasm and chromophobia not merely as concepts from art history that Jarman's work thematizes, but as still dominant assumptions in film studies that prejudice the critical reception of his colorful films. I will read the rich color schemes and surface effects of Jarman's Super-8 films as central to his queer politics to suggest some of the ways in which his attention to color articulates a refusal of film culture's chromophobic thinking. My title comes from art historian Jacqueline Lichtenstein, who, like Jarman, traces iconophobia from the classical era to European modernity. Describing the *disegno* versus *colore* debates in seventeenth-century France, in which rational line was widely held to be superior to sensual color, Lichtenstein outlines the perceived threat of color thus:

> The colorists threatened the mastery of discourse as much
> as the favor of drawing, the hegemony of a metaphysical
> conception of the image as well as the primacy of the idea
> in representation. They attacked the principles of morality
> and the pedagogical virtues of rules alike. Brash, they
> defended the purely material qualities of representation.
> Indecent, they advanced an apology for cosmetics,
> pleasure, and seduction. Libertine, they praised color
> for the incomparable effects that its simulacra produced.
> (Lichtenstein 1993: 3–4)

The practitioners of color trouble moral and sexual as well as aesthetic categories. Indeed, the lesson may be that the aesthetic is bound to the moral and the sexual. Something comparable happens in film – film theories repeatedly regard color as morally suspicious and secondary to the meaningful qualities of linear form. This inheritance from aesthetic history has often led to Jarman's exclusion or rejection from canons of value, but it also offers a way of conceptualizing his articulation of film aesthetics to sexual politics: Jarman's brash, indecent, libertine style allows us to conceive of him as a film colorist.

In film, chromophobia is part of a broader exclusion of the overly composed and decorative: aesthetic hierarchies that privilege word over image and line over color are inherited by modern film culture and added to a cinematic modernity that values openness, contingency and realism. In order to bring into view the sexual politics of this aesthetic discourse, I call these excluded modes "pretty." Thus, Hugo Münsterberg compares seeing the coloring of Mary Pickford to painting the cheeks of the Venus de Milo: the modernity of cinema is closely tied to ideas of colorless classicism that are themselves, ironically, a modern invention. A colored-in Pickford would have been too pretty, and this term describes those qualities of cosmetic surface effect and visual design that successive models of film theory and criticism must reject in order to produce a regime of value. Thus, while the anti-aesthetic theories of the 1970s and 1980s dismissed Münsterberg's aesthetic prescription, they maintained a rejection of the colorful and composed. And while these theoretical models themselves might be radical, they inherit the patriarchal sexual politics of classical and modern aesthetics. From classical film theory to the modernist Marxism and feminism of Jarman's era, aesthetic austerity remained preferable to pretty style.

I would argue that this anti-pretty structure explains Jarman's difficult position in contemporary film history. While he is clearly an important figure, his investment in theatricality and richly artificial colors has prevented him from being as widely valued as he might otherwise have been. Tony Rayns (1986: 46) calls Jarman "number one in a field of one." This sense of him as a misfit figures the institutional effects of prettiness even in a field as accepting of aesthetic difference as experimental film. One of the earliest scholarly studies of Jarman was a special issue of *Afterimage* dedicated to two "troublesome cases": Jarman and the 1930 film *Borderline* (MacPherson). The editors see both as nurturing their marginal positions, sharing a preoccupation with the borderlines of class, race, and sexuality: "If they do find a place in the traditions of British cinema, it is with the company of outsiders and intransigents that includes Powell and Pressburger at one end of the production spectrum, Margaret Tait and Jeff Keen at the other" (Field 1985: 3). Of course, all of these filmmakers might be seen as "national treasures" of one kind or another and their outsiderdom and awkwardness as a peculiarly British mixture of Romanticism and stubbornness. Nonetheless, despite recent critical interest in many of these artists, a sense of troublesomeness remains.

Jarman certainly felt himself to be outside of his contemporary avant-garde institutions: he describes using Super-8 as a way to evade the strictures of the structural film scene (cited in Dollin 1984: 42). A. L. Rees (1999: 100) finds a hostility between Jarman and the London Filmmakers Co-operative, seeing him rather as a high modernist, in the mode of Ken Russell, Lindsay Anderson and Michael Powell; filmmakers who "resisted the safer options and who were roundly attacked for their pains." But if Jarman has modernist qualities, his colorful style suggests other art historical categories that might lead to his rejection by the structuralists. A 1975 French introduction to his work defines it as aestheticist, painterly, and with a plastic sensibility (Anon. 1975: 73).[1] These are precisely the terms of a sensuality that his British contemporaries sought to expel from the cinematic. Think, for example, of Peter Gidal's aim to minimize film's content "in its overpowering, imagistically seductive sense" (1976: 2), his dubbing of people in film as "baroque appendages" (47), and his scathing rejection of the end of Michael Snow's *Back and Forth* (1969) as "rococo rubbish" (49). Gidal uses the vocabulary of art to promote an austerity of form that strongly rejects the imagistic, the baroque and the rococo. Jarman's sensual colorism was unlikely to be accepted in such a context.

But it is not only filmmakers who rejected Jarman's style. Even some of his most sympathetic and significant interlocutors find prettiness to be troublesome. Mike O'Pray sees the film *Imagining October* (1984) as ambivalent. He says, "the imagery is Stalinist and yet very beautiful at the same time. You seem to want to criticize certain things, but it's always tempered by beautiful imagery" (Field and O'Pray 1985: 46). Making a presumption typical of anti-pretty rhetoric, O'Pray finds that the film's beautiful painted images inevitably work against its political critique rather than forming an integral part of it. Rees goes further, seeing Jarman's experimental films as too theatrical, literary and symbolic. He finds that "their visual impact was chained rather than liberated by the preordained shooting strategies which they adopted" (1999: 100). This seems odd to me, since Rees valorizes filmmakers like Snow and Gidal who make highly arranged films. But where the pre-planned is also theatrically composed, then both cinematic modernity and art history are called upon to explain what is wrong: Rees proposes that the "films don't breathe: every inch of the screen has to be filled, like an academic canvas, but there is still too little work for the eye to do" (Rees 1999: 102–103). The excess of color, detail, and design is an affront both to the wind in the leaves of cinematic realism and to the austerity of 1970s modernism.

color as a politics of form (lessness)

If Jarman's experimental work fails to meet the formal demands of structural film, his features are more often read as political. Richard Porton argues that "in Jarman's work it is impossible to separate cinematic style from a decidedly undidactic political fervor; formal choices are simultaneously political choices" (1996: 135). And while we might respond that they always are, Porton helpfully isolates the way that Jarman's films are not usually thought of in a leftist counter-cinematic tradition even while they are explicitly activist. Thus, he points out how Jarman's pantheon of Powell, Pasolini and Cocteau "are united by their hostility to mainstream naturalism and their radical individualism – an individualism that does not foreclose the cultivation of collective, but non-dogmatic, radical hopes" (136). Whereas many Marxist critics find, alongside O'Pray and Gidal, that prettiness works against political meaning Jarman's example demonstrates that the opposite is true: to imagine a genuinely radical collective future, one needs a decorative eye.

James Tweedie finds a similar potential in Jarman's use of the tableau. For him,

> The foundational representational problem for Jarman's
> filmmaking is how to resolve the formal politics of political

modernism and the exigencies of the present, in particular
an oppositional queer politics centered on the archaeology
of past identity formations and a genealogy of the present.
(Tweedie 2003: 380–381)

This articulation is particularly fruitful as it identifies a conflict between
cinematic modernism and queer politics that is resolved through the composed surface of the image. I think a similar representational question
hangs over Jarman's colors: abstraction and politics, the image and the
word. Jarman's final color experiment, *Blue*, uses words centrally, whereas
the early Super-8 films are silent. Some critics see *Blue* as a late abjuration of
the image but I want to suggest that we don't have to keep reading this as
a binarized battle between reason and image, *disegno* and *colore*. Just as the
tableau in the narrative films negotiates between modernist form and
queer politics, so in Jarman's experimental films, color is a mobilizing
conceptual force.

1. indecent: queer color

Lichtenstein's categories form a guide for examining the stakes in Jarman's
color.

Color's indecency speaks most directly to a queering of the image: several recent color theorists have noted the association in aesthetic writing of
color with homosexuality. Color as a Platonic cosmetic is effeminate,
overly sexual and duplicitous. It exists on the surface, hiding the true face
underneath. For David Batchelor, artists like Andy Warhol use this idea of
the cosmetic to evoke drag and sexual indeterminacy in their colored
images, "playing with the order of nature and going Against Nature in a
very specific way" (2000: 62). Jarman, too, plays with this philosophical
association, referring to color in *Chroma* as "the bordello of the spectrum"
(1995: 52). In *The Art of Mirrors* (Jarman, 1973) and *Tarot* (Jarman, 1972),
deeply colored filters are combined with elaborate costuming to stage artifice and
cosmetics. Elegant outfits and feathered hats evoke a historical aestheticism, while the changing monochromatic setting of greens and reds
reminds us, as with Warhol's lino prints, that color is an object in its own
right and not a supplement to line. Thus, the sea-foam green in *The Art of
Mirrors* demands that we look at texture, tone and light. The effect of turning the mirror to the camera further focuses attention on color. It's an
oddly chiasmic effect – the mirror should make us look at a point, the
circle of the mirror flashing, but since that point is hard to look at (a bright
mirror, or a darkened screen) its real effect is outward, to make us look at
the entire colorful surface of the screen, at the tones and textures the
mirror light illuminates. (**See Plate 7.**)

Indecent color implies an erotics, and the immersive quality of these
filters is indeed pleasurable. But seduction is also a political question, as

dominant anti-aesthetics resist the charms of color, evincing patriarchal fears of overwhelming femininity, formlessness and the loss of straight male subjectivity. For Lisa Robertson, this borderless cosmetic is precisely a site of political change. She writes,

> Dangerously pigment smears. Artifice is the disrespect of the propriety of borders. Emotion results. ... To experience change, we submit ourselves to the affective potential of the surface. This is the *pharmakon*: an indiscrete threshold where our bodies exchange information with an environment. (Robertson 2003: 142)

In *Death Dance* (Jarman, 1973), the surface is color itself, the effect of filters forming the type of threshold that Robinson suggests between the sensual surface of the screen and the eroticized bodies in profilmic space. And that space is changed by its encounter with color, becoming at once an enchanted mise-en-scène and an immaterial surface. The blue filter here makes the ground and wall seem as much a flat color field as a real place. It doesn't look exactly like the abstract field of *Blue* but there's enough similarity to remind us that Jarman has always worked with the queer potential of surface color. (**See Plate 8.**) As Robertson puts it, "For Newton, of course, all color joined in the pure concept of whiteness, of light. But we are attracted to the weakness and impurity of the bond of pigment, because we can identify with nothing other than instability. This identification is admittedly a style of taste, but it also improvises a political alignment" (2003: 142).

Tony Rayns offers a fascinating analysis of the Super-8 films in which color is a figuration of sodomy, commenting that "these were the films of an anti-Eisenstein: languorous, formless reveries in which various theatrical and painterly ideas were subsumed into a never-ending flow of colors and visual textures that was finally pure surface" (1985: 61). The formlessness of pure color expresses an anxiety around passivity and the feminine threat of the bodily cavity. As color takes over from form, it operates as a subsuming void. Rayns sees the films as overly passive, concluding that "for viewer and filmmaker alike, they represent a perpetual state of arousal without the attendant climax" (1985: 61). For a reading that proposes sodomy as an organizing metaphor, this analysis exhibits an odd anxiety around the passive and the formless. Nonetheless, it is precisely illustrative of how Jarman's colors engage at the formal level the same sensual terrain that his iconography of naked, masked and bound men offers in the mise-en-scène. Thus, *Arabia* (Jarman, 1974) displays a man chained among lines of fire, a St Sebastian in a loin cloth and several naked boys lying on the ground. (**See Figure 8.1.**) The seductive qualities of bodily passivity and masochism refute the dominance of masculinist line and propose, instead, a visual and erotic economy of engulfment. As Brian Price has

Figure 8.1
Arabia (Derek Jarman, 1974) proposes a politics of masochism and formlessness.

argued (2006: 76–87) with regard to Claire Denis' *Beau Travail* (1999), formless color can contain sexually and aesthetically radical potential.

2. libertine: queer life

Lichtenstein's colorist libertines praised color for the incomparable effects that its simulacra produced. In other words, they found it a superior means to evoke life. Mimesis is hardly a controversial aim, but problems arise when the life in question is seen as libertine: wantonly sexual or lacking in proper social aims. In this way, queer lives are excluded from the healthy and open discourses of cinematic realism, which, like Adolf Loos's 1900 polemic against ornament, emphasize purity and reproduction as opposed to enclosure and death. Loos (1966: 225) describes a "Poor Rich Man" who decorates his house in art nouveau style and, being completely surrounded by ornament, realizes that he has to learn to live with his own death. As Rees says of Jarman, composed spaces don't breathe. This modernist parable vividly stages what aesthetics sees as the wrong kind of life, but it also alerts us to the possibilities for transvaluing color's libertine force. Jarman does, in his later work, have to learn to live with his own death, but his color nonetheless celebrates queer life as a détournement of aesthetic propriety.

In his introduction to the *Wittgenstein* (Jarman, 1993) scripts, Colin MacCabe says that the film's use of bright colors "illuminate[s] a queer life"

99

(1993: 2). The same can be said of the Super-8 films, which deploy bright colors to access a contingent experience of time and place. We jump across bodies, locations and quickly lost scenes in *It Happened By Chance* (1977), the rapid-fire encounter of the diary film intersecting with posed figures from *The Art of Mirrors* or *Arabia*. Punk icon Toyah stands against a pinky-red background; red, white and blue flags hang at a street party; and the pyramids are bathed in deep red. This sensory overload pointedly refuses to follow the rules of the formalist avant garde, constructing a discourse on colorful life at the same time that it eschews meaningful form. In *Chroma*, Jarman writes "red is a moment in time. Blue constant" (1995: 37). Here we see elaborated a relationship that spans from Jarman's earliest work to his latest: between color and cinematic temporality. The Super-8 films evoke the transient pleasures of life, while *Chroma* and *Blue* use color to negotiate the lack of time and the immediacy of death. But from the beautiful boys of the early films to the blank screen of *Blue*, Jarman bonds color to the potential of queer life in the face of homophobic forms.

Jarman is interested in color language – in what blue means for instance. Most theories of color language seem reactionary or naïve in their attempts to assign universal cultural associations. However, Jarman doesn't ascribe inherent meanings to colors but rather works with a history of inherited associations. In this sense, he expands Eisenstein's analysis of color in his theory of synaesthesia (1946: 143), in which he proposes that filmmakers engage the political histories that might make red signify revolution in one context and aristocratic reaction in another. Color's meaning is shaped by historical forces, which exactly dovetails with Jarman's project to construct a queer history. Eisenstein takes his place in this history as much as Plato, where the sexuality of the theorist subtends a revised orientation to color theory itself. What is useful about linking Jarman's project of queer historicity to color is that it demands a meaningful role for what is often seen as mere sensation.

We might compare Jarman's color theory to Henry Adams's notion that each era forms its own color world. Adams discusses the blues in the cathedral of Chartres, which, he claims, we no longer know how to make (Adams 1959: 152). For him, color could be the structuring force behind a space (a cathedral or a body of film); it could be the central organizing principle for how we experience it and a force that would not be simply an aesthetic choice but a historical one. In Jarman's films, color also provides a way to create an era, or rather, to create a counter-era. While the cathedral embodies a dominant site of repressive institutional space, the coercive force of art, Jarman's films elaborate the aesthetic imaginary of queer life. The vivid chromatic spaces of gay London and of a punk appropriation of the post-industrial Docklands conjured in *The Art of Mirrors* and *It Happened By Chance* represent both a counter-present and a counter-reading of aesthetic history. Prettiness perverts "art history," deforming form and demanding we find life instead in the richly colored and socially excluded. The somber monochrome of *Blue* speaks to the end of life and the incommensurability of living with AIDS, but across Jarman's career color also encodes the era in the imaginary of a different collective.

3. brash: mineral histories

Lastly, the brashness of the colorists lies in their defense of the purely material qualities of art and Jarman equally insists on the sensual pleasure of film color's visible qualities. An example of this quality is the dialogue between the colorful material of 8 mm film and the material remnants of ancient culture that occurs in *Ashden's Walk on Møn* (Jarman, 1973). Set on the Danish island of Møn which is known for its prehistoric stone structures, *Ashden* superimposes an image of the Milky Way onto shots of nature such as moving water and blades of grass. The blue is darker than that of *Blue*, closer to violet. It suggests a night sky, but the images are earthly, projecting a celestial immateriality onto the material world. (**See Plate 9.**) Next, an old cosmography of the sun and planets is superimposed onto a building, layering histories of the sky and its cultural manifestations onto Møn's material space. When we reach a prehistoric site, the materiality of grass and ancient hill is combined with a bright green filter and a lens flare that recurs, dancing across the surface of the screen (**See Plate 10.**) A relationship is forged between the filmic material that doesn't really exist (light effect, color) and the natural material (grassy hills) that is unchanging.

Such a natural scene might not seem fertile ground for politics, yet the interrogations by earlier avant gardes of cinematic material are understood as political as a matter of course. Jarman's abstractions are too pretty to join this masculinist discourse, and his color-work was only admitted to the cultural big time with *Blue*, the only one of his films that critics could redeem as iconoclastic and austere. Conversely, a more realist account of landscape such as Siegfried Kracauer's endlessness (1997) or André Bazin's ontology (1967) would find social engagement in the transparency of the profilmic. It is Jarman's decorative colors, superimpositions and light effects that preclude such validatory interpretations, along with a suspicion that standing stones make too hippyish a topic for serious cinema. But it is precisely in this mineral history that Jarman forges a utopian politics: brash color conjures an alchemical relation between pretty form and esoteric content.

Karen Pinkus (2008) has recently discussed alchemy as a figure of ambivalence, connoting both the transmutations of genius – the artist who can turn meager materials into aesthetic gold – and the hocus pocus of falsification, linked to toxic capitalism. Jarman is equally fascinated with both aspects of alchemy. On the positive side, it figures his artistic process, an *arte povera* that creates something out of not much more than nothing. It also enfolds a queer sense of secret knowledge, of outsiders who trade in occult glances and strange processes. Both of these senses are contained in *Ashden's* mysterious images. Pinkus's second sense of alchemy also leads us toward Jarman's political critique. To be sure, he, too, is interested in what goes wrong with capitalism, but the mobilization of alchemy as a queer visual technique troubles the stakes of alchemy's ambivalence. It is seen as unhealthy, unnatural, and mendacious, just as color and prettiness connote deceptive cosmetics and exclude proper and healthy life. To propose alchemy as a principle of color film is to make a transvaluative – indeed an alchemical – claim on the politics of color. We see this most clearly in *Blue*, a film that begins from nothing but the pure pigment of Yves Klein's International Klein Blue, and which uses its mineral surface to plumb the depths of life and death. Klein himself spoke of "an alchemy of painting," and found in his blue "the invisible made visible" (Klein cited in Charlet 2000: 100). It is such a work of visibility that Jarman's colors promise.

note

1. Michael O'Pray (1987: 7–10) speaks of Super-8 as "a rather despised medium for serious work" (8) in the context of John Maybury and Cerith Wyn Evans's influential show A Certain Sensibility in 1981. These filmmakers were part of Jarman's scene and, like him, their influences included both avant-garde artists like Andy Warhol, Kenneth Anger and Jack Smith and art cinema auteurs such as Pasolini, Jean Cocteau and Federico Fellini. These influences were rather looked down on, and we see that even in the avant garde, prettiness is associated with a love for the more middlebrow or bourgeois that can never accommodate modernist purity and austerity of form.

references

Adams, H. (1959) *Mont St. Michel and Chartres*, New York: Anchor Books.

Anonymous (1975) "Derek Jarman: Présenté dans le cadre des sélections étrangères", *Apec Cinema* 13, 3: 73–74.

Batchelor, D. (2000) *Chromophobia*, London: Reaktion Books.

Bazin, A. (1967) *What Is Cinema?*, vol. 1, trans. H. Gray, Berkeley, CA, and Los Angeles: University of California Press.

Charlet, N. (2000) *Yves Klein*, trans. M. Taylor, Paris: Vilo/Adam Biro.

Dollin, S. (1984) "Super 8 Artist", *Movie Maker* 18/7: 41–43.

Eisenstein, S. M. (1946) *The Film Sense*, trans. J. Leyda, New York: Harcourt.

Field, S. (1985) "Editorial: The Troublesome Cases", "… of Angels & Apocalypse", special issue of *Afterimage* 12: 2–5.

Field, F. and O'Pray, M. (1985) "Imagining October, Dr. Dee and other Matters: an Interview with Derek Jarman", *Afterimage* 12: 40–58.

Gidal, P. (1976) *Structural Film Anthology*, London: BFI.

Jarman, D. (1995) *Chroma: a Book of Colour*, Woodstock, NY: Overlook Press.

Kracauer, S. (1997) *Theory of Film: The Redemption of Physical Reality*, Princeton, NJ: Princeton University Press.

Lichtenstein, J. (1993) *The Eloquence of Color: Rhetoric and Painting in the French Classical Age*, trans. E. McVarish, Berkeley, CA: University of California Press.

Loos, A. (1966) "The Story of a Poor Rich Man", in L. Münz and G. Künstler (eds), *Adolf Loos: Pioneer of Modern Architecture*, New York: Praeger.

MacCabe, C. (1993) "Preface", *Wittgenstein: The Terry Eagleton Script and the Derek Jarman Film*, London: BFI.

O'Pray, M. (1987) "The Elusive Sign: from Asceticism to Aestheticism", in D. Curtis (ed.), *The Elusive Sign: British Avant-Garde Film & Video 1977–1987*, London: Arts Council of Great Britain.

Pinkus, K. (2008) "Nothing from Nothing: Alchemy and the Economic Crisis", *World Picture* 2. Online. Available at http://www.worldpicturejournal.com

Porton, R. (1996) "Language Games and Aesthetic Attitudes: Style and Ideology in Jarman's Late Films", in C. Lippard (ed.), *By Angels Driven: The Films of Derek Jarman*, Trowbridge: Flick Books.

Price, B. (2006) "Color, the Formless, and Cinematic Eros", in A. Dalle Vacche and B. Price (eds), *Color: the Film Reader*, New York: Routledge.

Rayns, T. (1985) "Submitting to Sodomy: Propositions and Rhetorical Questions about an English Film-maker", *Afterimage* 12: 60–64.

Rayns, T. (1986) "Unnatural Lighting", *American Film* 11, 10: 44–47 and 59–61.

Rees, A. L. (1999) *A History of Experimental Film and Video: From the Canonical Avant Garde to Contemporary British Practice*, London: BFI.

Robertson, L. (2003) *Occasional Work and Seven Walks from the Office for Soft Architecture*, Astoria, OR: Clear Cut Press.

Tweedie, J. (2003) "The Suspended Spectacle of History: the Tableau Vivant in Derek Jarman's *Caravaggio*", *Screen* 44, 4: 379–403.

the hues of memory, the shades of experience

color and time in *syndromes and a century*

j o c e l y n   s z c z e p a n i a k - g i l l e c e

Although Thai filmmaker Apichatpong Weerasethakul has been the subject of considerable acclaim since the late 1990s, his recent accomplishments have been the focus of greater attention, particularly following his win of the Palme d'Or at the 2010 Cannes film festival with *Uncle Boonmee Who Can Recall His Past Lives* (2010). In this and his other celebrated films, he employs a delicate imagery that is quotidian and mystical, wry and melancholic, to a degree arguably unmatched in contemporary cinema. Critics frequently herald Weerasethakul both for his fluid approach to time and his use of saturated color; meticulously cultivated, rich and sumptuous hues bleed from one film to the next to construct a sensibility, at once dreamlike and grounded and a cinematic experience, that is both hypnotically enigmatic and inherently recognizable. Color in his films, though, has a larger purpose than style: in helping to situate scenes between dream and reality, it also questions the intertwined positions of spatial depth and time, of personal and collective visual perceptions, and of experiences and memories in the cinema itself.

In Weerasethakul's *Syndromes and a Century* (2006), color's visual depth contributes to and resonates with an evocative, elusive approach to sensory time, helping to develop a narrative overtly concerned with space, visibility, and temporality in general. The film consists of two parallel segments that tell a semi-reconstructed story of Weerasethakul's parents' meeting: the first concerns Dr Toey, Weerasethakul's mother, in a village hospital while its second focuses on Dr Nohng, his father, in an urban medical center. Both segments repeat and refract one another in terms of character, dialogue, and setting, but also through a shifting color design that bears both consonances and transformations from one portion of the film to the next. In its considerations of memory and perception paired with a careful and flowing palette, *Syndromes and a Century* is a privileged site to consider the interplay between filmic time and color; what *Syndromes* provocatively proposes is that cinematic color vision may be thought of as something that divides temporality and sensory perception and brings them back together again, re-imagining the experience of time as a sensory cinematic form.

The question of where color should be placed in the realm of cinematic visual experience remains largely unanswered, perhaps unanswerable. Given filmic color's inherently speculative and transient nature, then, in the following essay I want to put forward some preliminary thoughts on how color operates in *Syndromes and a Century* to explore the possibility of thinking about color in the cinema in general. Although an undeniably powerful and evocative aspect of filmic form, color challenges spectators to think in terms neither entirely metaphoric nor symbolic. Defining color in cinema is at best a frustrating task – the slipperiness that makes color so appealing also makes it difficult to describe. Curiously, time enacts similar operations in film; both captured onscreen in indexical duration and impossible to grasp as a material entity, time flows through cinema. In *The World Viewed* (1979), Stanley Cavell illustrated this point when he argued for an implicit link between temporality and color.

For Cavell, color's first major uses on camera created filmic worlds ruled less by consistency and more by imagination. As filmic color technique became more familiar and more complex, color became a tool for establishing filmic space and time both as part of the spectator's extradiegetic reality and as expanding past everyday experience, suggesting that "the world created is neither a world just past nor a world of make-believe. It is a world of an immediate future" (Cavell 1979: 82). Cavell thus describes the world of color on film as not yet fully available, hovering just beyond the present moment but not entirely apart from it, an impression of a time at once experienced and defamiliarized. Following Cavell, the function of cinematic color, then, could be considered alongside the interval that exists between analogically photographed film frames, itself both an instrument of sensory movement perception and the absence of movement itself.

Similarly transitory and nearly untraceable, distinct from the more forceful components of line, movement, and shape, color's very elusiveness can be an aid in uncovering the sensory aspects of filmic temporal consciousness. The spectator might read color as sculpting cinematic time into a sensory experience; there, tints and traces illuminate time and perception as interval states akin to the liminality of color perception itself.

Brian Price argues that in certain examples of globalized contemporary art cinema, such as P. T. Anderson's *Punch Drunk Love* (2002) and Hou Hsiao-Hsien's *Millennium Mambo* (2001), abstract cinematic color fields extend meaning beyond the restrictions of an economically and politically standardizing narrative force, insisting upon specificity, subjectivity, multiplicity, and the force of cinematic eros (Price 2006). Excess, in the face of a strictly formal and thus depoliticized analysis, is color's guarantee against totalization. Despite its apparent containment on the rectangular screen or on the filmstrip, filmic color hints at this excess and at an expanded consciousness that ultimately confounds efforts at limitation and leaks beyond stringent lines. And while filmic time is similarly seemingly restricted and bounded – film was the first art object to successfully capture duration – color's visual force makes time into a phenomenon both enclosed and escaping.[1] Similarly, in *Syndromes*, color is a creative motion toward a fluid, sensory understanding of temporal consciousness. As the film's hues formulate an interval between perception and memory, an emptied moment fills with sensory possibility; as the two halves of the film slip away from one another and meet again, so perception and memory, clarity and color intertwine to frame the instant as an escaping moment of sensory experience. Temporal consciousness, consisting of both the fleeting nature of perceptual experience and extended life of memory, is braided with color's necessarily interval state.

Many discussions of color in cinematic and aesthetic theory, which tend to cluster around either color as evocative of emotion or color as aspect of design and form, reflect its temporary and variable state. In *Art and Visual Perception*, Rudolf Arnheim observes an inclination to align shape with masculinity and rationality and color with femininity and emotion. For Arnheim, rather than revealing some essential gendering of color, this highlights the difficulty of defining color's function. Compared to color, shape's more "efficient means of communication" easily conveys immediate symbolic information (Arnheim 1964: 323). Yet inherent to color on both a psychological and aesthetic level is a division both between perception and description and between subjects; color is not easily circumscribed, nor can one be sure the color one sees is the same another does (Arnheim 1964: 330). Arnheim thereby formulates color as within an interval, illustrated by the fact that identifying a specific color always requires the identification of the two colors it lies "between," and that a color "depend[s] greatly upon the context in space and time" (Arnheim 1964: 310, 331).

Cognitive science also explains that color in memory tends to be brighter than the original stimulus, demonstrating how color hovers between material and temporal poles (Davidoff 1991). This betweenness both complicates analysis and makes color a conceptual analogue to the cinematic interval and to the division between perceptive experience and memory.[2]

To filmically describe this division, which is at once a chasm and a bridge, *Syndromes* employs spatial metaphor in its two hospital settings, themselves architectures of liminal states, transitions, and intervals. Like the interval, which slips past before it can be grasped, experience can be described only in the moment of its passing. Perceiving a film is similarly a process of encountering experience as it slips into memory; the interval that is constitutive of the cinematic is both the interval between frames and that of the perception of a film as it moves past. The interval is neither entirely perceptible nor wholly nonexistent: what exists is the moment past and the moment yet to come, suggesting an analogy between the fluctuations of temporal experience and the constitutions of the cinematic. The filmic oscillation between experience and memory may therefore be considered as a constant tunneling through an escaping perceptual and sensory present. Experience functions as a state of flux and as the motion of being embedded and constituted in a discursive moment; it is a reflection of the state of constantly being-alive. Among the explanations of this is Derrida's *survivre*, the state of survival as the opposite of death that operates continuously in the face of death (Derrida 1987, Hodge 2007). In Derrida's description, immortality is much closer to death, as it is a state of constancy and immobility, than is survival; the true opposite of death is the flux of surviving despite death's constant presence. And where this state of survival might be most saliently located is in the between time and space of a hospital; *Syndromes* offers us two hospitals, not merely separated in space but also in time.

As *Syndromes* substitutes one hospital for the next, the narrative also transfers its position in time from past to present. Although both narrative segments must necessarily take place in the past, given that the memories on which they are based are several decades old, the second part's repetition of moments from the first segment, its location in the midst of a bustling city and up-to-date medical equipment mark it as present compared to the "past" of the first hospital.[3] Both times of the film highlight similar but accented stories and enclose narrative and visual moments both mimicked and transformed, while characters from the first segment, including Toey, Nohng, Ple the dentist, and the Buddhist monk Sakda, appear in the second, sometimes repeating dialogue and sometimes not. In this way, the film operates in a space both reminiscent and outside of normative time, a formless area of remembrance and imagination.[4] As temporalities confuse, commingle, and flow, *Syndromes and a Century*'s color palette also shifts so that visual perception becomes caught up in the perception of time. Provocatively, where the film's past tends to be saturated and vibrant, its present space is more whitened, depleted. Any existing moment is thus continually emptying, briefly frozen between its fleeting experience and successive memory. Drained or brightened color serves to mix perceptions of past and present in order to display, as Cavell would describe, a "world of the immediate future" and a world of the immediate past just beyond possession.

Jihoon Kim notes Weerasethakul's tendency to use a double structure of narrative that he terms the "interstice": "an abrupt extradiegetic gap that interrupts the spatiotemporal continuity of a film's narrative in such a way that it is not chronologically or causally justified by its diegetic elements" (Kim 2010: 132). Although Kim's interest is in how Weerasethakul's films and installations imply an aesthetic fluctuation among multiple disciplines – the future of cinema as multisensory and multiobject orientation – his argument points toward the gap of narrative also animate within *Syndromes'* solitary text, for the film's characters are always between spaces, times, and each other. Indeed, throughout the film Weerasethakul's parents, Drs Toey and Nohng, rarely cross paths, leaving the director's own unspoken origin to float as something ungraspable: if their relationship remains nonexistent, the author of the text remains unborn. As Kim notes the necessity of conceiving of Weerasethakul's narratives as both cinematic and architectural, so the two hospital spaces become essential visualizations of another kind of interval: that between good health and poor health, or between life and death.

Within the two temporally furtive hospitals, whiteness acts as a conduit for memory to funnel into a viewable present. Hospital spaces, particularly the transient areas of hallways in which visitors are asked to wait, are light-filled like projected images, or the brief click of white between slides; in this way, the hospitals are places of lightness and air, suspensions between present/past and moment of watching/moment of remembering. As much as this whiteness marks the hospitals as sites of cleanliness, order, and suspension, it also evokes analogous spaces like the white cube of the art gallery. Where the white cube in Western museum aesthetics affirms boundaries between art and not-art, here whiteness in a similar action suffuses the flexible borders between life and death, delineating and framing a space of interval.[5] And while whiteness appears to be the absence of color, it is instead the containment of *all* colors – these spaces then are both apparent nothingness and limitless potential, empty and full moments, the flux of an escaping present.

The palettes of the film's two hospitals thus help to position them as mid-points between life and death and between experience and memory. Yet within them, colors that might be expected to play vivid roles against the clinical whiteness of a hospital environment are nowhere to be found: no splashes of blood or other bright fluids, no bouquets at patients' bedsides, no multicolored pills. Rather, brightened color's role tends to be relegated to two significant elements: in environments outside the hospital boundaries, like the trees and grasses swaying just beyond the windows, or in clothes that break up the hospital's clinical white or subdued beige and olive tones, such as the running outfits of exercisers or a monk's saffron robes. (**See Plate 11.**) There is no emergency or crisis or visible marker of death in these hospitals, merely the ongoing business of perception and of being-alive. In these architectural arenas of both embodiment and potential disembodiment, memory and experience likewise flow into one another. Outside of the hospital, color is found particularly in moments of transition and in characters marked by their ability to cross boundaries: monks, who throughout the narrative are linked with reincarnation and dream-life, and hospital patients who exist between life and death. For these subjects, the perceptual interval, emptied of the linearity of chronological time, fills with the sensory awareness of color.

As noted, the interiors of both hospitals are frequently glowing white or beige, at once stripped of color and holding its continual visual promise. Visible beyond the first hospital, however, ridged, elephantine and jade-toned leaves nod just outside the windows of the dentist's office, and green fields extend far into the distance past the building's exterior boundaries. These deep emeralds visually establish an atmosphere of dreaminess and mythos, reflecting Weerasethakul's tendency to associate the natural world with timelessness, transformation, and mysterious knowledge accessible through the relinquishment of rationality and logic.[6] Yet the rich shades of green contrasted with the more austere interiority of the hospital also give shape to, if not entirely a history, then a pattern of continued existence outside the hushed corridors; the leaves constantly hovering outside the windows remind of the tenuousness of a constructed story and the directions lying just beyond a narrative's borders. These verdant tones, however, are lessened in the second segment, partially due to a shift in setting to the city. This considerable minimization of a defining color from the first segment also suggests the richness of memory in contrast to the starkness of the present – the present is ungraspable, less vivid than the blooming images of memory. Compared to the hues of memory, present experience operates in softened tints; through *Syndromes'* visualization of temporality, memory is privileged as more cinematic than the moment of occurrence.

Sensory perception in the film is thus linked as much, or at times more, to the past than the present; the memory of a time gone rather than the experience of the instantaneous moment. This seemingly paradoxical association complicates the evidentiary nature of experience, the dichotomy between perception and memory, and a past/present binary. Toey's recollections of meeting her ex-lover Noom and his mother Pa Jane are filled with comparatively rich hues and reference to such saturation: deep greens of hanging plants and grassy meadows, murky brown waters, an orchid that glows in the dark, an orange, a story of a lake filled with gold and silver. In the second hospital, the spatial environment is paler, bleached; even Ple, who in the first half works in a room with multiple although muted shades and wears a green jacket outside of work, is only seen covered in white scrubs and working in a whitened office. This is not to say that the film's present is colorless. *Syndromes and a Century* complicates the assumption that sense perception exists only in the immediacy of experienced time and that moment and memory may be separated from one another. Glimpses of the exterior of the second hospital reveal fewer deep greens; what is visible blossoms, mostly from pruned shrubbery and cut grass outside, delimited and bounded compared to the lush plant-life of the first hospital's surroundings. Inside the hospital, however, the monks' golden robes and the blues, yellows, greens, and reds making up patients' clothing coalesce into a visual bridge between the first segment and the second, performing as spots of instantaneous memory that continually emerge in the present. In this section, these colors appear frequently in corridors, or spaces of transition – here, *Syndromes* posits sensing as a function of memory as much as it is a function of experience. The apprehension of *Syndromes'* non-linear temporality depends upon the discursive fluctuations of chromatic perception; the formlessness of color signifies the subjective nature of filmic time.

Clearness and transparency are also essential building blocks of the film's temporal/sensory paradigm. Both segments of the film open with Nohng's interview by Toey, who asks if he prefers "triangles, squares or circles?" "Circles," Nohng responds. "Which color?" Toey inquires. "Clear [...] like the bottom of a glass," Nohng answers. At the opening of the film's second segment, the same interview occurs nearly word-for-word. The present, here, repeats and erases itself as does the lingual image of the circle: clear, but invisible, approachable, but ungraspable, operating in a moment of both existence and reference. The division of clarity from saturation constructs an absence from temporal perception, suggesting a time that slips both forward and back. The film's second segment visualizes time in fields of transparency, color, and simulated cross-fade; in one late image, Toey gazes out a window (like a hallway, a marker of transition), framed between spaces and times, surrounded and constructed by layers of objects, images, and lines. (**See Plate 12.**) This kind of play between color and transparency hints at how, in film, the sensory illuminates levels of temporality; color reminds of the presence of memory within experience, and the impossibility of approaching clarity without the tempering factor of its darkened complement. The filmic moment cannot entirely last and exists instead in an escaping present moment, both perceptible and vanished.

Below the clinical brightness of the urban hospital is a crumbling area accessible only by rickety stairway; Nohng is warned to "be careful, these steps are old" as he walks downstairs. Moving into the building's belly,

Nohng watches as the film's colors become darker, denser, and more mysterious; walls are speckled with the mottled dust of age. Close to the end, the camera drifts through the lower level of the urban hospital, finally wandering into a room filled with ducts, glowing fluorescent lights, and mist enveloping lurking, strange machines. At the end of the ductwork a round black opening mirrors an earlier shot of solar eclipse from Toey's memories of Pa Jane and Noom. This hanging vacuum sucks in the mist with a loud drone that overwhelms the soundtrack, and the camera hovers for well over a minute, observing the devouring of moments that have come before both in the film and in its greater network of incomplete narratives. (See Plates 13 and 14.) Here, it is as though all the stories and layers of memory housed within the hospital are slowly being dragged into the past, the upstairs urban hospital's present inevitably wending its way into disjuncture and dissolution. In this sense, the hospital's space and time continually becomes part of the past and formulates futurity. It is fitting that these moments are filled with deepened color as well as deepened time; as present and past commingle, the shot lingers on inanimate objects and spaces, implying a perceptual interval filling with the strata of multiple forms of knowledge. Color is the brightest of these layers, offering a creative means of discernment outside the boundaries of typical cogency and suggesting that temporality itself likewise expands past the gates of logic.

Syndromes' final question, then, is whether cinematic color can represent the unrepresentable. For Jacques Rancière, however, unrepresentability implies in turn its own representation.

> In order to assert an unrepresentability in art that is commensurate with an unthinkability of the event, the latter must itself have been rendered entirely thinkable, entirely necessary according to thought. The logic of the unrepresentable can only be sustained by a hyperbole that ends up destroying it. (Rancière 2009: 138)

Regimes of artistic representation are therefore inescapable even when they appear to be avoided. Bearing this in mind, I do not mean to suggest that *Syndromes and a Century* achieves an escape velocity sufficient to escape the boundaries of what is currently representable. Yet I think it does, in some small and subtle way, succeed in pointing toward the limits of filmic representation by intimating a temporal consciousness potentially accessible in the sensory realm. In citing the importance of color to creating an experience of filmic time, *Syndromes and a Century* proposes that film can reconfigure the rationality of the visual and insist upon the productivity of the ephemeral moment. This reliance upon a mode of sense perception so intrinsically braided with excess theorizes cinematic time as equally excessive, spilling over into a state of interval. Weerasethakul's work, then, is at once as filmmaker and as theorist discovering how color and time operate in film in general. In *Syndromes*, as much a bright and saturated recollection of its own conception and making as an actual filmic experience, colorful hints of cinematic memory suspended in spaces between unveil evidence of a subjective sensory time.

notes

1. For a clear description of duration in cinematic form, see Doane (2002).
2. The divide between memory and experience constitutes too long a philosophical discussion to describe here. As just a few examples, Joan Scott describes experience as discursive, both mediated and needing to be mediated rather than accepted as objective truth. Dominick LaCapra also explains that "what we refer to as experience is typically the memory of experience." For Maurice Merleau-Ponty, the nebulousness that relegates color perception to the fringes of rational consciousness makes the sensory realm so productive for uncovering other kinds of knowing (see Scott 1991; LaCapra 2004: 66; Merleau-Ponty 1964).
3. Weerasethakul's mother also worked at a village hospital like the film's first for much of his childhood. See Weerasethakul (2006).
4. Fully establishing one segment as "past" and one as "present" is an impossible task as is determining when each moment occurs chronologically in the greater narrative, reflecting the film's temporal confusion and play. In its approach to time the "past," "present," and "memory" are always subjective terms.
5. Here I follow Lundemo (2006).
6. Such use of the natural world often occurs at climactic moments that mark the dawning of a revelation for the characters involved. See, for example, the second half of *Tropical Malady* (2004), when the two lovers embark on a shape-shifting journey through the forest's unbounded wilds, or the nighttime walk through the luminescent cave with ghostly companions in *Uncle Boonmee Who Can Recall His Past Lives* (2010).

references

Arnheim, R. (1964) *Art and Visual Perception: A Psychology of the Creative Eye*, Berkeley, CA: University of California Press.

Cavell, S. (1979) *The World Viewed, Enlarged Edition*, Cambridge, MA: Harvard University Press.

Davidoff, J. (1991) *Cognition Through Color*, Cambridge, MA: MIT Press.

Derrida, J. (1987) *The Post Card: From Socrates to Freud and Beyond*, trans. A. Bass, Chicago: University of Chicago Press.

Doane, M. A. (2002) *The Emergence of Cinematic Time: Modernity, Contingency, the Archive*, Cambridge, MA: Harvard University Press.

Hodge, J. (2007) *Derrida on Time*, London: Routledge.

Kim, J. (2010) "Between Auditorium and Art Gallery: Weerasethakul's Films and Installations," in R. Galt and K. Schnoover (eds) *Global Art Cinema: New Theories and Histories*, Oxford: Oxford University Press.

LaCapra, D. (2004) *History in Transit*, Ithaca, NY: Cornell University Press.

Lundemo, T. (2006) "The Colors of Haptic Space: Black, Blue and White in Moving Images," A. Dalle Vacche and B. Price (eds) *Color: The Film Reader*, New York: Routledge.

Merleau-Ponty, M. (1964) "Eye and Mind," in J. M. Edie (ed.) *The Primacy of Perception*, Evanston, IL: Northwestern University Press.

Price, B. (2006) "Color, the Formless, and Cinematic Eros," reprinted in A. Dalle Vacche and B. Price (eds) *Color: The Film Reader*, New York: Routledge.

Rancière, J. (2009) *The Future of the Image*, trans. G. Elliott, London: Verso.

Scott, J. (1991) "The Evidence of Experience," *Critical Inquiry* 17: 773–797.

Weerasethakul, A. (2006) "Interview," *Time Out London.* Online. Available at http://www.timeout.com/film/features/show-feature/3509/apichatpong-weerasethakul-interview.html (accessed 8 December 2010).

from *psycho* to

pleasantville

the role of color and black-and-white

t e n

imagery for film experience

philipp schmerheim

The juxtaposition of color and black-and-white imagery belongs to the arsenal of cinematic narrato-aesthetic strategies. In particular, juxta-position within the film frame, or across different versions of the same film, offers a viable strategy for producing "haptic" film experiences in spectators with the audiovisual means of cinema. Recent research in syn-aesthesia by authors such as Cretien van Campen, as well as the work of film scholars Vivian Sobchack and Laura U. Marks on embodied film per-ception, provides a theoretical basis for understanding this "haptic" effect of cinema, which this chapter argues can operate in both single films and across films such as Gus van Sant's color remake (1998) of Hitchcock's (1960) *Psycho*.

Remakes play on the familiar and unfamiliar of image and narrative through a shift from a color to a black-and-white version, which inadver-tently provokes an analytic, detached mode of spectatorship that prohib-its, rather than fosters, a haptic impression on a spectator. The narrative use of the juxtaposition of color and black-and-white can also be found in *Pleasantville* (Gary Ross, 1998) where the presence or absence of color influences the behavior and emotional states of the film characters (and not only of the spectator). In turn, *Sin City* (Robert Rodríguez, Frank Miller, 2005) represents an extreme instance of an aesthetic use of color inserts in a black-and-white world which, in contrast to *Pleasantville*, is exclusively aimed at eliciting haptic effects in the film audience. The case studies align with the current tendency in film studies to "'turn aside' from a strictly visual reading of the filmic image to the multisensorial or plurisensorial complexity of cinema" (Laine and Strauven 2009: 253).

cinema's direct and indirect address of the senses

Film perception as an embodied process opens a space in which the presence or absence of color in a film affects not only visual perception but the overall sensory perception of the film as well. Film directly affects the senses of hearing and vision, and in some cases the sense of touch (e.g. qua vibrations caused by the volume of modern Dolby surround sound systems), while the senses of smell and taste are not affected directly. However, filmmakers and theatre owners early in cinema history had already attempted to address more than hearing and vision. They followed two general strategies in order to go beyond cinema's audiovisual dimension. Firstly, they added sensory stimuli that directly address at least one of the other senses. Examples are techniques such as the Smell-O-Vison technology used in Jack Cardiff's film *Scent of Mystery* (1960), which works with the injection of distinct odors into screening rooms, or Motion Seats which move according to the action on screen similar to an effect used in popular features in amusement parks, such as *Star Tours* at Disneyland parks in France, Japan and the US. The second indirect strategy is to employ imagery, sound and montages of conventional films in such ways as to create the illusion that the missing senses are affected as well.

While the direct strategy expands the range of senses involved in the polymodal perception of films, the indirect strategy can be regarded as an attempt to provoke synaesthetic perceptions, such as actual perceptions that transgress the traditional boundaries between the senses, or at least synaesthetic impressions as the (imaginary) associations between stimuli. For instance, camera shots of a pile of rotting fish would induce associations with the smell of decay, and if the impression made is vivid enough, it might actually induce a sensation of such smells.

As a neurological phenomenon, however, synaesthetic perceptions are exceedingly rare.[1] Brain scans suggest that only synaesthetes sustain such intermodal neural connections even though they experience their senses separately and thus are able to say that they "smell" colors, or taste the sound of an instrument.[2] In literature, synaesthesia is often used as a "literal mode" of writing that aspires to an "as if"-effect, for instance, by employing such metaphors that the reader is supposed to imagine the described phenomena as if she actually perceived them. Indirect synaesthetic strategies in film differ from such literary synaesthetic modes in a crucial respect: the audiovisual information delivered by a film generates actual sensory perceptions that can test the established boundaries between the senses, even though the majority of a film audience is only able to experience synaesthetic impressions.

One of the most ambitious recent examples for the indirect strategy is Tom Tykwer's 2006 adaptation of Patrick Süskind's 1985 bestseller *Das Parfum — Die Geschichte eines Mörders*. Süskind's novel narrates the life of the synaesthete Jean-Baptiste Grenouille who possesses a superior sense of smell which dominates his overall sensory experience. *Das Parfum* had been regarded as non-adaptable because Süskind created a writing style which at least metaphorically invokes in his readers the smells and odors whose presence is an integral part of the story's diegesis. Süskind's novel is an attempt to simulate synaesthetic experiences with the means of literature. Tykwer, by contrast, develops an entire catalogue of images, sounds and cinematographic strategies which are supposed to render audio-visual counterparts to specific smells and odors, most obviously in the fish market scene which is crowded by footage of rotting fish corpses and dirt, or in the synchronization of color palette, lighting and score for each of Grenouille's female victims.

An examination of this indirect strategy identifies a number of films that juxtapose color with black-and-white imagery, producing "haptic experiences" of various sorts for film spectators. In the case of *Psycho*, the spectator may be affected by a comparison between the presence of color in the remake and their memory of the impression of the black-and-white original. *Pleasantville* juxtaposes color and black-and-white within the same film frame, but uses it not only in order to induce a special film experience in the spectator but also as a narrative device which changes the way in which the film characters behave, perceive and experience their world. In the third case study, *Sin City*, color is juxtaposed with black-and-white imagery within the same film frame, but is only used as an aesthetic element for affecting spectatorship, while assuming no significance for the film characters themselves.

Through the work of theorists such as Michel Chion, Vivian Sobchack or Laura U. Marks, classical film theory's ocularcentrist paradigm has been supplemented by a growing understanding of cinema's direct and indirect address to all of a spectator's senses, and by the acknowledgment that (film) perception is an embodied rather than a merely cognitive process (Chion 1994 and 2009; Marks 2000; Sobchack 2007). While the image and sound track of a film directly affect the spectator's senses of hearing and vision, these dimensions also indirectly address the other senses as they interact with each other.

A second tendency can be seen in Laura U. Marks' model of haptic cinema and Vivian Sobchack's account of embodiment and film perception, each of which relies on the assumption that synaesthetic phenomena, understood as an interaction between traditionally separate sensory channels, at least implicitly form a part of the process of film perception. Laura U. Marks not only acknowledges the interplay of the senses but the interconnection between sensing and thought as well:

> haptic cinema appeals strongly to a viewer perceiving with all the senses. [...] Tactile epistemology involves thinking with our skin, or giving as much significance to the physical presence of an other as to mental operations of symbolization. This is not a call to wilful regression but to recognizing the intelligence of the perceiving body. Haptic cinema, by appearing to us as an object with which we interact rather than an illusion into which we enter, calls upon this sort of embodied and mimetic intelligence. (Marks 2000: 190)

While "perceiving with all senses" does not automatically include interplay *between* all the senses, films appeal to hearing and seeing more directly. Perceiving with all senses in the cinema thus does demand the interplay of senses, in the form of image and/or sound as they address the spectator's capacity beyond vision and audition.

Sobchack follows a similar direction in writing about the carnal dimension of film experience: "we do not experience any movie only through our eyes. We see and comprehend and feel films with our entire bodily being, informed by the full history and carnal knowledge of our acculturated sensorium" (Sobchack 2007: 63). The screened events involve all of a spectator's senses, not only hearing and vision. Sobchack writes: "As 'lived bodies' [...] our vision is always already 'fleshed out'. Even at the movies our vision and hearing are informed and given meaning by our other modes of sensory access to the world" (Sobchack 2007: 60). Sobchack describes film perception as an essentially embodied experience that is not merely reduced to the visual and the aural: "When we watch a film, all our senses are mobilized" (Sobchack 2007: 80). In such accounts, film perception is not constituted by a cluster of independent sense perceptions but rather an integrated phenomenon, a kind of network of senses, which is constituted by the interplay between different sensory perceptions and higher-level cognitive faculties. Changes in one of the parameters of the network can also affect the overall function of the others: shifts in the imagery of a film thus influence other sensory dimensions.

Filmmakers' decisions to use color or black-and-white imagery in their films will affect a spectator's entire perception of the film. But what exactly happens in a spectator if the same film or scene is screened — one time in color, one time in black-and-white? A change in coloring within a film, as either paradigmatic (within the same frame) or syntagmatic (from frame to frame) shifts between black-and-white and color, can be extended to a reading of instances where a black-and-white original is remade as a color film. Shifts within a single film can be seen in *Pleasantville*, and *Sin City*, while a paradigmatic example of the alterations that can be perceived between original and remake is Gus van Sant's 1998 color reworking of Hitchcock's *Psycho* (1960). Van Sant's version reproduces the cinematography and mise-en-scène of its pretext almost identically, with differences in color, lighting and actors' performances.

color as hyper-reference: from *psycho* (1960) to *psycho* (1998)

Gus van Sant introduces two major deviations to his remake of Alfred Hitchcock's thriller *Psycho*, one of which – an altered cast – was necessary due to the 38 years that had passed since the time of its first making. Most significantly, van Sant and his cinematographer Christopher Doyle decided to shoot the film in color. Hence, the juxtaposition of color and black-and-white operates across two films. The rest of the film's elements aspire to the highest degree of fidelity possible. For instance, the film is based on Joseph Stefano's adapted screenplay and Bernard Herrmann's original score. This comparability of two film versions finds an analogue in that of old films that were originally colored but that are predominantly known through their surviving black-and-white versions. An additional complication is introduced with the subsequent color restoration of films such as *Nosferatu*.[3]

The change of color is already apparent in Saul Bass' title sequence, in which the bright grey lines have been replaced by bright neon green, quickly indicating the film's non-standard color palette. In Hitchcock's black-and-white original, the sequence draws on gray tones rather than high contrasts which could be comparable to this effect. Cinematographer John L. Russell predominantly used soft light; the actors often blend with the color composition of the background. In contrast, the bubble-gum-pop pastel colors of van Sant's remake, with its dominating pink, orange and bright green, are emphasized by cinematographer Christopher Doyle with a hard lighting scheme that sometimes obfuscates areas of the background. This is most evident before and after the shower murder scene, when Norman Bates shows the bathroom to Marion, and later when he disposes of her corpse, placing her on the shower curtain lying on the floor of the bedroom. The visible details of the bathroom dissolve in bright neon light when seen from the bedroom, its unnatural appearance fore-shadowing the murder. The deliberate inclusion of washed-out, cold neon lights – the sign of the motel which ironically includes the lines "Newly renovated. Color TV" (**see Plate 15**), the bathroom scenes, Arbogast's phone call to Marion's sister Lila (Julianne Moore) from a public phone booth – also remind the viewer of Doyle's earlier work for Hong-Kong-based director Wong Kar-Wai in *Chungking Express* (1994), *Fallen Angels* (1995) or *Happy Together* (1997).

Considering the reception history of Hitchcock's version, it is perhaps unsurprising that the shower murder scene remains central in the 1998 film. Legend has it that some viewers of the black-and-white version vividly recall red swirls of blood rather than the film's grey tones. Apart from budget considerations, Hitchcock shot the film in black-and-white in order to limit the goriness of the shower murder scene on the audience, who at that time were not used to such direct incidents of violence on screen. The comparison of the shower murder scenes shows that a mere advance in photorealism via the inclusion of color does not necessarily correspond to a more realist impression on a spectator; there is no direct correlation between use of color in film and a heightened realistic impression of events occurring on screen.

The film's composer Bernard Herrmann decided to record a score that is entirely played with strings in order to capture the "film's stark mono-chromatic visual style" (Totaro 2004). By changing the style of lighting and introducing a color palette for the remake, this close, latently synaesthetic connection between score and imagery is lost. In effect a reading which operates across the two versions of *Psycho* finds that the original remains open to a more haptic spectatorial experience. With prior knowledge of Hitchcock's *Psycho*, a reading of van Sant's film is informed by background memories and feelings that can be derived from the 1960 original. Van Sant's version invites meta-spectatorship; by using color while staying faithful to all other basic components of the original film, it constantly pushes the spectator into a mode of film perception that explicitly engages the cognitive dimension of spectatorship. This altered spectatorship is played out in an intermediate realm between a haptic film experience and spectatorship as a rational cognitive enterprise.

The synaesthetic experience provided by the film is – if at all – an indirect one. It deliberately invokes the memory of films as a facet of spec-tatorial experience. Indeed, the whole point of van Sant's efforts is lost if one does not experience the 1998 version as a colored yet reconfigured mirror-image of Hitchcock's 1960 film. It directs attention to the interplay between shifts in style of representation, film movements and viewing conventions.

narrative function of color in *pleasantville*

In contrast to *Psycho*, a number of contemporary Hollywood films such as *Pleasantville* and *Sin City* explore the paradigmatic juxtaposition of color and black-and-white imagery by experimenting with a co-presence of both color schemes within the same film frame. In *Memento* (Christopher Nolan, 2000), color and black-and-white imagery serve to distinguish the chronological from the alternating retrograde plot line. The different color schemes support the audience in distinguishing the film's different plot lines, while the presence or absence of color is not an intrinsic element of the diegesis or plot structure. Color does not assume an intra-diegetic narrative function.

This, however, is the case with *Pleasantville*. In Gary Ross' 1998 sitcom parody the presence or absence of color in a black-and-white world becomes a deciding element for the attitudes and behavior of the film characters. *Pleasantville* takes place in the 1990s and tells the story of the two siblings David (Tobey Maguire) and Jennifer (Reese Witherspoon) who are accidentally transported into a television screen, where they become part of the black-and-white world of a 1950s TV serial called "Pleasantville," as two of the serial's main characters Bud and Mary-Sue. Their very un-1950-ish behavior literally as well as metaphorically introduces colors to the village which is a projection of WASP ideals of idyllic American small-town life. After Jennifer spends a night at Lover's Lane with the captain of the local basketball team, things start to turn colored in Pleasantville: at first, it is only a single rose; later the lips and tongues of the girls, who quickly follow Mary-Sue's example, gaining a red tone. The film revolves around the conflict between the innovative highly colored part of Pleasantville and the conservative, mostly male inhabitants who are worried about the vanishing of their hitherto "pleasant" lifestyle, which is threatened by the Coloreds' new way of life. *Pleasantville* uses color as a device for an allegorical reenactment of traditional generational conflict between parents and their children, where the world of the young people is seen as "colorful" and "vibrant," while the old order represented by the generation of parents and grandparents is seen as "dull" and "colorless." At the height of the conflict between "black-and-whites" and Coloreds, there are even shop window signs reading "No Coloreds." By this, the film explicitly invites comparisons to the history of racial segregation and the conflicts surrounding the US Civil Rights Movement in the 1950s and 1960s. In *Pleasantville*, color thus not only functions as a literal device for the film's narrative structure but includes metaphorical and political discourse on color as well.

Apart from the "politics of color," *Pleasantville* explores the metaphorical interrelations of color and emotion. Only characters that fall in love or experience other profound emotional reactions become colored. Seeing colors completely changes the distanced behavior of the inhabitants of Pleasantville towards each other. Couples openly show their affection and love, they actually touch and stop treating each other in the former distanced, formalized manner. Lover's Lane becomes a hotspot for one-night stands. The change in the visual dimension of the characters' world influences the way in which they use their other senses: seeing things in color incites them to pay more attention to their other senses such as touch and smell. Seeing things in color has a haptic effect on the town's inhabitants.

Pleasantville exposes this haptic effect in a double way: first, on the level of film spectatorship, the film confronts its audience with color and black-and-white versions of the diegesis and characters, and thereby offers different ways of experiencing the film. Second, on the level of the film diegesis, it is the film characters themselves who react to the changing coloring of the world.

aesthetic function of color in *sin city*

Unlike *Pleasantville*, the film adaptation of Frank Miller's *Sin City* graphic novels does not use color as a narrative device that motivates its film characters' behavior, but is prima facie used in order to highlight certain character traits, objects, situations or emotional states, and to direct the attention of the spectators to these. In *Sin City*, characters are not aware of the peculiar color scheme that structures their world. Color does not assume a narrative function within the diegesis of Basin City, even though it supports and directs narrative comprehension and affects a spectator's interpretation of the film. In terms of the diegesis: While in *Pleasantville* the presence or absence of color is an element of the diegesis which the film characters are aware of, this is not the case in *Sin City*. Color presence or absence, then, is a narrative tool in *Pleasantville*, but not in *Sin City*, but in both films is used as a tool for steering the film audience's comprehension of the film.

Sin City is a neo-noir style episode film that explores the violent adventures of a number of characters whose disillusioned, nihilistic world view by far surpasses that of traditional film noir characters. Rodríguez's attempt to "translate" rather than merely adapt Frank Miller's graphic novels results in a high-contrast black-and-white film that integrates a limited number of colored objects. The panels of Miller's stories provide the storyboard for the film. With the exception of Kadie's Bar, which appears on screen as a sepia-toned environment, the locations of the film scenes are represented in high-contrast black-and-white. Only single objects, such as signposts, backlights, cars or linen, and characteristics specific to some characters are colored, such as the hair of the prostitute Goldie, who is the dead love interest of one of the film's main characters Marv (Mickey Rourke), or the lips and the robe of The Customer in the exposition.

Apart from its aesthetics and stylistics, color, which is limited to a palette of ruby red, yellow, gold, green and turquoise blue, assumes a semiotic function throughout the film to signal the emotional states of the characters. This is most apparent in the character of Goldie with her shining golden hair, red lips and bronze complexion. The bed in which Marv and Goldie spend a night together is heart-shaped and covered with ruby red satin sheets. (**See Plate 16.**) During his search for Goldie's killers, Marv meets Goldie's twin sister Wendy (Jaime Smith), who, despite her looks, is entirely represented in black-and-white, since she is not Marv's love interest. When Wendy visits Marv in the death-row cell, he first mistakes her for Goldie and sees her as having gold-colored hair and red lips. Once he becomes aware of his mistake, Wendy fades to black-and-white suggesting a shift in emotion.

The film's aesthetics of unnaturalness suggests a kind of hyper-real space which is partially removed from the laws that govern the normal world. It is represented by the omnipresence of violence: The film characters constantly hit, shoot, and otherwise injure each other; acts of violence are a part of their everyday life. Interestingly, this everydayness of violence is suggested to the film audience through the use of white as the color of blood. In the gray-scale environment, it does not attract as much attention as it would in a standard-colored environment. This removes "the gravity of the violence from normal human terms" (Burley 2010) and thereby facilitates the viewing experience of extreme representations of violence such as decapitation, amputation, extreme injuries to all parts of the bodies and torture. If represented in a realist, non-comic fashion, *Sin City*'s scenes of violence would be too "haptic" in nature as to allow for a wide screening. As part of Basin City's "natural" environment, blood is an unremarkable element presented to the audience in a non-haptic way, which makes the isolated red-colored representations of blood all the more haptic. One instance is the *The Hard Goodbye* sequence, in which Marv's blood is sometimes represented in red. In these scenes, he is in the middle of seemingly dangerous situations and suffers injuries that for normal human beings would be life-threatening. Marv, however, is represented as an almost invincible character – and the red color of his wounds becomes a marker of his invincibility.

While the comparative analysis of Hitchcock and Van Sant's *Psycho* suggests that the presence or absence of color can constitute an important element of spectatorship between the present film experience and another that is remembered, *Pleasantville* shifts the focus of the effects of the juxtaposition from the spectators to the film characters themselves. In *Sin City* the juxtaposition is exclusively aimed at the film spectators (and not noted by the characters). However, even though its handling of color and black-and-white as an aesthetic element is rather traditional, the film's overall style is unique. What remains for future research is a more extensive investigation of the strategies of using of the presence and absence of color in contemporary cinema.

notes

1. Aleman et al. (2001), quoted in van Campen (2008: 5). This account of synaesthesia is informed by van Campen's book.

2. An overview of current research on clinical synaesthesia can be found in Robertson and Sagiv (2005).
3. Odo (2010) provides a detailed comparison of the public domain version with the 2006 restored version of *Nosferatu – Eine Symphonie des Grauens*.

references

Aleman, A. et al. (2001) "Activation of Striate Cortex in the Absence of Visual Stimulation: An FMRI Study of Synaesthesia", *Neuroreport*, 12, 13: 2827–2830.

Bordwell, D. (2009) "Color, Shape, Movement ... and Talk". Online. Available at http://www.davidbordwell.net/blog/?p=4374 (accessed 29 December 2010).

Burley, S. (2010) "Understanding Color in *Sin City*". Brighthub.com. Online. Available at http://www.brighthub.com/arts/movies/articles/67469.aspx (accessed 29 December 2010).

Campen, C. van (2008) *The Hidden Sense: Synaesthesia in Art and Science*, Cambridge, MA: MIT Press.

Chion, M. (1994) *Audio-Vision: Sound on Screen*, New York: Columbia University Press.

Chion, M. (2009) *Film, a Sound Art*, New York: Columbia University Press.

Laine, T. and Strauven, W. (2009) "Introduction. The Synaesthetic Turn", *New Review of Film and Television Studies*, 7, 3: 249–255.

Marks, L. U. (2000) *The Skin of the Film: Intercultural Cinema, Embodiment, and the Senses*, Durham, NC: Duke University Press.

Odo (2010) "*Nosferatu* – Eine Symphonie des Grauens". Online. Available at http://www.schnittberichte.com/schnittbericht.php?ID=4112494 (accessed 3 January 2011).

Robertson, L. C. and Sagiv, N. (eds) (2005) *Synaesthesia: Perspectives from Neuroscience*, New York: Oxford University Press.

Schmerheim, P. (2008) "Paradigmatic Forking-Path Films: Intersections between Mind-Game Films and Multiple-Draft Narratives", in Gächter, Y. et al. (eds), *Erzählen. Reflexionen im Zeitalter der Digitalisierung/Storytelling. Reflections in the Age of Digitalization*, Innsbruck: Innsbruck University Press: 256–270.

Sobchack, V. (2007) "What My Fingers Knew. The Cinesthetic Subject, or Vision in the Flesh", *Carnal Thoughts: Embodiment and Moving Image Culture*, Berkeley, CA: University of California Press: S3–84.

Süskind, P. (1985) *Das Parfum. Die Geschichte eines Mörders*, Zürich: Diogenes.

Totaro, D. (2004) "Appropriating Hitch. *Psycho* Redux". Offscreen.com. Online. Available at http://www.horschamp.qc.ca/new_offscreen/psycho_van.html (accessed 29 December 2010).

aesthetics

part three

the illuminated

fairytale

the colors of paul

e l e v e n

fejos's *lonesome* (1928)

j o s h u a   y u m i b e

> *The monotony of this life is demonstrated in many striking*
> *details. Only kitsch, which momentarily illuminates the*
> *grayness, is able to interrupt it.*
>
> (Siegfried Kracauer, review of Lonesome, 1974: 204)

> *Millions go every night to the motion picture theatres of the*
> *world. They go there always seeking the elusive mood of a child*
> *listening to a fairytale; seeking, in other words, the photoplay,*
> *which will for a few brief hours lift them out of the monotony of*
> *their own humdrum existence into the enchanted realm of*
> *make-believe.*
>
> (Paul Fejos 1929)

Paul Fejos's *Lonesome* contains three tinted, stenciled, and hand-colored sequences that occur in the middle of the film during scenes at Coney Island. The film's story is relatively simple, taking place over the course of a single day. It begins on a Saturday morning with a half day of frantic, alienating work in New York City, where the film's lonely protagonists Jim and Mary toil, strangers to one another. She is a switchboard operator, he a punch-press machinist. The film shows their afternoon escape from the city to Coney Island to, as an intertitle explains, "recover from the stress of a daily routine." Situated in this liminal space of leisure and entertainment, they meet randomly, and in the magnificent glow of the dreamland, they fall in love. In a series of overlapping dissolves, the red neon lights of a ferris wheel illuminate the blue-tinted sky, and the sunset throws its golden rays over them in the film's first colored sequence. Caught in the visual and sonic swirl of the amusement park, they make their way through its attractions of fun houses and in the second color sequence a music hall awash in golden and pink tinting and stenciling, only to lose one another when the utopian space of fun and distraction becomes a nightmare. A rollercoaster catches fire in the same hues that previously colored their romance (the final colored sequence) and separates the lovers. A storm blows in to further impede their search for one another. At the end of the day, they return home more alone then ever—until the sound of a phonograph, like the wisp of an arrow, penetrates the adjoining wall of their apartments, and the lovers discover themselves to have been by chance neighbors all along.

In his review of Lonesome, Siegfried Kracauer draws attention to the fairytale nature of the film, specifically the ending (1929: 202–204). Shifting generic registers from the urban realism that the film opens with and returns to after Coney Island, a fairytale ending emerges in the film's final moment. This miraculous ending, however, casts the narrative in an ambivalent light. It unites Jim and Mary who as neighbors should have met long ago, yet the improbability of this coincidence negatively illuminates the resolution: these two lovers, separated from one another by accident, would in all likelihood never have met again. Even when they finally embrace, one cannot forget the bitterness of the more probable reality. This then for Kracauer is the value of fairytales: given the hopelessness that threatens to overwhelm modern life, one needs a means of imagining a better world if anything is to change. Rather than weakening the film, the ending's ambivalence provides this by imaging modernity's utopian dreams of unalienated intimacy without hiding its traumas.

I wish to explore the ambivalent relationship that Kracauer notes between fairytales and modernity by focusing on one specific aspect of Lonesome: its use of color, for I take it to be a formal aspect of the ambivalence Kracauer delineates in the film. Color and fairytales have long been entwined, from vibrantly illustrated children's books, to the magical stage colors of the féerie plays of the nineteenth century, to the spectacular hand-colored and stenciled féerie films of Georges Méliès and Segundo de Chomón during the first decade of the 1900s. From the féerie to the fairytale of Lonesome, color plays a pivotal role in the emergence of mass culture, yet color has not yet been sufficiently explored in relation to the cultural context of modernity. This is evident, for instance, in John Gage's magisterial studies of color, *Color and Culture* (1993) and *Color and Meaning* (1999), which, despite their depth and range, collectively spend but two inadequate paragraphs on the question of "popular culture" (Gage 1999: 33). In discussions of color in film, this has also proven to be a blind spot due to the fact that the cultural history of color has largely been overlooked as questions of realism in relation to natural, photographic color have dominated the history. In actual practice, color in mass culture and in the cinema has been aligned generically with spectacle, which forms a counterpoint to the prevailing emphasis on photographic realism. Color's generic association with spectacle has marked film aesthetics from the earliest uses of color in the cinema of the 1890s through Technicolor to the various digital grading effects of the present day.

In 1928, the applied-coloring techniques deployed in *Lonesome* were growing less common in Hollywood productions. By the latter part of the 1920s, color was proving difficult to apply in ways that did not interfere with soundtracks on prints, and in the films that still used color, Technicolor's two-color, imbibition system was more aggressively supplanting applied-coloring techniques. In the face of these issues, Universal actually promoted *Lonesome*'s use of color. In the company's publicity journal *Universal Weekly*, it advertised the film as "The first talking picture with color sequences," and in the same issue highlighted a review by the *San Francisco News* noting, "The color scenes in *Lonesome* are unusual, and greatly enhance an already beautiful story" (*Universal Weekly* 1928: 4–5, 11). To understand how color enhances this story, I wish to trace the ways in which the film uses color in conjunction with intermedial topoi deriving from urban mass culture (Coney Island, advertising, neon lighting) and modernist color theory and practice (color abstraction and synaesthesia). I am interested in how this use of color elaborates not only Kracauer's fairytale reading of the film but also what Miriam Hansen has theorized as the "vernacular modernism" of classical cinema: that is, that the cinema not only reflected the modern world but also offered audiences a vernacular horizon in which to negotiate modernity in ways akin to the sensory-reflexive practices of high modernist works (Hansen 1999). The modern, fairytale colors of *Lonesome* haptically engage one's senses: illuminated in the colors of Coney Island, the characters and the surrounding crowds in the film model a form of spectatorship that reflexively suggests a broader reading of the influence of color on the viewer of the film. Color saturates not just the people in the film, but it also reflects from the screen to envelop the audience, and in these movements, the *féerie* modernism of color illuminates the cinema.

Lonesome's first colored sequence begins on the beach at Coney Island and runs into the following scene depicting the park's amusements, lasting for approximately three and a half minutes. Beginning the sequence, a medium shot of Jim and Mary dissolves into three superimposed images: 1. a blue-tinted medium shot of the protagonists; 2. Jim and Mary again, doubled in long shot at the bottom of the image, illuminated in a stencil-colored golden light; and 3. amusement rides with stencil-colored red lights framing the right and left of the entire image. **(See Figure 11.1.)** The superimposition gives way to a stenciled medium shot of the protagonists for the second talking sequence of the film, which lasts until Jim and Mary realize that the sun is setting (shown in long shot against the ocean, tinted blue and stenciled gold) and that everyone else has already left the beach. In the next scene, Jim and Mary return to the crowds of Coney Island, and for the length of the remaining colored sequence, they are almost indistinguishable from the mass. As the camera moves through the throng, it explores the attractions of Luna and Steeplechase Parks, dissolving one colored attraction into the next in rapid succession. The crowd dissolves back and forth into the famous lights of Coney Island, stenciled and tinted in reds, golds, and blues, while colored balloons mingle with the lights above the people's heads. The film then returns to black-and-white, and Jim and Mary emerge from the crowd.

Given the overlapping histories of cinema and amusements parks, it is significant that all three of *Lonesome*'s colored sequences occur at

Figure 11.1
Lonesome (Paul Fejos, 1928): Jim and Mary superimposed at the beach. Stencil-colored in film print.

Coney Island. The first sequence in particular calls attention to the topos of the amusement park that recurs so often in silent cinema: from early films such as Edison's *Shooting the Chutes* (1896), *Rube and Mandy at Coney Island* (1903), *Coney Island at Night* (1905), through later films such as *Sunrise* (1927), *It* (1927), and *The Crowd* (1928). One of the defining visual features of Coney Island, often referenced in films, was its lighting displays. (**See Figure 11.2.**) When night would descend, hundreds of thousands of lights stretched in patterns outlining the buildings would illuminate the park. These lighting displays not only lit the night for revelry but also served as a glamorous icon of American modernity in photographic, song slide, and filmic representations of the illuminated park.

In its use of this lighting topos, the first colored sequence of *Lonesome* is exemplary. Against the illuminated background of Coney Island, Jim and Mary's romance sparks and flourishes. Through multiple dissolves, the lights both envelop and move through their bodies, creating complexly layered, abstract images. When Jim and Mary leave the beach, this abstraction is then carried into the crowds through which they move. The lights of the sequence not only illuminate the night but also absorb the revelers in colored hues. This circulation of lights—overlapping and dissolving, spinning and falling—abstractly mimics the circulation of bodies that

Figure 11.2
Lonesome (Paul Fejos, 1928): The lights of Coney Island. Stencil-colored in film print.

dissolve back and forth through the various shots. Rather than alienating, the dissolving abstraction models a potential relationship between people and things: one that can playfully bring them together to and through technology. As liminal spaces, amusement parks—and by reflexive extension the cinema—sit on the peripheries of the everyday, yet in their nearness to it, they possess the potential to reimagine it by shifting the boundaries between technology and the bodies found therein. This first colored section of *Lonesome* provides a utopian vision of modernity: a contingent space where strangers can still meet and fall in love, and where modern technologies are harnessed for intimacy within the crowd.

The second colored sequence of the film lasts for approximately 90 seconds and follows Jim and Mary into a music hall at Coney Island. A stencil-colored sign fills the screen in gold and pink, flashing the word, "Dancing." **(See Plate 17.)** A dissolve seemingly pulls the screen out immersively toward the audience as the camera tracks through the sign and into a close-up of a brass horn; the horn dissolves and through its circumference the camera continues to track into a red-tinted medium shot of a band performing the film's theme song, "Always." The words and music of the song are superimposed over the bottom of the screen while the song plays on the soundtrack. The film then begins to dissolve the various instruments of the band together creating a synaesthetic montage of sounds: the horns, the drums, the banjos illuminated by pink stencil colors and tints. This is then intercut with medium shots of Jim and Mary dancing in alternating tints of pink, lavender, and gold. A number of abstract dissolves leads to a long shot of the crowd with Jim and Mary in the mid-foreground in a gold and then lavender tint. A match dissolve to their bodies isolates them from the crowd, and as on the beach, they are once again alone in an elaborately colored fantasy space. They dance beneath the yellow crescent moon. A shimmering golden palace appears to the right, and as they waltz through the clouds, rotating celestial orbs mark the passage of time. **(See Figure 11.3.)** Another match dissolve returns them to the dancing crowd in the hall at which point the film returns to black-and-white.

As suggested earlier, the interaction between the crowds and the modern lighting of Coney Island refigures human intimacy through technology. In his review of *Lonesome*, Kracauer uses the language of artificial lighting to emphasize the film's fairytale quality in his emphasis on the film's "glimmering reflection [*Abglanz*] of a better life" and in his discussion of kitsch, which interrupts and illuminates the gray monotony of the modern world (1929: 204). Kracauer draws attentions to these aspects of *Lonesome* to illustrate how the cinema, as a technologically mediated form of kitsch, can grant one a new perspective: a fleeting glimpse of a better life.

Throughout his Weimar writings, Kracauer frequently calls attention to modern lighting effects, in particular colored ones—e.g. the tiny red lights on a rollercoaster; the red gleam of advertisements on the boulevards

Figure 11.3

Lonesome (Paul Fejos, 1928): Jim and Mary's daydream in the dance hall. Stencil-colored in film print.

(see especially his two essays on artificial lighting in which he again deploys the term *Abglanz* to refer to modern technology, "Lichtreklame" [1927] and "Ansichtspostkarte" [1930], reprinted in 1990: 19–21, 184–185). Kracauer's interest in artificial lighting reflects the growing significance of color in commodity culture. Modern lighting began to be colored and used in advertisements, and in marketing handbooks from the period it is commonplace that colored lighting is useful because of color's aesthetic influence over spectators' moods and emotions. The roots of such discourses on the power of color are ancient and have historically revolved around debates over the role of color in cognition, as epitomized in Goethe's polemic against Newton in his *Color Theory*. In the late nineteenth and early twentieth centuries, research into the affective powers of color was abundant and had affinities with Symbolist and occult color aesthetics, which stressed the related notions of correspondences and synaesthesia to explain color's mood-inducing powers. In the realm of early abstract art, interest in synaesthesia was commonplace, as in the Theosophically inflected paintings and writings of Wassily Kandinksy and in the experiments with projected, color-music by composers such as Alexander Scriabin and Thomas Wilfred (on this history, see for instance Elder 2008: 1–201). These influences have most obviously seeped into film through the experimental works of artists such as Oskar Fischinger, Harry Smith, and Paul Sharits.

Bringing this history to bear then on the second colored sequence of *Lonesome*, one can recognize the affinity the colors display with both advertising lighting and modernist color abstraction. The film's use of color invokes and adapts the affective powers attributed to color in these various media practices, and in this process of adaptation, the film demonstrates Hollywood's intermedial affinity with modernism. However, this is not a passive move but rather is indicative of Hollywood's active appropriation of cultural tropes, topoi, and imagery into a vernacular modernism of its own.

The second colored sequence of *Lonesome* in particular foregrounds this process of vernacularization. The moving dissolve from the colored "Dancing" sign into the horn and then into the band suggests the synaesthetic power of colored film to mimic the rhythms and tones of music. The abstract montage of sound and image synaesthetically conveys the whirl and attraction of the amusement park. The addition of color—the neon glow—to this equation underscores the transformative power of the park's amusements: the glamorous hues from the neon sign saturate the crowd and facilitate its interaction with the abstractions of modernity. At the same time, this collective innervation leads to a private fantasy world for Jim and Mary as they dance out of the crowd and into their romantic dreamscape. When they return to the crowd, the two are now one, together intimately part of the larger whole.

It is worth teasing out the reflexive implications of the technologically mediated intimacy in the scene. The movement of the camera into the neon sign at the beginning of the sequence seemingly pulls the screen out into the audience through the track in. In doing so, it suggests a broader, more reflexive reading of the crowd in the dance hall. Shifting focus from the screen to the theater space, an attention to color projection allows for the theorization of a process through which cinema spectators both absorb and are absorbed by the images on the screen. As the crowd in the film moves within the warm, colored glow of the "Dancing" sign, the ambient light of the film's projection reflects off the screen and into the crowd in the theater (a reflection doubled by the camera movement). The synaesthetic illuminations that saturate the collective of the dance hall in *Lonesome* can also be read as reflexively enveloping the theater audience, expanding the colored abstraction of Coney Island into the cinema space. The images of the film then are not only to be gazed at, but they reflect back and saturate the audience, projecting not just to the eyes but also immersing the bodies, the seats, floors, and walls of the space. This saturation of the theater must not be essentialized; however, calling attention to it usefully foregrounds the haptic nature of cinematic experience (see Lant 1995: 45–73). It expands the screen into the world, collectively tinting the audience. While the effects of this saturation can be read positively (the unification of a collective and amorous subjectivity), its potentials also have more disquieting implications, as the final colored sequence of the film demonstrates.

After leaving the dance hall, Jim and Mary move on to their next amusement: a rollercoaster. In the crowded line, they end up separated, riding in two parallel trains. At first they slowly move along the tracks, smiling and waving back and forth to one another. As the ride picks up speed, point-of-view shots blur the lights of Coney Island, and with the ride's dips and turns both protagonists and spectators are sensually hurtled through the ride. Thirty seconds into the mayhem, Jim looks back and realizes that the wheel of Mary's cart has caught fire. After the intertitle announces this, the camera cuts to Jim's point of view, and the final colored sequence of the film begins. The golden-orange hue that had previously colored the sunset on the beach and the fairytale palace of the music hall now illuminates a fiery disaster. Shots of Jim and Mary in their carts are intercut with point-of-view shots of the fiery hand-colored wheel. Overcome with fear, Mary faints, and the last color sequence ends after only 30 seconds. The carts roll into the station and pandemonium ensues, which keeps Jim and Mary separated and lost to one another for the rest of their time at Coney Island.

If the previous two colored sequences can be read as utopian visions of modernity, the final colored sequence underscores a more apprehensive attitude. It does so by calling attention to the disastrous potentials harbored by modern technologies. Significantly, these dangers are epitomized by a rollercoaster disaster that evokes a train wreck. Wolfgang Schivelbusch has written about the ambivalence surrounding train transport in the nineteenth century (1986: 129–133), and in a parallel move in *Disenchanted Night*, he traces the latent dangers found in networked technologies of lighting such as the explosive and poisonous hazards of gas (1995: 33–40). As Schivelbusch clarifies, modern technologies both productively transform and threaten everyday life. Similarly, through the near disaster of the rollercoaster fire, *Lonesome* illustrates the malleability of color meaning and in this suggests a more skeptical reading of entertainment technology.

The inherent ambivalences of these technologies can be theorized in terms of the emerging commodity culture of the time. Though less physically dangerous, the technologies of lighting and color as applied in advertising and commodity production have their own set of destructive associations. The culture industry's application of these technologies greatly expanded the potential to market commodities through the production and manipulation of desire. Such uses of color and lighting reinforce the groundwork of consumer culture and adversely contribute to the formation of homogenous, consuming subjects.

These negative facets of technology dialectically balance the more utopian moments in *Lonesome*. Rather than illuminate the inequalities of the everyday, technologies of lighting and color collectively divert spectators' attention to the nonessential, thus establishing a compensatory logic for the color in the film. In so doing, color functions as part of a structure that systematically petrifies the status quo through the regimented control of spectatorship. To reframe the analysis of amusement park lighting and by extension of *Lonesome*, these color illuminations bear the force of commodity desire, and the libratory moments found therein are thus but a step away from the compulsive mimesis to cultural commodities that Adorno and Horkheimer discuss in their critique of the culture industry (1947: 136). Similar to advertising illuminations, the colors in *Lonesome* reflect over the revelers at Coney Island and onto the cinema audience continuing this intermedial circulation of desire.

But then this is a point that Fejos's film makes remarkably clear. The color sign in the film's second sequence directly advertises the entertainments of the park, and when Jim and Mary enter the dance hall, it is within the rosy hues of neon advertising that they dance into a fantasy world. However, though *Lonesome* motions toward a utopian union for Jim and Mary in the first two colored sequences, it quickly ruptures this harmony with the rollercoaster. The same colors that cast a utopian hue over the film reoccur here to illuminate their misfortune. With the ride's change of hue from grayness to fiery orange, the utopian entertainments of Coney Island become ominous and alienating.

To return to Kracauer on the fairytale, Jim and Mary begin in the loneliness of their boarding house and return to it even more alone. If the film does assert its miraculous powers in the end by drawing them back together, it does so only by first dwelling on the dystopic side modern life and then evacuating plausibility from the plot in its shift from realism to fairytale. In so doing the film displays its ability to enchant and disenchant at the same time, to paraphrase Kracauer elsewhere on rollercoasters (1992: 58–60). *Lonesome* ambivalently acknowledges and pushes beyond a compensatory logic by recognizing both the promises and failures of modernity. But this is more than just ambivalence: it is a dialectical move through cinema that uses the medium's glimmering powers to suggest a chance of intimacy in the face of overwhelming alienation. By lodging this suggestion in the guise of a fairytale, though, the film refuses to lapse into ideology about it: intimacy is possible but implausible, at least for now.

The film makes this dialectical move not only narratively but also at the level of form. In its use of color, *Lonesome* displays its affinity with a network of related claims about color in the early twentieth century: from idealistic assertions about its harmonizing ability to attempts to marshal such possibilities for the mimetic formation of subjectivity and desire. Such affinities, however, are not just passively absorbed into the matrix of classical

Hollywood cinema; rather, it actively appropriates them into its vernacular. In the case of *Lonesome*, it is possible to frame this as a critical appropriation. The hues that cast a utopian glow over the film in the first two colored sequences reoccur in the third illuminating the film's rollercoaster accident. The polarity among them inscribes a modern fairytale: one that dialectically places its utopian potentials under erasure. Color thus sustains and builds the fairytale character of the film: for through its glimmer, a better life is glimpsed and effaced.

acknowledgements

For Miriam Hansen, who not only introduced me to *Lonesome* but also taught me how to look, feel, and think my way through color's glimmering reflections. For the research, my references are to the colored, sound print prescorred by the George Eastman House, and I am grateful to Anthony L'Abbate of the GEH for details on the most recent restoration. An earlier version of this essay was published in 2004.

references

Adorno, T. W. and M. Horkheimer. (1947; trans. 2002) "The Culture Industry: Enlightenment as Mass Deception," in *Dialectic of Enlightenment*, trans. E. Jephcott, ed. G. S. Noerr, Stanford, CA: Stanford University Press.

Elder, B. R. (2008) *Harmony and Dissent: Film and Avant-garde Art Movements in the Early Twentieth Century*, Waterloo, ON: Wilfrid Laurier University Press.

Fejos, P. (1929) "Illusion on the Screen," *New York Times*, 26 May: x3.

Gage, J. (1993) *Color and Culture: Practice and Meaning from Antiquity to Abstraction*, Berkeley, CA: University of California Press.

Gage, J. (1999) *Color and Meaning: Art, Science, and Symbolism*, Berkeley, CA: University of California Press.

Hansen, M. B. (1999) "The Mass Production of the Senses: Classical Cinema as Vernacular Modernism," *Modernism/Modernity* 6.2: 59–77.

Kracauer, S. (1929, reprinted 1974) "*Lonesome*," in Kino: *Essays, Studien, Glossen zum Film*, Frankfurt: Suhrkamp.

Kracauer, S. (1990) *Schriften*, vol. 5.2, ed. I. Mülder-Bach, Frankfurt: Suhrkamp.

Kracauer, S. (1992) "Roller Coaster," trans. T. Levin, *Qui Parle* 5.2: 58–60.

Lant, A. (1995) "Haptical Cinema," *October* 74 (Autumn, 1995): 45–73.

Schivelbusch, W. (1986) *The Railway Journey: The Industrialization of Time and Space in the Nineteenth Century*, Berkeley, CA: University of California Press.

Schivelbusch, W. (1995) *Disenchanted Night: The Industrialization of Light in the Nineteenth Century*, Berkeley, CA: University of California Press.

Universal Weekly (1928) 28.11.

Yumibe, J. (2004) "Das Illuminierte Märchen: Zur Farbästhetik von Paul Fejos's *Lonesome*," in *Paul Fejos: Die Welt macht Film*, trans. W. Astelbauer, ed. E. Büttner, Wien: Verlag Filmarchiv Austria.

color unlimited:

amateur color

cinema in the 1930s

twelve

charles tepperman

In 1928 when natural color photography was still a rarity in commercial movie theatres, amateurs claimed color filmmaking as their own terrain for aesthetic experimentation and discovery.[1] That year, Kodak introduced their Kodacolor process and amateurs encountered a new technology that set their medium apart from the commercial cinema. For over a decade, from 1928 until the end of the 1930s, amateur filmmakers explored color film aesthetics, first with Kodacolor, and later with the much-improved Kodachrome process, introduced in 1935. An editorial titled "Color Unlimited," published in 1935, articulated the amateur's position in explicit terms:

> While sound movies were a definite product of the theatri-
> cal motion picture industry, it is indisputable that a wide
> use of color movies has been a specific product of personal
> filming ... Amateurs are several jumps ahead in the intel-
> ligent use of color in cinematography, because their
> employment of it has been so extensive. As amateur sound

has been aided by Hollywood pathfinding, so can amateurs
extend to their professional friends a helping hand in this
new color field which will rapidly engage Hollywood's
interest. (*Movie Makers* 1935a: 193)

These claims prompt a consideration of the role of the amateur in the history of color film technology and aesthetics. What *were* the creative uses
and limitations of use of amateur color film processes in the 1930s? Did the
amateur use of new color formats extend beyond the novelty of natural
color recording?

This essay examines how amateurs incorporated Kodacolor and
Kodachrome into their discourse and practice during the 1930s. The focus
of this discussion is not so much "home movies" as "advanced" amateur
filmmaking, a category that encompassed individuals and organizations
that treated amateur filmmaking as a serious hobby and encouraged the
production of personal, experimental, and documentary filmmaking.
These advanced amateur filmmakers distinguished themselves from
typical home moviemakers by doing pre- and post-production work on
their films (not just point-and-shoot filming), developing sophisticated
technical and aesthetic strategies, and joining organizations like the
New York-based Amateur Cinema League (ACL), which organized annual,
international competitions for amateur work. To elucidate the amateur's
fascination with the possibilities of color film aesthetics in the 1930s, this
essay will focus on some films that received awards and attention from the
ACL publication, *Movie Makers* magazine, and especially those of the prominent Danish-American amateur filmmaker John Hansen. In 1932, Hansen's
film *Studies in Blue and Chartres Cathedral* was named in the Amateur Cinema
League's list of the year's Ten Best films, and Hansen also published several
magazine articles about color perception and composition in films. These
writings, along with other articles and editorials about color filmmaking,
further extend the discourse around amateur color moviemaking and
illuminate a shared effort to expand the cinema's aesthetic vocabulary and
elevate the medium's position in relation to other more established
art forms. While working to accomplish this, amateurs and writers also
articulated methods for developing color perception, with benefits both
for producing effective film compositions, as well as for the revitalized
experience of everyday life these color compositions conveyed.

kodacolor: the promise of color filmmaking

Color filmmaking played an important role in the Amateur Cinema
League's prognostications for motion pictures from its founding in 1926. In
the first issue of the ACL's *Amateur Movie Makers* magazine (later simply *Movie
Makers*), founding President Hiram Percy Maxim predicted a time when

color motion pictures would be transmitted like the radio and permit the home viewing and exchange of color films by people around the world (Rowden 1926: 24). While Maxim's vision of personal, color broadcasting would have to wait until the arrival of the Internet, the magazine also published articles about how amateurs could employ existing color techniques such as tinting and hand painting (Nicholson 1928a: 314; Nicholson 1928b: 466). When the 16mm Kodacolor film process was introduced to the American market in 1928 it was greeted by *Movie Makers* magazine with a great deal of excitement. An editorial touted the significance of Kodacolor as an expressly amateur innovation, developed and marketed just for them: "[By] the very fact of his existence in large numbers, the amateur has been responsible for the development of a new kind of color photography in motion pictures" (*Movie Makers* 1928: 567). Kodacolor also promised new aesthetic possibilities for amateur filmmaking. "Here is something that is their very own," the editorial pronounced. "From their comments upon it, their experiments with it, and their suggestions concerning its betterment and expansion will come the brilliant future for it that MOVIE MAKERS confidently expects." With the arrival of Kodacolor came a new aesthetic terrain for amateur filmmakers to experiment with and explore.

The introduction of Kodacolor was a timely arrival for amateurs, corresponding with discussions about the fate of film art with the coming of sound.[2] By the end of the 1920s, popular film was shifting away from the artistic achievements and style of the silent era. Roy Winton, Managing Director of the ACL, noted in 1930 that this shift presented an opportunity for the amateur:

> The events of the last two years in the professional movie world have put the movie amateur in a very novel position. To put it bluntly, the commercial producers have gone out of the movie business into the stage entertainment business and their present product of talking movies is fare not for the devotees of movie art but for patrons of stage entertainment. The movie amateur is the inheritor of the silent films … (Winton 1930: 85)

Winton's remarks reproduce what has become the canonical account of the transition from silent to sound film aesthetics: if silent film embodied a young art of plastic movement, sound film appeared to be becoming little more than a handmaid of stage drama. Color filmmaking presented a unique opportunity for amateurs to develop silent film style further, and in a new direction, in contrast to commercial cinema's increasingly stage-bound style. Appearing at a time when the transition to synchronized sound occupied commercial filmmaking, the arrival of Kodacolor marked a distinct path for amateurs. Though mute, amateur cinema would be claimed as the terrain for continued development of film aesthetics, understood as an essentially visual art form, now with the addition of color. But what did amateurs *do* with color cinema, and how did they advance new directions for film art?

Developed by Kodak specifically for 16mm amateur use, Kodacolor was an additive, lenticular process. In an additive process, the presentation of color is not intrinsic to the film stock's photochemistry, but is the result of a system of filters attached to the camera in filming and the projector in exhibition. Kodacolor film stock also employed minuscule lenses embossed directly onto the base of the film stock. To the naked eye, a strip of developed Kodacolor film is monochrome in appearance, and when projected without the appropriate filter it is indistinguishable from black-and-white film except for the presence of fine vertical stripes. When projected through the appropriate red, green, and blue-striped Kodacolor filter, however, the embossed lenses on the film combine the three hues to reproduce the appearance of natural color. Writers expounded the values of the color system for travel films, and even Hollywood cinematographers called it "a natural-color process far more perfect than anything available to the professional" (Boyle 1934: 86).

Despite the excitement with which amateurs greeted Kodacolor, the format was not as user-friendly and easily adopted as originally touted. The use of filters and embossed film stock created problems with obtaining correct exposure, as it required very bright lighting conditions. As a result, Kodacolor was most commonly used by amateurs for exterior filming. And although Kodacolor equipment was adapted in 1933 to function in more diverse lighting conditions, including indoor shooting, the format still required more careful calculation of exposure than many amateurs were prepared to accommodate (Gilks 1933: 23; Hansen 1933: 320; Hansen 1934: 61). Articles written to convince amateurs that filming in Kodacolor was "worth the trouble" betray a general acknowledgement that the format was not widely embraced. Though technologically capable of producing strikingly colorful images and providing home moviemakers with greater realism in their personal or travel records, Kodacolor's technical challenges appear to have dissuaded most casual filmers from adopting its use.

But there were some amateurs who persevered with more thorough explorations of Kodacolor's possibilities. The more successful attempts to use Kodacolor can be found in the ACL's annual "Ten Best" amateur film contests.[3] Each year, starting in 1930, ten films were selected for the list along with several other honorable mentions. Though most of these films are now lost, their descriptions, printed in *Movie Makers*, provide valuable information about a vast corpus of amateur filmmaking.[4] These contests acted as annual evaluations of the progress and development of amateur filmmaking, and serve as indications of the ACL's shifting critical norms and aesthetic aspirations for the medium. To trace along purely statistical lines, these lists reveal only one Kodacolor film received an award in 1930 and 1931, two in each of 1932 and 1933, and three in 1934. One of these Kodacolor award winners was the retired engineer and avid film hobbyist, John Hansen. Before turning to color filmmaking, Hansen had already demonstrated his skill as a filmmaker with his 1931 black-and-white travel film about Egypt, *Tombs of the Nobles*, which was named one of the Ten Best of that year. In 1932, Hansen turned to color filmmaking with the afore-mentioned reel *Studies in Blue and Chartres Cathedral*. Described in its award citation as a "cerulean cinema achievement" the film was evidently both a travelogue and a meditation on the use of color in amateur filmmaking (*Movie Makers* 1932: 538).

While Hansen's *Studies in Blue* appears to be a lost film, his sequences of the Chartres Cathedral survive, and are stunning meditations on one era's medium of light and color as seen through another's. The film begins as a typical travelogue, presenting exterior shots of the town of Chartres and the cathedral from a distance. The film cuts to a closer shot, and the camera tilts down the exterior of the cathedral's tower, presenting the stained-glass windows as they appear from outside, dull and reflective. This silent film's intertitle reads "Enter and behold the glorious beauty of the famed, old stained glass windows. For the first time faithfully repro-duced with aid of Kodacolor." From points of shimmering light, the camera gradually cuts in to closer and closer shots until indistinct color forma-tions reveal themselves as shapes and images. While we never get a per-fectly clear view of the stained-glass images, the film provides a faithful experience of the glass's shifting light effects and its play on the eye. (**See Plate 18.**) This is a travel film that transports an aesthetic experience for the audience, while simultaneously reflecting on the cinema's own mimetic capacities. The film appears to ask if cinema is any different than a mobile version of stained-glass. The award citation from *Movie Makers* magazine for the film reads:

> Here, [Hansen] succeeded in capturing that peculiar, deep
> dyed transparency found only in the colors of old stained
> glass. It is questionable if any other method of reproducing
> color can give such a real and beautiful rendition of stained
> glass windows as the motion picture. Certainly no color
> printing process can compete … (ibid.)

In both Hansen's film, and the commentary upon it, we find a self-conscious and illuminating commentary on color cinema's relationship to other media.

In a similar vein, Hansen's next award-winning Kodacolor film, *Venice* (1934) – which is again considered lost – also explored color cinema's capacity for presenting an older art form. Like a typical amateur travel film, *Venice* chronicles some of the city's attractions and artworks; but according to its description in *Movie Makers* Hansen's treatment of Andrea del Sarto's mosaics at St. Mark's "exemplifies in a new way the amazing versatility of the amateur color medium in the hands of a master craftsman" (*Movie Makers* 1934: 534, 545). In this account, it is not just Hansen's technical skill in capturing the mosaics under unfavorable lighting conditions that marks him a "master craftsman," it is also his sensitivity to the original artwork's texture and tonality, and his use of this work to explore Kodacolor's expressive range. "Mr. Hansen succeeded in registering the tones and colors," the award citation continues, "from the most subtle pastel shades to the brilliant yellow of metallic gold. This latter quality, so difficult to simulate in any other medium than the real thing, here is shown with the rich luster of the metal itself" (ibid.: 545–546). In the hands of a "master craftsman," the range of possible tones and colors from Kodacolor was perhaps indeed unlimited. The *Movie Makers* award citations repeatedly compared Hansen and other filmmakers to the great artists of other media, not just for their reproduction of their artworks, but for recognizing and mastering Kodacolor's range of aesthetic expressions in personal motion pictures. For example, the award citation for *Venice* concludes:

> Turneresque interpretations of Venice in another section
> of the reel are equally beautiful, if less obvious accom-
> plishments, while studies of colors of buildings, as reflected
> in the shimmering water, succeed in preserving what
> otherwise would be the most elusive memories of beauty.
> (ibid.: 546)

If Hansen's color films seem primarily concerned with the faithful reproduction of artworks from other media, we can shed further light on his aesthetic objectives by examining the articles he wrote about Kodacolor filming for *Movie Makers* magazine between 1932 and 1934. In these articles, Hansen notes the broad range of potential subjects for color filmmaking, a range that far exceeds "personal, flower and sunset opportunities" (Hansen 1932: 295). In addition to these familiar topics, he also suggests some subjects that might be otherwise overlooked: "Even the big cities of America overflow with subjects worthy of color delineation. The dull everyday street scene is brightened with painted vehicles" (ibid.). In this context, color filming could be just as much a strategy for refreshing one's view of familiar places as a presentation of the distant or the exotic. Indeed, Hansen's articles seem more concerned with color filmmaking that pursues primarily aesthetic goals than films about specific subjects, and to this end he proposes strategies for improving color perception and productive experimentation arguing that, "attention may be directed to a sadly neglected branch of cinematography, namely, experimentation with light and composition" (ibid.). While Hansen's remarks confirm the sense that

Kodacolor had not, by 1932, been widely adopted by either casual or artistic filmmakers, he urges the readers of *Movie Makers* to explore its artistic possibilities. "As for the question of artistry," he writes, "the door stands wide open to anyone who cares to enter and enjoy this fascinating and absorbing branch of photography, which, if approached in seriousness and with intelligence, can be counted on to reward the experimenter with revelations in novel and beautiful color combinations" (ibid.).

Hansen's award-winning films used artworks like stained glass and mosaics as starting points for color experimentation. In his advice to other amateurs, however, he proposes everyday ways for filmmakers to attune their eye to color. Hansen outlines exercises for training one's perception of light and color under different circumstances, such as the observation of different shades of blue sky visible on a bright morning, the variations in tint and intensity of hue of a flower seen from different angles. "Through this procedure," Hansen writes, "in a short time will be acquired a new sense of light appreciation which will be found most helpful later on in selecting special subjects and choosing the right camera position for bringing out desired details and combinations in color values, rarely seen by the average person" (ibid.: 308). Here, Hansen suggests how attentiveness to light and color lead to keener perception of these qualities, and productively direct the composition of a film. In another article, Hansen draws on this sharpened color perception to encourage the use of "transmitted light," or light which has visibly passed through another substance, in color filming (Hansen 1933: 320). While less common than films using reflected light as a source of illumination, Hansen suggests that "[transmitted] light and color rendition can be woven into striking and fascinating compositions. … Closeups of translucent orchids or the large petals of other flowers are obvious possibilities" (ibid.). Hansen doesn't mention the effect of filming light transmitted through stained glass, as in his film of Chartres Cathedral where there is no use of reflected light in the interior scenes at all. But he suggests a number of other natural sources for filming transmitted light, such as the foliage of trees, particularly during fall when they change color and produce something like a natural stained-glass effect.

Though Hansen offers some additional guidelines for effective composition in Kodacolor filming, it is, he argues, ultimately the *function* of this composition and more general experimentation with color that is most striking: "Composition is the result of the skill and artistry expended in arranging a picture or electing a point of vantage. It should reveal to others the lure of strange places or a new attraction in familiar things" (Hansen 1932: 310). Effective color composition, therefore, passes along to viewers an experience of the light and color of even quotidian objects that many people overlook. In this way, color filmmaking could be seen as enhancing and expanding the amateur filmmaker *and* viewer's sensorium, attuning them to new ways of seeing the world, from familiar subjects like family, to defamiliarized settings like the city, to compositions of pure light and hue. But this result could only be accomplished through technical skill and pragmatic experimentation with the medium. For advanced amateurs like Hansen, Kodacolor presented many more possibilities for creative color filming than was generally acknowledged and explored among amateurs.

kodachrome: expanding color experimentation

Although some amateurs did experiment with Kodacolor, it was not until the arrival of 16mm Kodachrome film in 1935 that amateur filmmaking cemented its advantage over professional filmmaking in the area of color moviemaking. The Kodachrome subtractive color process required no special filters for filming and projection and marked a major advance for amateur filmmakers in terms of its ease of use and vividness of results. Indeed, according to *American Cinematographer*, "[m]any connected with the motion picture profession in Hollywood hail it as even better than Technicolor" (1935: 208–209).[5] Because Kodachrome film stock employed a "reversal" developing process, through which the same reel exposed in-camera became a projectable film print, it was not adaptable to the commercial industry's requirements of mass reproducibility. Among amateurs, however, anyone could now produce high-quality natural color images, especially once 16mm Kodachrome was followed in 1936 by Kodachrome 8mm film stock (*American Cinematographer* 1936: 264). *Movie Makers* magazine heralded the arrival of the new film process with its usual hyperbole: "The year 1935 will be marked in the history of personal movies as that in which the era of unlimited color filming began" (1935a: 193). This time *Movie Makers'* hyperbole was matched by Kodachrome's rapid and broad acceptance among amateurs. But the editorial also points out the important role that users of Kodacolor had played:

> That color filming is capable of developing into a definitely artistic form has been demonstrated already by those amateurs who have worked in the more limited medium … They have made the pioneer experiments in bringing color movies up to the status of accepted art. Their efforts and discoveries have erected a basic esthetic philosophy about color filming that is as applicable to the less limited new conditions as it is to the older. (ibid.)

Whether it was due to these "pioneer experiments" or not, Kodachrome films were quick to appear on the annual Ten Best lists. While 1934's Ten Best list included only three Kodacolor films, in 1935 five Kodachrome films were already listed among the Ten Best and Honorable Mentions. In 1936, this number more than doubled to eleven, and by 1937, less than three years after its introduction, more color films were listed than black-and-white films. This trend would continue through to the end of the decade.

Color filmmaking rapidly became a normal practice among amateurs, and by the end of the 1930s, an award-winning film's use of color was not always remarked upon. John Hansen continued making noteworthy color films, but because he became a Director of the ACL in 1936 he was no longer eligible for awards. Hansen made the transition to Kodachrome with ease, and gained further attention for his films of *Denmark in Color* (1937), which were widely shown in Europe and the United States (*Movie Makers* 1937: 128).[6] So well-known was Hansen for his use of color that he was even the subject of a gently satirical film called *Dabblin' in Moods* produced by his own Washington D.C. movie club:

> the film is an amusing impersonation of the Hansen cine manner, but with results entirely different from those of the famous original. Mood Indigo croons a title, to be followed by a deep blue underexposure. Mood Pastel claims its running mate, to give way to nearly blank over-exposure. The Mood Inverted piques your interest, then discloses a debacle of scenes spliced wrong side up. The Mood Dynamic promises a masterpiece, only to perpetrate as dizzy and delirious a sequence of "pans" and tilts as ever struck a silver screen. The first definite burlesque of a distinctive cine style, *Dabblin' In Moods* strikes us both as a lot of fun and some sort of milepost in the progress of amateur movies. (*Movie Makers* 1938: 332)

In its presentation of over- and under-exposure, sloppy editing, and haphazard camera movement the film offers a tongue-in-cheek primer of common amateur mistakes. The satirical slant of this film also highlights Hansen's own reputation for expressive and experimental color use at the opposite end of the amateur spectrum.

The Amateur Cinema League *did* continue to promote experimentation in color use, pushing its aesthetic development still further. In 1935, ACL president Hiram Percy Maxim predicted an ongoing link between color film and experimentation. He wrote:

> [Color] comes at the same time that a modernistic tendency appears among us. Shots made at unusual angles and shots made under unique lighting conditions seem to be driving the shot taken from the conventional point of view and with standard lighting into the limbo of the old fashioned. This modernistic tendency will unquestionably cross breed with color. (Maxim 1935: 513)

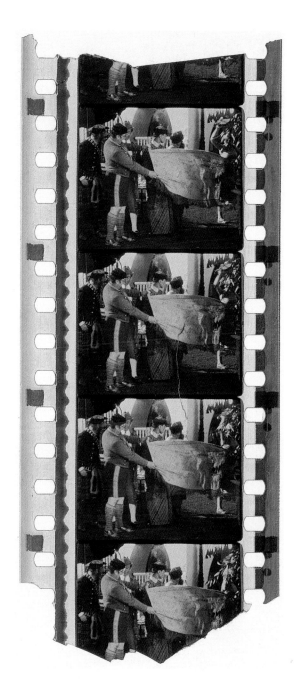

Plate 1.

Images from the presumed lost film *Jazz Mamas* (Mack Sennett, 1929). Courtesy of George Eastman House, Motion Picture Department Collection, Rochester.

Plate 2.

The "Golden Swan", emblematic shot in *The Glorious Adventure* (J. Stuart Blackton, 1922). Frame enlargements from restored print, BFI National Archive.

Plate 3.

"Lady Beatrice Fair" (Violet Virginia Blackton), star of *The Glorious Adventure* (J. Stuart Blackton, 1922).

Plate 4.

Flickering, framed flames in *The Glorious Adventure* (J. Stuart Blackton, 1922).

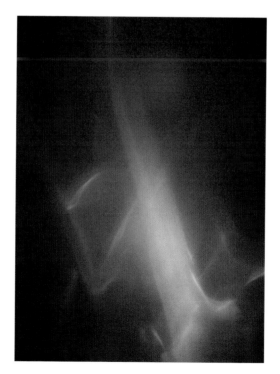

Plate 5.

Thomas Wilfred, *Untitled Opus 161* (1965–66) (courtesy of the collection of Carol and Eugene Epstein).

Plate 6.
Stencil applied color circa 1906, showing damage.

Plate 7.

In *The Art of Mirrors* (Derek Jarman, 1973), the flash of reflected light in a mirror illuminates a bright green screen.

Plate 8.

Death Dance (Derek Jarman, 1973) combines a flattened blue color field with an erotics of formlessness.

Plate 9.

Ashden's Walk on Møn (Derek Jarman, 1973) uses superimposition to explore materiality.

Plate 10.

In Ashden's Walk on Møn (Derek Jarman, 1973), a lens flare juxtaposes immaterial light with material place.

Plate 11.
Syndromes and a Century (Apichatpong Weerasethakul, 2006).

Plate 12.
Syndromes and a Century (Apichatpong Weerasethakul, 2006).

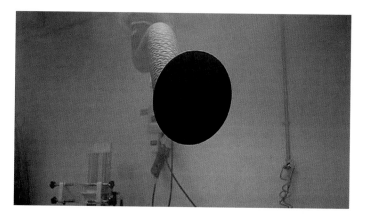

Plate 13.
Syndromes and a Century (Apichatpong Weerasethakul, 2006).

Plate 14.

Syndromes and a Century (Apichatpong Weerasethakul, 2006).

Plate 15.

Motel sign in *Psycho* (Gus van Sant, 1998).

Plate 16.

Heart-shaped bed in *Sin City* (Robert Rodríguez, Frank Miller, 2005).

Plate 17.

Lonesome (Paul Fejos, 1928): The stencilled music-hall sign, superimposed onto a horn. Stencil-colored.

Plate 18.

Studies in Blue and Chartres Cathedral (John Hansen, 1931) Human Studies Film Archives, Smithsonian Institution (99.10.15).

Plate 19.

The restricted color palette of costume in *L'Ami de Mon Amie* (*My Girlfriend's Boyfriend*, Eric Rohmer, 1987).

Plate 20.

Drums Along the Mohawk (John Ford, 1939). Lana and Gil in the tavern, after the villain Caldwell has been revealed in the background.

Plate 21.

Drums Along the Mohawk (John Ford, 1939). Lana, Gil and Blue Black in red and blue in front of the cabin's yellow fire.

Plate 22.

Drums Along the Mohawk (John Ford, 1939). The soldiers march into town in the background under heavy, diffusive rain.

Plate 23.

Drums Along the Mohawk (John Ford, 1939). Gil relates the story of the battle in the foreground, while General Herkimer's leg operation proceeds in the background.

Plate 24.

Close up of Cary (Jane Wyman) in *All that Heaven Allows* (Douglas Sirk, 1955).

Plate 25.
Red suffusion in *Marnie* (Alfred Hitchcock, 1964).

Plate 26.
Red suffusion in *Marnie* (Alfred Hitchcock, 1964).

Plate 27.

Yvonne contemplatively sips her drink in the lower left corner as the Nazis sing in the background. *Casablanca* (Michael Curtiz, 1942).

Plate 28.

The color passage between Yvonne and her surroundings diminishes her presence the colorization. The colorized *Casablanca*.

Plate 29.

The 1988 colorization of this black-and-white still creates strong color passage between Ilsa and her surroundings. *Casablanca.*

Plate 30.

The 1988 colorization of this black-and-white still creates a high contrast color harmony, in which Ilsa's yellow blouse and red waist sash contrast with the blue drapes behind her. *Casablanca.*

Plate 31.

A tinted and toned frame from the nitrate print of *Die Molens die Juichen en Weenan* (Alfred Machin, 1912). Courtesy EYE Film Institute.

Plate 32.

Still photograph of Aladdin's Cave (blue tone and pink tint). From the BFI National Archive 2010 digital color grade of *The Great White Silence*. Ponting incorporated still images such as this into his 1924 edit of the expedition footage.

Looking into the latter half of the 1930s, we can observe the results of this cross breeding with an experimental impulse in a little more detail.[7] Films that emphasized non-naturalistic color use were particularly noted. For example, one Ten Best winner, *These Bloomin' Plants* (1936) treated the familiar color subject of flowers, but this time through time-lapse photography: "Through this device of time condensation, buds are seen bursting open before one's eyes, often in cascades of beauty which vividly suggest fireworks against a night sky" (*Movie Makers* 1936: 542, 551). As this description suggests, the effect of color combined with time-lapse filming here denaturalizes a familiar image, so blooming flowers take on the appearance of fireworks. Writers and amateur filmmakers also drew on metaphorical associations between cinema and the other arts in order to describe some of the ways the medium exceeded a purely naturalistic recording of reality. In this vein, Robert Kehoe's award-winning *Chromatic Rhapsody* (1939) used a musical metaphor to organize, and render more expressive, scenic footage of autumn foliage:

> This beautiful picture can only be described as a scenic – a scenic held together rather tenuously by editing to create a symphonic arrangement of color and to associated scenes with the seasons … One is so impressed with the flawless color that he is inclined to suspect that nature puts on a special show for Mr. Kehoe. The truth is probably that Mr. Kehoe has a special understanding of nature and an intuitional sensitivity to light and color. For the rest, as Mr. Kehoe would say, he simply follows exposure instructions. (*Movie Makers* 1939: 634)

In this description we see further indications of how amateurs used color film in order to push aesthetic exploration of the medium and familiar surroundings further. While these films may seem to be a far cry from the pure modernist abstractions of Oskar Fischinger, for example, they are still experiments with the purely graphical dimensions of color cinema. Like Hansen's advice in his articles, there is a blend of the experimental and the pragmatic here. Kehoe's film appears from this description to push beyond the typical amateur scenic through both its musical analogy and the filmmaker's careful color composition and skillful exposure of the Kodachrome stock.

The films and discourse examined in this essay suggest that colorful recordings of personal events provide only one part of the history of amateur color cinema. In the 1930s when color films were still a rarity in commercial theatres, amateurs claimed color filmmaking as their own terrain for aesthetic experimentation and discovery. For many users, color film was appealing primarily for the opportunity it presented to produce more lifelike representations of the world than black-and-white film. But for

147

some amateur filmmakers and writers, it was color film's more evidently aestheticizing qualities, such as the ways it required specific kinds of perception or compositional skills, that was most appealing. These different aesthetic tendencies additionally reveal some of the fascinating tensions within amateur filmmaking between more traditional aesthetic strategies, and experimental – occasionally even modernist – ones. Consistent with these tendencies, however, was the idea that color filmmaking, like amateur filmmaking more generally, relied on craftsmanship and pragmatic experimentation, and presented an opportunity for anyone with a movie camera to deepen their aesthetic experiences of the everyday.

notes

1. The author would like to thank Kaveh Askari, Simon Brown, Lee Curruther, and Buckey Grimm for their assistance at various stages of the writing of this chapter.
2. Other natural color formats, such as Vitacolor, were also marketed to amateurs during this period (Du Pont 1929: 33; Crespinel 1939: 443). Kodacolor and Kodachrome were the two most widespread natural color film processes in North America, and so are the focus of my discussion here.
3. Kaveh Askari has also written recently about Kodacolor films made by early cinema pioneer and Amateur Cinema League member Alexander Black. In this fascinating work, Askari links Black's Kodacolor filmmaking with his proto-cinematic illustrated lectures and his editing of the *Sunday World*'s color supplement (Askari 2009: 150–163).
4. For a list of the annual Ten Best winners, see Kattelle (2003: 238–251); detailed descriptions of the Ten Best and Honorable Mentions appeared annually in the December issue of *Movie Makers* from 1930 until the ACL's demise in 1954.
5. Some also viewed Hollywood as aesthetically inferior in its use of color film: a writer in *American Cinematographer* presented *Becky Sharp* as an example of clashing color composition that amateurs should avoid (Hale 1935: 312).
6. "*Denmark in Color* is a six reel cine document, largely in Kodachrome, which, in addition to the exquisite color compositions for which Mr. Hansen is famous, includes light, genre studies of Danish life." A New York screening of this film was sponsored by World Peaceways, an organization that presented media images to counteract the glorification of war and promote international understanding (*Movie Makers* 1937: 128).
7. Though sometimes these developments occurred in directions that don't correspond to our traditional expectations for experimental cinema; *Keratoplasty*, for example, was "a beautifully perfect" "experimental and demonstrative operation on the eye of an anesthetized rabbit." Here, scientific and aesthetic experimentation are conflated (*Movie Makers* 1935b: 515, 550).

references

American Cinematographer (1935) "Eastman's New 16mm Color Film Sensational", May: 208–9, 220.

American Cinematographer (1936) "8mm Kodachrome", June: 264.

Askari, K. (2009) "Early 16mm Color by a Career Amateur", *Film History*, 21, 2: 150–163.

Boyle, J. W. (1934) "Kodacolor Gives Life to Travel Films", *American Cinematographer*, June: 86, 95.

Crespinel, W. T. (1939) "Cinecolor Makes Contribution to Color", *American Cinematographer*, October: 443.

Du Pont, M. B. (1929) "Color for the Amateur", *American Cinematographer*, May: 33.

Gilks, A. L. (1933) "Kodacolor Comes Indoors", *American Cinematographer*, May: 23, 34–35.

Hale, K. (1935) "Learn About Shooting Color from 'Becky Sharp'", *American Cinematographer*, July: 312.

Hansen, J. V. (1932) "Kodacolor, Unlimited", *Movie Makers*, July: 295, 308, 310.

Hansen, J. V. (1933) "Color Counsel", *Movie Makers*, August: 320, 342–343.

Hansen, J. V. (1934) "Joseph's Coat Indoors", *Movie Makers*, February: 61, 72.

Kattelle, A. D. (2003) "The Amateur Cinema League and its Films", *Film History*, 15, 2: 238–251.

Maxim, H. P. (1935) "From our President", *Movie Makers*, December: 513.

Movie Makers (1928) "Editorials", September: 567.

Movie Makers (1932) "The Ten Best", December: 537–538, 560–562.

Movie Makers (1934) "The Ten Best", December: 513, 534, 545–548.

Movie Makers (1935a) "Color Unlimited", May: 193.

Movie Makers (1935b) "The Ten Best for 1935", December: 515, 534, 550–551, 553, 555.

Movie Makers (1936) "The Ten Best for 1936", December: 523, 542, 548–552.

Movie Makers (1937) "Practical Films", March: 128.

Movie Makers (1938) "Closeups – What Filmers Are Doing", July: 332.

Movie Makers (1939) "The Ten Best and the Maxim Memorial Award", December: 634.

Nicholson, C. F. (1928a) "Tinting Motion Picture Film", *Movie Makers*, May: 314.

Nicholson, C. F. (1928b) "Coloring Film With Brushes", *Movie Makers*, July: 466.

Rowden, D. (1926) "Colored Home Movies By Radio?", *Amateur Movie Makers*, December: 24–25.

Winton, R. W. (1930) "A Defense Inherited: What the Amateur Can Learn from Hollywood's Mistakes", *Movie Makers*, February: 85, 112.

filmography

Hansen, J. V. (1932). *Chartres Cathedral*, John V. Hansen Travel Films Collection, Acc. No. 99-10, Human Studies Film Archives, Smithsonian Institution, Washington, DC.

color and meaning

in the films of

eric rohmer

f i o n a   h a n d y s i d e

Eric Rohmer (1920–2010) is a filmmaker whose wide body of work, made over a fifty-year period, is famous for its critical engagement with the tenets of cinematic realism. With a few important exceptions, Rohmer's films, according to Joël Magny's detailed analysis of his style, are marked by transparency, where cinematic technology is in service of as clear and unmediated as possible a view of empirical, observable reality (Magny 1986: see especially 14–19: see also Crisp 1988: 8–11). Direct sound, natural light and long shots are used alongside focal lengths, camera heights and angles that echo those of standard human visual perception to respect the intrinsic reality of what is being filmed, in a gesture which harks back to André Bazin's desire that film should record perceptual reality as closely as possible. So great is Rohmer's interest in capturing the effects of natural light that his long-term collaborator as director of photography, Nestor Almendros, reports that when they were filming *Pauline à la plage/Pauline at the Beach* (1982), Rohmer would often delay shooting by several hours in order to capture certain lighting effects (Desbarats 1990: 19). Such an aversion to interfering with the effects of natural light, and seeking through technology to allow the cinematic apparatus to approach the rendering of things as they are ontologically, has important repercussions for Eric Rohmer's color filmmaking. First, Rohmer's work in and on color is indebted to broader debates concerning realism and the image, to the extent that we can see his theoretical discussions of cinematic color as bound up in wider discussions of realism. Second, Rohmer's decision to attempt to preserve the effects of natural light through his color work has important repercussions for filmic meaning. Last, Rohmer develops a paradoxical use of color, where it both hides and reveals the presence of the film-maker through a play of "invisibility" (color transcribed through natural light) and "presence" (color as part of a carefully controlled palette decided by the film-maker). This paradox of presence and invisibility echoes the theological argument of Rohmer's filmmaking and color comes to have a key role in explicating his films' meditation on the place of God in the world of his characters.

color and/as monochrome in eric rohmer's films

The ordering role of color in Eric Rohmer's films is signaled to us by its decisive use in the *Contes moraux/Moral Tales* (1962–1972). The first three *Contes moraux* were released in black-and-white, the last three in color. However, this order is out of sequence in their production as *La Collectionneuse* (1967), which is in color, was filmed third but is placed fourth in the series. The decision to respect choice of film stock rather than production order in the numbering of his *Contes moraux* demonstrates that Rohmer regards color as key to his developing style and themes. Notably, *La Collectionneuse* takes place in the summer, on the Côte d'Azur, linking its predominant hues of rich, warm brown and pink tones to sunburned flesh and its limpid blues to the sea and sky. Almendros pushed his Eastman film stock to its limits during night for night shooting, and shot in the shade during the day to avoid the harshest effects of the light, establishing the color cinematography for which both he and Rohmer would become recognized.

As Rohmer comments, it is ironic that the only film he deliberately chose to film in black-and-white, *Ma Nuit chez Maud/My Night at Maud's* (1969) (rather than such stock being imposed through economic circumstance, as for his early 1960s films), was filmed just at the time when European cinema was finally embracing color photography as the standard. Rohmer's decision was taken because he felt he did not have the ability to manipulate color stock successfully in this film. Clermont-Ferrand's dark grey buildings, built from local volcanic rock, would appear beige, violet or yellow on color stock. Furthermore, the film took place during winter, in white snow, allowing Rohmer to reinforce his black-and-white palette even when shooting on location, a linkage of setting, seasonality and color that

Rohmer carefully develops throughout his work. In other words, rather than considering *Ma Nuit chez Maud* a black-and-white film, Rohmer argues we should consider it a color film whose palette is black and white (Legrand, Niogret and Ramasse 1986: 19). Rohmer used the classical technique of filming on a black-and-white-set and clothing his characters in black-and-white, so that the color the spectator experiences is not a false transcription because of film stock, but a rendering of the perceptual reality of the location.

As Paul Coates notes, "the terms 'colour' and 'black-and-white' enact a dialectic of simultaneous opposition and prickly supplementation, as white and black may also be seen as 'colours' and their supposed 'opposition' to colour be a trick of language, ideology, or history" (Coates 2010: 45). In *Ma Nuit chez Maud*, Rohmer moves between these two opposing conceptions of the monochrome palette. On the one hand, he seems to characterize his monochrome palette as functioning in opposition to color stock, which would have been too harsh, bright and distorting, and he avoided what he terms "the detail of color" which he felt would be distracting to the viewer (Rohmer in Legrand, Niogret and Ramasse 1986: 19). On the other hand, he asserts the way in which black-and-white function in this film as part of the color spectrum, and the colors that characterize this film happen to be black-and-white. In this way, his choice of black-and-white illustrates the highly complex and nuanced account Rohmer gives of the relation between cinema and reality. Rohmer acknowledges that black-and-white film stock, far from being opposed to cinematic realism, can be seen to be in service to it. At the same time, the careful control over every aspect of the set that monochrome film stock demands alerts us to the way in which, far from being a transcription of a pre-existent reality, realism is itself is a manipulated, aesthetic construct.

Key to our understanding of how this paradox works in *Ma Nuit chez Maud*, and the complex role the conception of black-and-white as both opposition to and supplement of color plays, is the film's penultimate scene. Our final view of Clermont-Ferrand and of Françoise and the narrator occurs here. The couple stand on a hill overlooking the town from which we have a fine panoramic view, including a prominent church spire of a very dark grey stone, and a modern block of flats built of a pale white material, possibly concrete. As Françoise and the narrator talk, she wearing a dark coat, carrying a delicate white lace shawl, and with pale blonde hair, and he wearing a dark coat and with dark brown hair, soft snow falls around them, gradually changing the landscape behind them from predominantly dark to increasingly pale. There is absolute tonal harmony here between the weather, the landscape, and the couple. The monochrome palette employed here functions as color, shaped by Rohmer to create a harmonious and realist composition of season, landscape, and character. Furthermore, the conversation between the couple – where the narrator lies to Françoise and pretends to have slept with Maud, as she confesses to an affair – adds further layers of meaning, through dramatic irony, to the harmonious color scheme, in which the perfect match between the couple and their environment highlights through contrast the differences between them that they willfully ignore. However, if the monochrome palette seems to share some of color's functions here, it still remains in opposition to color, deliberately simplifying and purifying the landscape, and rendering it more abstract than a color composition would have done, lending a "Jansenist" absence of color to this moment where the narrator deliberately betrays his Catholic principles.[1]

considering color in theory

Rohmer's interest in color and film predates his experience as a filmmaker and he wrote several pieces considering the role of color in the cinema when he was working as a cinema critic; especially relevant are *Reflections on Color* (1949) and *Of Taste and Colors* (1956). In these pieces, Rohmer develops his theory of color in line with changing cinematic technology, praising it for its inherent "greater fidelity" to external reality than black-and-white. In *Reflections on Color*, Rohmer argues that the reason audiences "cannot bear" color is because what we have seen so far is not really color and "therein lies the problem, which it is up to technology to resolve" (1989a [1949]: 39). Rohmer advocates color cinema, provided that technology is used in such a way that the reproduction of color is as accurate as possible (filters and chemical correction are to be avoided). Rohmer argues then that the color film should aim for a pure reproduction of color as close as possible as that to be found in the world in natural light conditions. For Rohmer, it is here that the image captures the beauty of the world. By 1956, technology had improved sufficiently that Rohmer could note that, "color is slowly but surely conquering film" (1989b [1956]: 67). He praises films that make pictorial harmonious use of color through tonality, which implies a collaboration between the director, the set designer, the photographer and the costume designer. As Paul Coates points out, this idea of color is typical of the classical Hollywood style, and recalls Natalie Kalmus's Technicolor technical guides advocating color harmony and control (Coates 2010: 16). Rohmer, however, prefers another category of color film: those where color is "unquestionably in charge," singling out the power of such objects as Harriet's blue dress in *The River* (Renoir, 1951) or the green dress of Miss Lonelyhearts in *Rear Window* (Hitchcock, 1954). Rohmer specifies that "it is not enough for a blue or a green to bolster the film's expression; they bring with them new ideas, their presence at a specific moment evokes an emotion sui generis" (Rohmer 1989b [1956]: 68). Ironically, then, a filmmaker whose own style is usually regarded as classical here seems to favor the Romantic notion of color providing an overwhelming excess and generating an emotion beyond the neat confines of "tone" and "harmony." Rohmer's own filmmaking combines both these perceived cinematic qualities of color, with Rohmer paying scrupulously close attention to color in his films through his control of costume and setting in order to achieve an overall tonality, but also allowing color at certain moments to take charge of the film and impose its own complex symbolic layers of meaning. This most classical of directors, working primarily within a neo-Bazinian idiom of strict location-shooting based realism, indulges in color as a melodramatic element that is used to symbolize emotion. Color is ambiguous within Rohmer's films. It is both realist and expressive, both classical and melodramatic, and, as I shall explore in my next section, both figurative and abstract.

color, abstraction and figuration: painting(s) in/and eric rohmer's films

In a posthumously published interview, Rohmer asserts that the Fine Arts (primarily painting, but also drawing and to a certain extent sculpture) are the most important arts of the twentieth century, as they have managed to negotiate the challenge modernity has thrown down concerning the role and purpose of attempts at reproducing reality. Painting has found itself in a paradoxical position where it no longer depicts the world in a realistic fashion through mimesis, but nevertheless offers us new ways to perceive the reality of the world. Rohmer argues that painting is born from a desire to imitate reality, even when it seems purely abstract, such as the works of Klee, Kandinsky or Mondrian: "if one is not capable of figurative painting, as it was taught in fine art schools, I don't think one can be an abstract artist. Abstraction always carries the memory of figuration, otherwise it is simply decoration" (quoted in Fauvel and Herpe 2010: 45).

Rohmer uses color in his films to examine this complex and paradoxical relationship between abstraction and figuration, which he characterizes as a constant exchange. In *Of Taste and Colors*, Rohmer argues that modern art "has given color a life of its own [and ...] made it the absolute ruler of the canvas [...] the green of a fruit spills onto a table, or to a face, if harmony so demands" (1989b [1956]: 69). In other words, color both belongs to a "realistic" representation of the world, but also leads toward abstraction, and existence for its own sake: green exists as color, harmony, and composition, rather than (or as well as?) the quality of an apple.

Rohmer references painting for both figurative and abstract purposes in his films. He uses paintings as part of the decorative verisimilitude of his films, thus alluding to the figurative past that all paintings "remember": the painting is simply a piece of furniture and therefore in a sense figurative by its very presence (within the filmic diegesis it attests to the reality of a given character). However, he also uses painting in a far more abstract way, to give his entire film a palette, such as the reference to Matisse's *La Blouse romaine* in *Pauline à la plage*, with its tricolor palette of red, white and blue. The color of the film works to bring about a unity between setting, season, character and theme, or sometimes exists in and of itself to provoke a new set of emotions or ideas. References to paintings and color are thus both realistic and figurative (the desire to reproduce as closely as possible the color of the world, including paintings that may be found within it) and abstract and symbolic (the color as a guiding motif for the film; the emotions, desires and feelings connoted by the use of certain colors). Rohmer, often using painting as a reference (Matisse in *Pauline à la plage*; Mondrian in *Les nuits de la pleine lune/Full Moon in Paris* (1984)) develops a complex tricolor palette in his *Comédies et proverbes/Comedies and Proverbs* (1981– 1987), in which two dominant colors are complimentary and a third color clashes with them, and he had his shooting scripts bound in the appropriate colors. In *La Femme de l'aviateur/The Aviator's Wife* (1981), for example, the dominant colors are blue and yellow, echoing François's job as a postman (the corporate colors of the post office are yellow and blue). Into this environment, which blends into the green of the park where the characters spend an afternoon, come small bright flashes of red, such as the necklace worn by Lucie, or the goldfish in Anne's apartment. These small vivid splashes can work precisely because they are so restrained, adding balance to the overall scheme of blue, yellow and green. Within a complex plot bringing together different couple formations, both actual and virtual, color works to impose harmony and order; but also possibly suggests entrapment and suffocation within precisely this order (the goldfish trapped in their bowl; François's job that robs him of sleep; even the carefully managed verdure of the urban park in its pale imitation of nature).

Color works to enhance film's primary vocation of realism: this color palette is provided using "realistic" means (locations, clothes, props). In this way, it would seem to differ from the use of color in modern art as analyzed by Rohmer, which saw color as primarily an abstract quality rather than attached to specific objects in the world. Nevertheless, cinema and painting both move between abstraction and figuration in their use of color, although in differing degrees. Within the cinematic verisimilitude of colored objects, there lies in Rohmer's films a more abstract use of color for purposes of composition and form. Color is both part of a pre-existing object world to be mechanically reproduced, minimizing the role of the director, and also of a carefully controlled palette in which every object has multiple meanings, and in which the presence of the director is crucial.

the theology of color

Given Rohmer's dedication to location shooting and use of color for verisimilitude, color is an important tool in Rohmer's rendering of the world

155

as truthfully and carefully as possible. However, color is also used to express Rohmer's ideas, for symbolic purposes. Furthermore, part of this symbolic use of color draws its power exactly from the fact that this symbolic meaning is hidden, or masked, behind the verisimilitude of the color palette — we are not meant to notice the symbolic impact of the color behind the realistic decors, unless we look carefully. *L'Ami de mon amie/My Girlfriend's Boyfriend* (1987) is an exemplary film to illuminate my argument here and I shall now discuss its use of color in some detail.

Color is used to advance the argument that in an unprepossessing New Town, there is the possibility of hope and transcendence. While Paris's cinematic and cultural appeal is certain, Rohmer is militating against the view held by such influential urban theorists as Henri Lefebvre that life in the New Town is sterile, arid and trivial (Lefebvre 1962: 129). Robin Tierney argues that Rohmer's film "provides a visual interpretation of the ville nouvelle that supports the views of [...] Lefebvre" (Tierney 2006: 124). He claims that Lefebvre's assertion of "triviality" is exemplified by the concluding shot of the film, where two couples come together in co-ordinated green and blue clothing. Tierney therefore concludes that "the potentially passionate plot of the film, which revolves around romantic intrigue and betrayal, is belittled by the final scene, which foregrounds the utter exchangeability of characters and the simple legibility of color" (Tierney 2006: 126). Tierney's analysis ignores the way that Rohmer's colors function not as legible signals, but as a very carefully constructed system designed to reveal essences, in a belief that blue and green can symbolize beyond themselves within a narrative system in which color takes charge. The use of green and blue as dominant colors is not new to the final scene of the film but is part of a carefully developed color palette of greens and blues with the contrasting flash of yellow or white used throughout the film. In the film's opening sequence, for example, Léa is wearing a mid-green cardigan and pale blue jeans and Blanche is wearing a royal blue jacket. At the swimming pool, Blanche wears a green swimming costume with a blue hat and yellow goggles, and Léa a blue costume with a white hat and yellow goggles. (**See Plate 19.**) At a later party, Blanche wears a navy dress and Léa a blue skirt. Controlling the color of his characters' clothing is particularly important to Rohmer, and chimes with his film-making method both in that it allows the assertion of artistic control within the "found" environment of location shooting, and second because it is a simple, economical solution. As he asserts:

156

> in front of lac d'Annecy, you've got the lake, the trees, you
> can't do anything, the color is there. You can choose the
> time of day, of course, but on the other hand, you can
> bring the clothes you want, and I think the pictorial nature
> of film begins with the clothing. And as Nestor Almendros

says, "when you're shooting a film, you can think the most important thing is to tune your projector, choose your aperture, place filters, perhaps, but there is something that is even more important, and that's choosing the clothes".
(Rohmer in Desbarats 1990: 116)

How, then, might we interpret the particular color palette in *L'Ami de mon amie*? Partly, of course, the dominance of blue and green works to integrate the characters into the design of their environment – Cergy-Pontoise is a town dominated by blue and green in the carefully planned site of parks, lakes, and buildings including the famous modernist Tour Bleue. Setting and season (the film takes place during summer) privilege a palette of blues and greens, which are also the colors of the town's emblem. No color is haphazard within the space of the planned new town, just as Rohmer's ordered, controlled color scheme points to the design of his film. The color scheme point points precisely to the ordered nature of design, and alerts us to the order that may lie behind the natural world as well as the manufactured one. As Bert Cardullo expresses it, Rohmer's Catholicism means that for him, design – the very power intelligently to conceive it – is a chief spiritual clarity, and the chief manifestation of the Spirit, amidst the physical chaos of existence [...] hence the providential design of Rohmer's cinema as opposed to the mechanical one of farce. (Cardullo 2001: 103) Rohmer's controlled color palette, especially in a film which works to draw our attention to the ordered nature of the environment in which the characters live, asks us to consider the forces behind the reality in which we live. Rohmer's realism in his choice and filming of colors points precisely to the contingent nature of that real, and the way in which this constructed reality is the result of choices. Furthermore, given his Catholicism, it suggests the possibility of a divine order behind the real in which we live – the colors of nature are themselves designed and ordered.

Further symbolic resonance is acquired by each individual color through this sensibility. As Keith Tester argues, "the most interesting – and extremely deliberate – use of colour to suggest Christian essences is found in *L'Ami de mon amie*" (2008: 38). In Christian symbolism, green is the color of hope and joy, and blue sincerity. In Rohmer's theologically inspired filmmaking, the colors' implication "seems to be that love as a real relationship with another is the coming together of these values" (Tester 2008: 39). This reading suggests that at the end of the film Blanche and Léa have found fulfillment, especially as the palette has been cleansed of the yellow of (self) deception. Tester further advises that Rohmer's use of color could withstand a much closer investigation of the relationship between his use of color and Catholic liturgical practice, which I shall now very briefly use to suggest why it is that the color green is so important in Rohmer's filmmaking in general.

Color plays a profound role in the Catholic Church's ordering of the mass in relation to the seasons (and such an impact on Rohmer's work cannot be underestimated, given his attention to seasons in his later series). The prevalent liturgical colors are white, green, red, violet, rose and black. In the rituals of the modern Roman rite, green is worn for the Seasons of the Year and on ferial days, and therefore is a color of the everyday, one that celebrates God's presence in the world even in the humdrum, banal days not earmarked for particular celebration (Elliott 2004: 48). As such, it is a color perfectly suited to Rohmer's modest and questioning filmic project, in which life and hope is present even at the least auspicious occasions, if only we look for it. Green symbolizes the possibility of divinity within the banality of the everyday round, if only we know how to find it. We can read Rohmer's green, via liturgy, as a reassuring sign of God's presence throughout the seasons and in all places. We can also, given the sheer ubiquity of green in Rohmer's location set films, read green as a disquieting anxiety that we are according the color too much significance. It remains ambiguous and unsettling even as it offers the possibility of grace.

Rohmer's writing sets up a division between color as artistic expression, associated with painting, and color as part of the ontological real of the world that cinema must record as faithfully as possible. However, his films' rich, symbolic use of color overcomes this rather arbitrary divide. Rohmer's films record color as faithfully and accurately as possible in order to reproduce the real world upon the screen. However, they also reveal this real world as one that is a result of choices. In Rohmer's world view, some of these choices may be made by people, but some of these choices have been made by God. In paying attention to the order and harmony of color in the world, the filmmaker reveals a truth beyond the truth of color coding – his truth that God is there, lurking, if only one can read his signs. The filmmaker who records outside locations has little control over his palette, but through exercising careful choice over set design, photography and costume, Rohmer gives his films a strong palette. In the real of Rohmer's filmic universe, color reveals an ordering presence, behind the camera and behind the world.

note

1. Jansenism is a branch of Catholicism founded by the Dutch theologian Cornelius Otto Jansen in 1616. It was condemned by Pope Urban VIII as heretical in 1643. It differed from Papal theology in its rejection of free-will: salvation is predestined and achieved through divine grace rather than good works. It shared some similarities then with Calvinism, and had a similarly austere and pessimistic view of humanity. It lends itself to an aesthetic asceticism that André Bazin ascribes to the "Jansenist" William Wyler and that he claims is marked by a "styleless style": a cinematic style that is marked by an *absence* of any kind of stylistic intervention (see Bazin 1997 [1948]: 1–22).

Bazin, A. (1997) "William Wyler, or the Jansenist of mise-en-scène [1948]", *Bazin at Work: Major Essays and Reviews from the Forties and Fifties*, trans. Bert Cadullo and Alain Piette, London and New York: Routledge.

Cardullo, B. (2001) "Hot and Cold, or Seasons Change", *Hudson Review*, 54, 1: 101–109.

Coates, P. (2010) *Cinema and Colour: The Saturated Image*, London: BFI.

Crisp, C. G. (1988) *Eric Rohmer: Realist and Moralist*, Bloomington, IN: Indiana University Press.

Desbarats, C. (1990) *Pauline à la plage d'Eric Rohmer*, Crisnée: Yellow Now.

Elliott, P. (2004) *Ceremonies of the Modern Roman Rite*, n.p.: Ignatius Press.

Fauvel, P. and Herpe, N. (2010) "Entretien avec Eric Rohmer: Le souvenir de la figuration", *Positif*, April: 44–46.

Lefebvre, H. (1962) *Introduction à la modernité*, Paris: Minuit.

Legrand, G., Niogret, H., and Ramasse, F. (1986) "Entretien avec Eric Rohmer", *Positif*, November: 15–19.

Magny, J. (1986) *Eric Rohmer*, Paris: Rivages.

Rohmer, E. (1987) "Les Citations picturales dans les *Contes moraux et Les Comédies et proverbes*", paper given at "Peinture et Cinéma" conference Quimper 1987, reprinted in Desbarats, C. (1990) *Pauline à la plage d'Eric Rohmer*, Crisnée: Yellow Now.

Rohmer, E. (1989a) "Reflections on Color" [1949], *A Taste for Beauty*, trans. Carol Volk, Cambridge: Cambridge University Press.

Rohmer, E. (1989b) "Of Taste and Colors" [1956], *A Taste for Beauty*, trans. Carol Volk, Cambridge: Cambridge University Press.

Tester, K. (2008) *Eric Rohmer: Film as Theology*, Basingstoke: Palgrave.

Tierney, R. (2006) "'Lived Experience at the Level of the Body': Annie Ernaux's *Journaux extimes*", *Substance*, 35, 3: 113–130.

the cameraman and

the glamour-puss

technicolor cinematography

and design in john ford's

drums along the mohawk

h e a t h e r   h e c k m a n

From a stylistic perspective, John Ford's reputation as an *auteur* can be neatly summarized in the now famous John Wayne quotation, "Pappy was a painter with a camera." Effectively awarding him cinematographer status, Ford's scholars and critics have carefully analyzed the director's compositions as though each shot were an individual work of art. Yet, commentators have tended to overlook the role of color, by both favoring the director's black-and-white works, and privileging line, shape, and scale in his chromatic ones. The recent 20th Century Fox restoration of Ford's first color feature, *Drums Along the Mohawk* (1939) provides an opportunity to explore the role of color in the compositional system familiar to his other works. This essay argues that *Drums* is an experiment in color cinematography that weds Ford's late 1930s high contrast black-and-white aesthetic to developing norms of Technicolor mise en scène.

Drums was the only color feature Ford made between 1935, when the Technicolor three color system first became available to filmmakers, and 1948. Compared to the reception of both Ford's later color works and the other productions of his fertile 1939–1941 period, *Drums* has been described as lackluster by biographers and Ford scholars including Tag Gallagher, Joseph McBride and, to a lesser extent, Scott Eyman (Gallagher 2007: 215–217; McBride 2004: 306–308; Eyman 1999: 212–214). There are several factors at play in the film's lukewarm critical reception, not least the enduring appeal of Ford's more famous 1939 releases, *Stagecoach* and *Young Mr. Lincoln*. However, this essay focuses on the tendency of scholars to caricature *Drums*'s Technicolor design. For example, Gallagher's analysis appears to be rooted in his understanding of two Technicolor design traditions: first, what Scott Higgins has labeled the "assertive mode" of design, and second, the practice of composing a color score around the costumes of the female lead:

> compared to *Young Mr. Lincoln, Drums* is artful naiveté, airy and bright in its use of Technicolor (Ford's first film in color and his least expressionistic since talkies began), and seemingly a particularly commercial enterprise for Ford – why *does* Claudette Colbert wear full glamour-puss makeup even while raking hay? (Gallagher 2007: 215–216)

However, describing the film's color as assertive, or "airy and bright," is inaccurate. The assertive mode is characterized by hues at high saturation (Higgins 2007: 19–20), whereas Ford prefers pastels for women and bleached or dark shades for men. Compared to *The Adventures of Robin Hood* and *The Wizard of Oz*, which are the canonical late 1930s examples of the assertive mode, *Drums* has a relatively muted palette. It is more accurate to align Ford's film with the low saturation color scores of Higgins's "restrained mode," which was associated with outdoor melodramas throughout the 1930s (Higgins 2007: 105–107). Indeed, contemporary reviews in *Variety* and *The Los Angeles Times* both emphasize *Drums*'s "outdoor" setting and photography (Anon. 1939a; Schallert 1939).

Despite the fact that Colbert sports rather neutral make up and fabrics in the hay raking sequence Gallagher singles out, his accusation of "glamour-pussery" is somewhat more defensible than his description of the overall palette. *Drums*'s color design does tend to revolve around its leading lady. Here again, though, Gallagher and others appear to have failed to properly contextualize the director's use of color. I would therefore like to more carefully locate *Drums*'s position within two distinct, yet overlapping, aesthetic systems in the late 1930s: Technicolor and Ford.

Technicolor aesthetics were partially shaped by its technological limitations as a color process. The Technicolor camera required a great deal of light to expose the three strips of film that ran through it, making deep focus effects a challenge. The sharpness of the film image was further limited by the dye imbibition printing process, which tended to soften lines. Technicolor aesthetics were also influenced by the company's market driven desire to smoothly integrate its product with the norms of the studio system's highly redundant, classical style (Bordwell 1985b; Higgins 2007). In practice, because color aesthetics were built largely out of costuming and set design, and because male costuming was often significantly less elaborate than female costuming, color palettes were usually developed around the costumes for the female lead, making the starlet the most salient chromatic point in frame (Higgins 2007: 37, 74, 99, 125).

From the cinematographers' perspective, Technicolor could easily be seen as a problem. After all, its technological shortcomings limited lighting options, which constituted their chief creative input. Throughout the 1930s, since very few features were made with the Technicolor system, most directors of photography could simply avoid the attendant restrictions. Some, however, must have seen appealing challenges and opportunities. From the beginning of Technicolor live action production, cinematographers and directors sought to achieve black-and-white cinematography effects in color (Higgins 2007: 98; Keating 2009: 210). These included low key lighting schemes and deep staging, even when the latter meant sacrificing sharp focus in all planes of action.[1] Light sources themselves could be colored, as well, either through under correction of their natural color temperature or through the use of colored gels and filters. Colored light techniques, which also dated to the earliest Technicolor films, particularly popular in low key lighting set ups, replacing, perhaps, some of the options lost to technological restrictions particular to this process.

Although it has often been caricatured as a conservative force in the shaping of film style (Merritt 2008), the Technicolor Company was invested in these same effects. In 1938, the firm met the demand for faster camera stock with reformulated film stocks for its three strip system. Cinematographer Ray Rennahan, who worked on *Drums*, claimed the improved film stocks were considerably faster than their predecessors in artificial light, allowing him to reduce the average illumination from 500–600 foot candles to a mere 250 (Anon. 1939b: 355). Rennahan was a Technicolor man and probably exaggerated the capability of the new materials; in fact, his "average" level of required light seems to have been closer to a *minimum* level of required light. In 1950, when Technicolor debuted the third (and final) generation of three strip negatives, average illumination levels for the generation Ford used were reported at 400–500 foot-candles, or double the amount Rennahan cited (Allen 1950: 414). And there is even evidence that this, too, was an underestimation: as late as 1951, Robert Surtees reported, "The standard basis for exposure of Technicolor film, established by Technicolor's London lab, is 750 foot candles at a stop of T-1.2." For his work on *Quo Vadis* (1951), Surtees said he was able to shoot at illumination levels as low as 150 foot-candles – but for some effects, he was forced to go as high as 5,000 (Surtees 1951: 473). Nevertheless, while the second generation of Technicolor film stocks may not have been a panacea for cinematographers, it certainly constituted an improvement over the first generation.

In the years leading up to the release of second generation Technicolor film stocks, Ford was becoming increasingly invested in the very photographic effects that were so difficult, if not entirely impossible, to achieve in color. As a result of his collaborations with cinematographers Arthur Miller, Bert Glennon, and Gregg Toland in the late 1930s and early 1940s, Ford was a participant in a larger black-and-white cinematography trend (one more often associated with Welles and Wyler) that we might loosely label the "hard-style."[2] Like other films made in the hard-style, many of Ford's works from this period (e.g., *Wee Willie Winkie* (1937), *Young Mr. Lincoln* (1939), *The Long Voyage Home* (1940), and *How Green Was My Valley* (1941)) favored deep, crisp focus, long takes, and high contrast lighting schemes (Gallagher 2007: 243). These were added to other compositional elements typifying Ford's films as early as the 1910s, including aperture framing, darkened foregrounds against brightly illuminated backgrounds, and deep staging (Gallagher 2007: 27–34).

Although low key lighting and deep staging characterized many Technicolor productions prior to 1938, improvements to the sensitivity of the camera negatives may have been requisite for Ford to even consider working with the color system. The first film to be produced with the improved negatives was not *Drums*, but rather *Gone with the Wind*, for which Rennahan served as Technicolor associate. Notably, Ford had at one point been slated to direct *Gone* (McBride 2004: 282). However Ford elected to make *Drums* for Fox instead, and because of the Civil War epic's lengthy production timetable, Ford's Revolutionary War film was distributed before *Gone with the Wind*.[3]

Drums was made by Ford for 20th Century Fox, where he had made his larger budget, more commercial, 1930s works. For the studio, *Drums* was a big budget production that headlined a major female star in her first color film. It was shot by Technicolor's Ray Rennahan and Ford's hard style collaborator Bert Glennon, both of whom had a vested interest in pushing the limits of the new negatives. For Rennahan and Technicolor, *Drums* was one of a handful of films that could demonstrate the viability of a new product, whilst for Glennon and Ford it was part of a larger experiment with high contrast lighting schemes and deep focus.

A first approximation of the way these goals are reflected in the final work can be seen relatively early in *Drums*, when the newly wed couple of Gil (Henry Fonda) and Lana (Claudette Colbert) stop at a tavern on their way from her city home to his Mohawk Valley homestead. Passably glamorous treatment of the leading lady is required in this early scene not just for Colbert's sake, but also for proper characterization of Lana, who undergoes a transformation from ornamental city girl to hardened frontierwoman. Lana and Gil enter, sit uncomfortably together as man and wife at a table frame right, are gently teased by the innkeeper, and then are startled by the appearance of the film's villain, the one eyed Tory Caldwell (John Carradine), who, it turns out, has been lurking with his dog by the fire in the back all along.

The tavern set is constructed from pale neutrals, the emphatic color accents being arranged to frame Lana who is also bathed in light that spills in through the window. The innkeeper's dark reddish brown vest almost exactly matches her auburn hair. Her Cobalt dress, meanwhile, is echoed by the pale blue beams and other painted woodwork in the background, and intensified by a cluster of bright objects on the table: two aquamarine glasses, a yellow cream stick of butter, and two brilliant yellow ears of corn. Though small, the objects are highly saturated and so take on greater compositional weight in contrast to the neutrals of the set. Along with the reddish auburn of Colbert's hair, the set is dressed to form a loose triad of primary colors that intensifies their chroma. The combination of contrast of saturation and the triadic scheme (Zelanski and Fisher 1999: 44, 112) make Colbert the most emphatic point in frame; and even when Caldwell appears he sports a yellow gold vest. This scene typifies Technicolor leading lady design. The set and other characters' costumes have all been coordinated with the female star. Yet, the overall palette of the sequence is far from assertive and its photography, with no true close-ups and little facial modeling is not particularly glamorous.

Perhaps more importantly, the tavern sequence is also about depth and the surprise reveal of the eye patch wearing Tory and his faithful canine in the background. The establishing shot flaunts the deep set, which extends from an empty table situated in soft focus in the extreme left foreground through Lana and Gil in the plane of focus in the right midground to a second anteroom at the back. The innkeeper moves through the space, from soft focus in the back, into the plane of focus with Lana and Gil. For the second shot, the camera is moved much closer to the young couple and to the right, so that Lana occupies center frame. The innkeeper stands frame left; Gil sits frame right. Whereas in the first shot the camera was angled to the right, in the second shot it is angled slightly to the left revealing a new space, the fireplace. Caldwell the Tory, however, remains concealed behind the innkeeper.

In the second set up, Technicolor design not only highlights the female star, it also helps distract us in service of a surprise effect, even as it keeps the depth activated due to the coordination of the yellow fire with the accents surrounding Colbert. After a shot reverse-shot exchange between the innkeeper and the newlyweds, Ford returns to the second set up, reactivating the fireplace. The innkeeper retreats and reveals Caldwell who turns in his chair to face the camera (**see Plate 20**), a position he holds, giving the audience ample time to register his presence by the fire in an area of the image that is out of focus; this pose is held until Lana looks back at him. Ford does subsequently cut in to properly introduce the villain in focus, but we are first introduced to him by the director's deft handling of staging and movement in depth. The tavern sequence, then, conforms to the norms of Technicolor design, but it also features deep staging in a deep set, patterned cast shadows, an emphatically foregrounded object, and surprise – all of which are hallmarks of Ford's filmmaking in the late 1930s.

What Ford cannot achieve in the tavern sequence is truly sharp focus throughout his large set, regardless of the advancements in Technicolor film stock sensitivity. Instead, the director begins to articulate a functional equivalent to the hard-style that he had used in his black-and-white films when Lana and Gil finally arrive at their frontier home. The single roomed log cabin, hand built by Gil himself, proves severely disappointing to the exhausted Lana. She enters it for the first time in the dead of night as a thunderstorm rages outside and she encounters her first Native American within. Blue Back proves to be a friendly, dim witted stereotype, but the unexpected meeting in the shockingly bare interior disturbs Lana. At the advice of his Indian friend, Gil strikes Lana to quiet her screams.

The emotional charge of this scene, amplified by its overt sexism and racism, may have authorized Ford's experimentation with much bolder color and lighting design. The costumes and set design are essentially reduced to a blue dress, a red blanket, and a yellow fire against a black background, while the lighting set up juxtaposes cool blue "moonlight" with warm yellow red "firelight." (**See Plate 21.**) Both the color and lighting design, therefore, are constructed around the visually arresting, high-contrast, painter's primary triad of red, yellow, and blue. The exaggerated contrast which characterizes the overall design is further amplified by a lightning effect, which periodically interjects brilliant flashes of white light that briefly illuminate a classic Technicolor neutral background only to suppress it again in favor of black.

The cabin sequence negotiates a kind of Technicolor hard-style through strong color and lighting contrasts. The sequence is also an incarnation of two hallmarks of the color style Ford was to develop when he returned to color filmmaking beginning in 1948: primary hues in costumes and colored light. However, Ford's late 1940s works reversed the relationship between these two elements. In *Drums*, the saturated red and blue of Lana's and Blue Back's costumes take up a large area of the frame, whereas in his later color films Ford seems to prefer bold accents instead. Consider, for example, the pops of red and yellow provided by the bandanas and military stripes in *She Wore a Yellow Ribbon* (1949).

On the other hand, compared to *She Wore*, the colored light in *Drums* is relatively subdued. In the cabin scene, the light is clearly sourced. It is directional, and reflects, in the case of the moonlight, a long standing Hollywood norm, and in the case of the fireplace, measurable color temperature.

Ford's interest in colored light may begin with *Drums*, but it does not approach the excesses of the cemetery sequence in *She Wore*, where a sunset suffuses everything in frame with rich, thick magenta, red and orange. Lest too much be made of the expressive lighting in the cemetery sequence, though, it is worth noting that Ford and cinematographer Winton Hoch are careful to cast balanced, white light on John Wayne's visage, adhering to what Patrick Keating has called the "number one priority" of most Technicolor cinematographers: "appropriate skin tones" (Keating 2009: 220). Ford's taste for colored light may sometimes approach the boundary of normative Hollywood practice, but to my knowledge, it never crosses that boundary.

Perhaps the boldest cinematography in *Drums* can be found not in the cabin sequence, but rather in the sequence depicting the soldiers' homecoming. While Lana and the other women anxiously wait, the men begin to return from their battle with the British. In the sequence's first two long shots, the men march back into town. (**See Plate 22.**) Here, the organization of a color scheme around the female star recedes. Colbert's costume harmonizes with the rest thanks to the restraint of the overall palette, but it hardly organizes the palette. Against these neutral objects, the colored light becomes more assertive, contrasting the women bathed in warm light emanating from the windows with the long line of soldiers under a blue moonlight key light and a stark white backlight. As in the cabin scene, white lightning strikes are a prominent lighting effect, but here they are accompanied by heavy rain. In addition to further muting the colors in frame, the rain has the paradoxical effect of diffusing the stark backlighting. Thus, the exterior shots in the scene depicting the soldiers' return are characterized by spectacular cinematography.

The celebrated shot of the homecoming sequence is the three minute, ten second long take of Fonda's battlefield monologue. Colbert's Lana nurses Fonda's Gil in the foreground, while, out of focus in the extreme depth of the cavernous space, General Herkimer's gangrenous leg is sawn off. (**See Plate 23.**) Initially a long-shot, the composition features many elements common to Ford's films: deep staging and minimal editing, as I've already noted, but also tiny primary accents such as blood, a darkened foreground against a background illuminated with yellow light, and an aperture frame. An ostentatious camera movement reframes the composition around a two-shot of Lana and Gil, but even in the closer set-up, while Fonda continues to speak uninterrupted on the soundtrack and as extras pass in and out of frame, the yellow glow of Herkimer's surgery bed remains evident in the background.

The soldier's homecoming is unquestionably the scene that most forcefully advertises the advantages of the improved Technicolor negatives, and it is also the sequence that best anticipates Ford's compositions after his return to color filmmaking with *3 Godfathers* (1948). As an experiment with a new product for Technicolor and with a new element of design for Ford *Drums* is less unified than his later color works. Nonetheless, many of the techniques that are first introduced in *Drums* resurface in Ford's more assured color films a decade later such as *She Wore a Yellow Ribbon* (1949) and *The Quiet Man* (1952). For example, his experience coordinating color accents around Lana (Colbert) anticipates the sumptuous compositions centered on Mary Kate (Maureen O'Hara) in *The Quiet Man*. The hues that will recur in his later films are already present in *Drums*: pastels for women's costumes and deep or bleached hues for men's, and saturated reds, blues, yellows, and greens, even though the latter is admittedly less prominent in *Drums* than in the Irish landscapes of *Quiet Man* or the masculine interiors of the Cavalry films. The diffusion of light through dust, sand, rain, sunsets and lightning storms. Whether natural or simulated, become typical motifs in Ford's films and are used right through to his last production, *7 Women* (1966). The director's taste for colored backlight in high contrast, low key sequences, meanwhile, is most prominent in *She Wore* and *What Price Glory* (1952), but can equally be found in films of all genres from the last two-and-a-half decades of his career, from *3 Godfathers* to *Donovan's Reef* (1953).

Furthermore, while it may initially seem that Ford's limited color filmography in the 1930s and 1940s attests to his distaste for the medium, the opposite argument could easily be made. Only thirty full color feature length films, made by as few as twenty four directors, were produced in the 1930s (Higgins 2007: 229–235); one of those films was Ford's *Drums Along the Mohawk*. During World War II, Ford's documentary unit, like many other United States propaganda units, worked routinely in color. In 1942, Ford himself directed *Torpedo Squadron* and *The Battle of Midway*, both in color. Furthermore, if we expand our definition of "color film" beyond three color Technicolor, the number of color films Ford made prior to 1948 quickly multiplies. Not only were his silent films regularly tinted and toned, but his *Wee Willie Winkie* (1937), one of the foremost examples of his monochrome experiments with the hard-style, was also sepia toned. Sepia toning boosts contrast, offering a tantalizing suggestion that the *Drums* cabin sequence was not an isolated early experiment toward a color hard-style.[4]

In interviews, Ford downplayed the role color played in his work. Color, he boasted, is:

> Much easier than black-and-white for the cameraman; it's a cinch to work in, if you've any eye at all for color or composition. But black-and-white is pretty tough – you've got to know your job and be very careful to lay your shadows properly and get the perspective right. In color – there it is; but it can go awfully wrong and throw a picture off. [...Y]ou'll probably say I'm old-fashioned, but black-and-white is real photography. (McBride 2004: 306)

Yet as we have seen, close analysis of Ford's films contradicts his rhetoric. In fact, he paid just as much – if not more – attention to photography in his chromatic works. We can conclude that John Ford's reputation as a cinematographer's director is fortified, not threatened, by his color works.

notes

1. It is important to make this distinction between deep staging as function of mise en scène, and deep focus which is a function of cinematography. David Bordwell explains, "You can represent spatial depth through composition, setting, and light and shadow; and you can represent depth through choice of lens, amount of light, aperture, film stock, and optical process work" (Bordwell 1985a: 341).
2. The group style to which I refer is also known as "deep-focus cinematography" (Bordwell 1985a). However, I like the parallelism between "hard-style" and "soft-style," the latter being the label applied to the group style popularized by cinematographers in the late silent period. "Hard-style" has the additional advantage of more easily encompassing high contrast lighting schemes under its rubric.
3. According to the American Film Institute catalog (2003), *Gone with the Wind* went into production in December of 1938 and premièred in January of 1939, while *Drums Along the Mohawk* and *The Private Lives of Elizabeth and Essex* (also shot with the new camera negatives) both went into production in June of 1939 and premièred in November of 1939. *Drums* beat *Elizabeth and Essex* to national theaters by one day, premiering on the 10th rather than the 11th of November. However, the late September Los Angeles première of *Elizabeth and Essex* almost certainly marked the first exhibition of a film shot with second generation Technicolor stocks.
4. Toning increases density in the dark areas of the positive image, where there are many silver grains, but has little effect in the light areas of the positive image, where there are fewer silver grains. At the Haghefilm Foundation, I was able to see firsthand the difference introduced by toning in experiments conducted with step wedges. The contrast increase is both perceptible and objectively measurable with a densitometer.

I wish to thank Lea Jacobs and the members of her spring 2008 "John Ford & Classical Cinema" seminar at the University of Wisconsin-Madison (particularly Mark Minett) where this paper was born. Thanks also to Uli Ruedel and the wonderful staff at the Haghefilm Foundation for sharing their knowledge of early color with me.

references

Allen, L. (1950) "New Technicolor System Tested by Directors of Photography", *American Cinematographer* (December): 414–415.

American Film Institute (2003–2011) *Drums Along the Mohawk, Gone with the Wind, & The Private Lives of Elizabeth and Essex* catalog records. Online. Available at http://afi.chadwyck.com (accessed 4 January 2011).

Anon. (1939a) "Drums Along the Mohawk", *Variety* (8 November): 14.

Anon. (1939b) "Faster Color Cuts Light in Half", *American Cinematographer* (August): 355–356.

Bordwell, D. (1985a) "Deep-focus Cinematography", in D. Bordwell, J. Staiger, and K. Thompson (eds) *The Classical Hollywood Cinema: Film Style & Mode of Production to 1960*, New York: Columbia University Press: 341–352.

Bordwell, D. (1985b) "An Excessively Obvious Cinema", in D. Bordwell, J. Staiger, and K. Thompson (eds) *The Classical Hollywood Cinema: Film Style & Mode of Production to 1960*, New York: Columbia University Press: 3–11.

Eyman, S. (1999) *Print the Legend: The Life and Times of John Ford*, New York: Simon & Schuster.

Gallagher, T. (2007) *John Ford: The Man and His Films*. PDF online. Available at http://home.sprynet.com/~tag/tag/ (accessed 28 December 2010).

Higgins, S. (2007) *Harnessing the Technicolor Rainbow: Color Design in the 1930s*, Austin, TX: University of Texas Press.

Keating, P. (2009) "The Promises and Problems of Technicolor", in P. Keating (ed.) *Hollywood Lighting from the Silent Era to Film Noir*, New York: Columbia University Press.

McBride, J. (2004) *Searching for John Ford: A Life*, London: Faber and Faber.

Merritt, R. (2008) "Crying in Color: How Hollywood Coped When Technicolor Died", *Journal of the National Film and Sound Archive*, Australia 23: 1–16.

Schallert, E. (1939) "'Drums Along the Mohawk' Strong Pioneer Subject", *Los Angeles Times* (3 November): 10.

Surtees, R. (1951) "Filming 'Quo Vadis' in Italy, Part Two", *American Cinematographer* (November): 448, 473, 475–476.

Zelanski, P. and Fisher, M. (1999) *Color*, 3rd edn, Upper Saddle River, NJ: Prentice Hall.

chromo-drama

innovation and convention in

douglas sirk's color designs

s c o t t   h i g g i n s

Douglas Sirk's cycle of 1950s melodramas earned him recognition as one of Hollywood's preeminent colorists. Along with Vincente Minnelli and perhaps Nicholas Ray, Sirk raised the aesthetic profile of the domestic melodrama in the 1950s by innovating expressive forms of color lighting and mise-en-scène. These qualities were understood by the first wave of Sirk's auteur critics as generating a distancing, self-conscious artifice. Fred Camper commented in a 1971 issue of *Screen* that Sirk's films are "about their own style," "call attention to their own falseness," and that "objects and areas are never allowed to have the primary physical meaning which they have in real life" (Camper 1971 in Fischer 1991: 254, 255, 266). In the same issue of *Screen*, Paul Willemen listed "the use of baroque colour-schemes" among Sirk's six methods of introducing "a distance between the film and its narrative pretext" (Willemen 1971 in Fischer 1991: 270). More recently Russell Merritt singled out *All that Heaven Allows* (1955) for creating "an utterly transgressive color system" (Merritt 2008: 12). Sirk's colors do ring of artifice, but at the same time they exact emotion. Following Barbara Klinger's seminal observations on melodrama (1994), I want to suggest that the modernist argument can obscure the affective power of Sirk's color designs, the way that color answered the overt expressive demands of mid-century melodrama.

My goal in this chapter is to begin placing Sirk's work in a formal history of color aesthetics. I argue that against the background of Technicolor design, what stood out as opaque artifice to Sirk's late champions was also a nuanced engagement with craft practice. This is not to claim that Sirk's designs, the careful matching of costume and mise-en-scène or the intensive colored lighting were ever perceived as "natural." Rather, the kind of artifice they represent is part of a larger tradition. Attention to formal context allows us to better specify the nature of Sirk's innovations.

Sirk's color design tactics often draw on earlier models for deploying overt and determined organizations of color in melodramatic situations.[1] For example, Mervyn LeRoy's 1941 sentimental biopic of Edna Gladney and her campaign for orphans' rights in Texas, *Blossoms in the Dust*, showcases highly artificial color coordination to portray the happy moments in Gladney's (Greer Garson) life, usually just before tragedy. At the film's start, matching dresses and contrasting pink décor broadcasts the mood of innocent happiness before her best friend is driven to suicide [web illustration 1].[2] Similarly, the film's art direction carefully orders and echoes the colors of Christmas ornaments and new toys on the joyful morning before Gladney's son dies in a carriage accident [web illustration 2]. Production design in Sirk's *Imitation of Life* (1959), particularly the chromatic precision of Susie's (Sandra Dee) picnic, the matching cars at her graduation, or Lora Meredith's (Lana Turner's) New Haven living room and kitchen, follows the tradition of LeRoy's Christmas tableau; the mise-en-scène is impossibly polished, determined, organized, and too perfect to last [web illustrations 3–6].

To gain depth and specificity, I will focus on one of the most notable chromatic instruments in Sirk's color orchestration, colored illumination. Cinematographer Russell Metty's experiments with blue, gold, and multi-colored light in *All that Heaven Allows* are the best-known examples of projected color in Sirk's canon, though the practice persists in *Written on the Wind* (1956) and *Imitation of Life*. Mary Beth Haralovich suggests that Metty's lighting is both expressive and obtrusive. She notes that colored light intrudes "on the realist narrative space" and "functions as a signifier of the psychic and sexual energy that cannot be contained or expressed by the narrative in the usual ways" (Haralovich 1990: 66, 69). Russell Merritt echoes Camper and Willemen, concluding, "the blue swatches feel entirely cut off from the referenced world, operating entirely within the framework of … genre pastiche. … Light itself … is 'light' only in an approximate sense – an approximation of sunlight and an approximation of reading light" (Merritt 2008: 12). The apogee of the technique in *All that Heaven Allows* is the confrontation between Cary Scott (Jane Wyman) and her daughter Kay (Gloria Talbott), staged in multi-hued light motivated by a rainbow-colored window in the daughter's suburban bedroom. In its visual hyperbole, the scene is readily open to to modernist distanciation readings, but aesthetic historical context helps us to better grasp the relevance of Sirk's achievement.

Projected color, or colored lighting, has a long history in Hollywood. In fact, we can profitably see it as a continuation of the additive color techniques of tinting and toning which were more or less dominant during the silent era (Salt 1992: 78, 124, 150–151). Color laid over the image could have an overt semantic and representational function, but could also swell into an expressive register. Cecil B. DeMille seems to be doing something like this in his depictions of Hishuru Tori (Sessue Hayakawa) in the *Cheat* (1915) where red tinting combines with experimental lighting effects to sweep the frame in a hot sinister glow [web illustration 7]. A more complex example comes from Marshall Nielan's Mary Pickford vehicle of 1918, *Stella Maris*. Pickford plays two characters, the cockney orphan Unity Blake and the romantic, celestial Stella Maris. When Unity, secretly in love with Stella's boyfriend, swoons over his picture, Neilan delivers particularly cruel melodramatic cutting between Unity in sepia lamplight and Stella, with her beau, in spectacular moonlight blue [web illustrations 8 and 9]. The color is quasi-diegetic, it is applied from outside the film world, but it has conventional diegetic connections to lamplight and moonlight. Beyond denotation, the color is highly expressive, an emotional embellishment providing a graphic equivalence to counterpoint romantic desire fulfilled and denied.

This notion of color as an operatic accompaniment to emotionally charged situations informed three-color Technicolor's earliest aesthetic as conceived by its very first color designer Robert Edmund Jones. Jones was hired from Broadway to oversee production for Pioneer Pictures of three-color Technicolor's early prototype films in 1934. Jones viewed color not as an embellishment of the image, but as "a new form of dramatic art" (Jones 1935b: 3). He drew on the musical analogy to describe color's expressive power, explaining "the difference between a black-and-white film and a Technicolor film is very much like the difference between a play and an opera" (Jones 1935a: 13). I adapt Jones' concept of "operatic color" to describe an expressive approach to colored lighting, or what he called "mood lights." Three-color Technicolor's first short subject *La Cucaracha* is really a laboratory for projected color, testing various motivations and levels of interaction between colored light and performance.[3] As passionate lovers argue they stage themselves progressively closer to a red light bulb to build up emotion, and when the male dancer becomes murderously enraged he sweeps his partner backstage to an area flooded with red light, only moving into a cooler environment when the tension dissipates [web illustrations 10–15]. Likewise, the loneliness and jealousy of the spurned lover is registered as she backs into blue-green light, and then reemerges from it with new resolve [web illustrations 16–17]. This is an attempt at chromo-drama, where color, like music, begins as an accompaniment but then becomes at least an equal partner in emotional expression. Though the washes of color originate from within the story world, this sort of color retains some of the quasi diegetic charge of tinting and toning. Jones intends his color to reach beyond the story world in a direct sensory and emotional appeal, like music in opera.

Not surprisingly, Jones' aesthetic was short lived, deemed too intrusive on the standard production practices and on the narrative experience of filmgoers. Elsewhere I have charted the concerted efforts to develop a Technicolor look that harnessed color to the conventional demands of film style in classical cinema (Higgins 2007). After Jones' brief reign, colored lighting did not go away but developed in two directions, one strongly bound to the story world, the other more overt and stylized. On one hand, the technique was transmuted into the control of color temperature, usually justified by warm orange-gold lamp or firelight and steely blue moonlight. Probably the first instance of this device appears in the *The Flying Mouse* (1934), a Disney *Silly Symphonies* cartoon in which blue moonlight contrasts with golden lamplight when the warm hearth of mother mouse's pumpkin home beckons her wayward son to abandon his dreams of being a bat [web illustration 18]. Cool/warm contrast swiftly became the primary way of incorporating expressive projected color into a Hollywood production. This was encouraged by the technological fact that uncorrected high-intensity arc lights were rendered as cold blue and incandescents registered as warm yellow in the daylight-balanced Technicolor system (Greene 1937: 11). This color temperature mix underscored the threat of an outsider not allowed into the warmth of Tara in *Gone with the Wind* (1939), lent a romantic determination to Errol Flynn's Essex, and suggested that romance suffused Queen Elizabeth's (Bette Davis) cold chambers in *The Private Lives of Elizabeth and Essex* (1939) [web illustrations 19–24]. In a similar vein, projected color signaled the bittersweet prospect of young romance in *Meet Me in St. Louis* (1945), and contrasted the Smith household's warmth against the cold, moon-dappled snow-family in their back yard [web illustrations 25–28]. Conventionally, the balance of temperatures connoted the warmth and security of domestic spaces, as when it painted rural home life with a patina of affectionate nostalgia in *The Yearling* (1946) [web illustrations 29–30].

Perhaps the most important precedent for Sirk's work is John Stahl's 1945 Technicolor melodrama/noir *Leave Her to Heaven* with cinematography by Leon Shamroy. Shamroy, a noted master of colored lighting, balances blue tinged backlight against amber lamplight to lend an uneasy elegance to Ellen's (Gene Tierney) family home. As she seduces Richard (Cornel Wilde) in the first act, Stahl gives the whirlwind romance a disconcerting undercurrent through performance, dialogue, and lighting. Ellen and

173

Richard begin in the dark, a low-key effect evoked by the steely sidelight with which Shamroy dapples the set [web illustration 31]. As she begins to politely but insistently question Richard about his romantic life and family, Ellen takes control of the mise-en-scène and snaps on the end-table lamp, motivating a warm key light from off left. The new key glamorizes and centers the female star but also motivates chiaroscuro modeling on Richard, contrasting with the coolly lit back wall [web illustrations 32–34]. Ellen chillingly extols the pleasure of shooting wild turkeys that "are so big and clumsy that they hate to take wing ... it's a lot of fun" and invites Richard to join her hunt. She leaves him just as he realizes that she had carefully arranged their meeting, and he pauses in silence after snapping off the light [web illustrations 35–36]. The scene has an uncomfortable and disquieting quality, a love scene played in moody shadow with the characters separated by luminance and temperature. By 1945, this was a conventional, if beautiful, expressive use of a diegetic element. Colored lighting had nearly become a "fact of mise-en-scéne," a term Lea Jacobs uses to describe the developing conventions of artificial lighting in the teens when it ceased to require strongly marked motivation and became an accepted expressive device (Jacobs 1993: 416).

Shamroy's work here is at the subtle end of a spectrum, and is an excellent example of how Robert Edmund Jones' vision for projected color had been reduced and motivated, but also honed into a precise and nuanced tool by Hollywood cinematographers. Projected color flourished in another guise as well. Technicolor filmmakers of the 1930s and '40s also employed florid washes of chroma with minimal diegetic justification. Sunset and fire were favorite motivations in films like *Adventures of Robin Hood* (1938) and *Gone with the Wind* (1939) [web illustrations 37–38]. These effects could approach the uniformity of tinting or toning, but some cinematographers found ways of balancing other color temperatures within the wash of hue, extending the technique and helping it accord with codes of dramatic cinematography. Red for passion in *Gone with the Wind* is tempered by cold highlights mixed in as modeling light [web illustrations 39–40]. Selznick's follow-up epic melodrama, *Duel in the Sun* (1946) amplifies the device by mixing blood red with green highlights, leading a character to remark "there's a strange glow in the sky" [web illustration 41]. Adventurous filmmakers, throughout the era, would return to projected operatic color for expressive ends. In the opening of *A Matter of Life and Death* (1946), Michael Powell, Emeric Pressburger, and cinematographer Jack Cardiff press colored light into service when June (Kim Hunter), an air-base radio operator, contacts the dying pilot Peter (David Niven) [web illustrations 42–45]. Here, an unseen light source, presumably an emotionally sensitive radar tower beacon, pulses and swells in tandem with the scene's dramatic intensity, ultimately overtaking the frame. Powell and Pressburger do so very little to motivate the red suffusions that it would be a stretch to call this a normative use of color. Still, it testifies to projected color's relevance, for certain filmmakers, as choice for stylizing the image and seeking operatic accompaniment.

Against this aesthetic background, we might view Sirk's colored light in *All that Heaven Allows* in a similar vein to his color art direction; it is an expressive exaggeration or heightening of established techniques. On one hand, the looming swaths of blue, set off by warm orange lamplight that structure the space of Jane Wyman's home, are direct descendents of Leon Shamroy's Technicolor low-key in *Leave her to Heaven*. Russell Metty has saturated the blue a bit more, perhaps because shooting in tungsten-balanced Eastmancolor meant he would no longer rely on uncorrected arcs, but gelled incandescents. The intricate play of color temperature to separate playing areas and generate character juxtapositions is much the same [web illustrations 46–49]. In fact, love scenes between Cary Scott and Ron Kirby (Rock Hudson), staged in front of a picture window, cling closely to Technicolor precedent. Sirk and Metty use a subtle balance of temperatures and move figures between them in rhythm with the scene's development [web illustrations 50–51]. *All that Heaven Allows* follows the pattern set by *Gone with the Wind* in which tortured lovers seem to constantly find themselves standing next to windows, a tactic that helps cinematographers find color equivalents to the greater latitude of black-and-white cinematography [web illustrations 52–53].

Metty's penchant for monochrome low-key is powerfully displayed in *Touch of Evil* (1958), and he takes up equivalent color strategies when working on *All that Heaven Allows.* The embellishment of lighting-key with color informs the end of the film's second act when Cary sinks into her wintery depression and pools of blue overtake her home [web illustrations 54–55]. The lowest-key portion of the film coincides with the highest point in Cary's crisis. Sirk and Metty amplify the color-temperature schema, pushing the standard motivations for projected color toward the quasi-diegetic quality of Jones' mood lights.

The rainbow window scene in Kay's bedroom offers an elegantly staged ten shots to mark Cary's decision to break it off with Ron, and it sends the film off into its climax. Narrative and formal arcs have been building to this point. It is the morning after Cary's son Ned (William Reynolds) has scolded and rejected her amid low-key blue moonlight [web illustration 56]. Metty and Sirk need to extend and exceed the tone of that scene, but the diegetic motivation for moonlight is no longer available. Their solution is a complex use of projected color motivated by the window in Kay's room. Sirk and Metty scale the heights of chromo-drama, where color enters an operatic register and sweeps across the frame. We might read it as a distancing device, or as an example of what Thomas Elsaesser called "a sublimation of dramatic conflict into décor" (Elsaesser 1987: 52). Neither position does justice to the care and skill with which the effect is carried out.

Sirk and Metty likely recognized that this color effect was a reach for the diegesis, and so the sequence includes three shots showcasing the rainbow window (1, 4, 6). The establishing shot is crucial; as Kay crosses to her bed we are given a clear demonstration of the source and direction of the lighting [web illustrations 57–58]. Midway through the scene, Kay crosses back to the window, allowing a more full-bodied performance style, and an insert of Wyman's concerned close-up [web illustrations 59–61]. Editing and staging deftly carry the rhythm of the drama, but Metty and Sirk also sneak in a reminder of the light's origin.

Metty has achieved a meticulous balance of temperatures in the scene. Wyman receives only warm to neutral light from the window, while Talbott dips into less flattering blues and greens [web illustrations 62–64]. This fits with Metty's practice of obscuring and manipulating the lighting of characters around a somewhat better-lit lead actress, best seen in Cary's argument with her son, and her love-scene with Hudson [web illustrations 65–68]. It is not just a matter of keeping the star beautiful, or even legible, but of giving us access to her facial expressions and channeling our empathic investment. The craft of this scene has been under-appreciated; it exhibits a precise choreography of figure and light such that Cary remains undistorted while Kay is immersed in bands of chroma. Cary's close-ups, the linchpins of the sequence, are shaped around a heightened rendition of flesh tone. She seems to glow against the blue and red background [web illustration 69]. (**See Plate 24.**) Sirk and Metty innovate by inverting the approach to projected color used in *La Cucaracha* and *Duel in the Sun*; color permeates the world around the protagonist rather than being projected upon her. While the moment remains an outlier in Hollywood cinema, we should also recognize how it works with and within received practices, and how it is woven into the film's style as a whole. Sirk achieves his auteurist mark not at the expense of our engagement with character and emotion, but through the exaggeration and development of expressive color schemata and patterns that govern the history of color aesthetics.

Sirk's colored light is not bridled by literal meaning; this is not red of danger or green for jealousy. There is important semantic ambiguity here. Distanciation critics read this color as interfering with emotional trajectories, while a viewer seeking narrative containment might find the color to stand for the pressures of the outside world that isolate Cary. But we should also see this as an operatic accompaniment, and ambiguity may actually aid the expressive effect. Color shapes the image emotionally, if amorphously; the scene joins in a trend of direct sensuous engagement that dates back to silent additive color.

Sirk's experiments in the 1950s melodramas take place at the crucial historical juncture of the transition from Technicolor to Eastmancolor, as color was becoming more generalized and less strictly controlled. *All that Heaven Allows* was shot using Eastmancolor but processed by Technicolor labs in dye transfer. As Russell Merritt has argued, this is a period where technological change encouraged experimentation, as it had done in the 1930s with the innovation of three-color Technicolor, or with the current rise of Digital Intermediate. The ascension of Eastmancolor helped to broaden color's dramatic range in all genres. Leon Shamroy would drive his experiments in washes of color to impossible extremes in 1958's *South Pacific* where filters work in conjunction with lighting [web illustration 70–71]. Meanwhile, producer Ross Hunter would repeat and begin to conventionalize Sirkian projected color in Lana Turner vehicles like 1960's *Portrait in Black*, where red light follows Anthony Quinn's character as he kills for her love, or the 1966 remake of *Madame X* where rainbow windows connote Lana Turner's character's lurid descent [web illustrations 72–75]. Sirk's color designs participate in a moment when color was once again thrown into the spotlight, made novel. The power of color in the bedroom scene originates in the larger tradition of operatic color, but this power is contextual, depending on its identity as a special quality, apart from the norm. The history of color in the moving image is marked by such periods of expressive experimentation, perhaps aligned with technological and institutional change. Such historical moments, with Sirk's cycle chief among them, reveal the great promise of color; that even as it reaches ubiquity or becomes a routine fact of mise-en-scène, we find it waiting in the wings for perceptual and aesthetic renewal.

notes

1. For a discussion of color design in melodrama, see Higgins (2006, 2007, 2008).
2. Full color illustrations for this essay are available online at: http://shiggins. blogs.wesleyan.edu/2012/03/11/chromo-drama-innovation-and-convention-in-douglas-sirks-color-designs/
3. For a detailed discussion of colored light in *La Cucaracha*, see Higgins (2007, ch. 2).

references

Camper, F. (1971) "The Films of Douglas Sirk," *Screen* 12, n.2: 44–63; reprinted in Lucy Fischer (ed) (1991) *Imitations of Life*, New Jersey: Rutgers University Press: 251–267.

Elsaesser, T. (1987) "Tales of Sound and Fury" in Christine Gledhill (ed) *Home is Where the Heart Is*, London: BFI Publishing: 43–69.

Greene, W. H. (1937) "Creating Lighting Effects in Technicolor," *International Photographer*, January: 10–11, 25.

Haralovich, M. B. (1990) "All that Heaven Allows: Color, Narrative Space, and Melodrama" in Peter Lehman (ed) *Close Readings*, Tallahassee, FL: The Florida State University Press.

Higgins, S. (2006) "Blue and Orange, Desire and Loss: The Color Score in *Far from Heaven*," James Morrison (ed) *The Cinema of Todd Haynes*, London: Wallflower Press; New York: Columbia University Press.

Higgins, S. (2007), *Harnessing the Technicolor Rainbow: Color Design in the 1930s*, Austin, TX: University of Texas Press.

Higgins, S. (2008), "Color Accents and Spatial Itineraries," *Velvet Light Trap* no. 62: 68–70.

Jacobs, L. (1993) "Belasco, DeMille and the Development of Lasky Lighting," *Film History* 5 no. 4: 405–418.

Jones, R. E. (1935a) "A Revolution in the Movies," *Vanity Fair*, June: 13, 58.

Jones, R. E. (1935b) "The Crisis of Color," *The New York Times*, 19 May: 3(IX).

Klinger, B. (1994) *Melodrama and Meaning: History Culture, and the Films of Douglas Sirk*, Bloomington, IN: Indiana University Press.

Merritt, R. (2008) "Crying in Color: How Hollywood Coped When Technicolor Died," *Journal of the National Film and Sound Archive* 2, n.2/3: 1–16.

Salt, B. (1992) *Film Style and Technology: History and Analysis*, Second Edition, London: Starword.

Willemen, P. (1971) "Distanciation and Douglas Sirk," *Screen* 12, n.2: 23–29; reprinted in Lucy Fischer (ed) (1991) *Imitations of Life*, New Jersey: Rutgers University Press: 268–272.

scott higgins

color and containment

domestic spaces and

restrained palettes in

hitchcock's first color films

steven jacobs

This chapter deals with the construction of cinematic space in Hitchcock's first experiments with color: *Rope* (1948), *Under Capricorn* (1949), and *Dial M for Murder* (1953). These films are characterized by a rather restrained palette contributing to the creation of a claustrophobic interior, which is central to the plot of these films. Unmistakably in line with the contemporaneous "low key" genres of the Gothic melodrama and film noir, Hitchcock's earliest color films clearly differ from the glaring colors of his later films that established him as one of the great colorists of film history although only fifteen of his fifty-three films are in color.

Hitchcock's reputation as a colorist, no doubt, is largely based on films such as *Vertigo* (1958) and *Marnie* (1964), which are characterized by a highly expressive and symbolic use of color (Bellour 1995; Fiévet 1995; Allen 2006). In addition, many of his films of the late 1950s are marked by spectacularly dazzling colors and their original 35mm dye transfer prints have been called "true works of art" (Haines 1993: 85). With spectacular scenes comprising a flower market and fireworks, *To Catch a Thief* (1955) started Hitchcock's fascination for glorious colors. The film is set in the French

Mediterranean, an environment that had contributed importantly to the chromophilia of French modernist painting (Van Gogh, Derrain, Matisse). Shot in Eastmancolor by Robert Burks, the film won an Academy Award for best color cinematography and was also nominated for both costume design and art direction/set decoration – both categories which had separate black-and-white and color awards at the time. Moreover, *To Catch a Thief* started a series of Hitchcock films shot in VistaVision in which glorious colors largely contribute to the evocation of exotic or spectacular locales such as a Moroccan market (*The Man Who Knew Too Much*), the woods of Vermont in Autumn (*The Trouble with Harry*), the purple clouds near the Golden Gate Bridge (*Vertigo*), or Madison Avenue skyscrapers at rush hour (*North by Northwest*). On the one hand, this is perfectly in line with the tradition of Technicolor, which had been particularly deployed to evoke exotic and spectacular realms from its inception. At the time Hitchcock made these films, color in film was still overwhelmingly associated with specific genres such as the musical, the western, and the adventure film (Neale 2006: 19). On the other hand, Hitchcock's use of color first and foremost contributed to the cinematic establishment of spaces and places. In so doing, Hitchcock's colorful evocation of exotic sites can be situated in a tradition of color travelogues such as the Brown-Nagel films of the late 1920s and early 1930s shot in Multicolor. Moreover, with their fascination for the establishment of spectacular locales, Hitchcock's films of the 1950s are also connected to the new trend of location shooting and a fascination for the outdoors.

William Johnson (1966: 17–18) noted that Hitchcock often used a basic contrast between interiors and exteriors on which he created striking variations. In *Vertigo*, for instance, the exteriors are in subdued greens and blues, while the interiors are keyed to soft browns, oranges, and yellows. In contrast with his films of the later 1950s, in which color is first and foremost invoked to construct exterior public spaces, Hitchcock's earliest color films use color to create a specific atmosphere that is inherently linked to domestic interiors. In films such as *Rope, Under Capricorn, Dial M for Murder*, and *Rear Window* (1954), the narrative is largely or even exclusively situated in domestic spaces that become oppressive and claustrophobic (Jacobs 2007). This tallies with Hitchcock's Gothic melodramas of the 1940s that present the house as a place of confinement (Doane 1987: 123–154; Waldman 1991). In black-and-white films such as *Rebecca* (1940), *Suspicion* (1941), *Shadow of a Doubt* (1943), and *Notorious* (1946), a young female protagonist gets involved in a series of bizarre and astonishing events in which another inhabitant of the house increasingly frightens her. In these somber Gothic melodramas, the house is turned into a prison or a trap for the female protagonist and the intrusion of secret rooms (the bedroom of *Rebecca* or the wine cellar in *Notorious*, for instance) mark important moments in the narrative. In these films, as well as in some of Hitchcock's later works such as *Psycho*

(1960) and *The Birds* (1963), danger lurks in the house. By turning the familiar domestic environment into a place of fear, Hitchcock developed into a master of the uncanny. The color films *Rope*, *Under Capricorn*, and *Dial M for Murder* are variations on this Gothic theme, which are set in domestic spaces: a Manhattan penthouse, a Georgian country house in New South Wales, and an apartment in a London Edwardian Mansion House respectively. What's more, these houses are places where a murder takes place and/or where a character gets the impression that he or she will be killed by another inhabitant. Instead of a place of safety and domestic bliss, the house becomes a trap and an uncanny place of treason, suspicion, and danger. Light and color play an important part in this process.

rope

One of Hitchcock's single-set films, *Rope* is entirely situated in a midtown Manhattan penthouse containing a living room dominated by an impressive panoramic window. A grand piano, works of modern art, and books (which are used as a pretext for a morbid party) indicate the refined taste of the protagonists, who answer to the typical suave Hollywood penthouse dweller. Famously, Hitchcock explored this single set by means of a (supposedly) single take. Shifting its frame constantly, the heavy Technicolor camera moves through the rooms of the apartment. In order to enable Hitchcock to experiment with his notorious long takes, the set of *Rope*, containing a sophisticated system of mobile "wild walls," was a masterpiece of production design. In addition, the set included a cyclorama of the New York skyline "lighted by 8,000 incandescent bulbs and 200 neon signs requiring 150 transformers" (Hitchcock 1948: 277).

Rope was also Hitchcock's first color film. Together with cinematographer Joseph Valentine and Technicolor consultant William V. Skall, Hitchcock turned this film into a masterful study of light and color. Although the Manhattan penthouse in *Rope* does not have the dark and gloomy spaces of Manderley in *Rebecca* or the Bates house in *Psycho*, it is dominated by dark and subdued hues of brown and grey. Hitchcock stated: I never wanted to make a Technicolor picture merely for the sake of using color. I waited until I could find a story in which color could play a dramatic role, and still be muted to a low key. In *Rope*, sets and costumes are neutralized so that there are no glaring contrasts. The key role played by color in this film is the background. (Hitchcock 1948: 284)

Apart from some blotches in a painting by a "young American primitive," even all the artworks are characterized by muted colors. Also the vista on the metropolis offers mostly grayish blue to brownish red – the same colors that mark the costumes of all the characters. Furthermore, the lofty penthouse is decorated in a way that neglects its own architectural language of light and openness. The wood paneling in the dining room, the rather heavy imitation antique furniture, the numerous table lamps, statuettes, and candelabra indicate a rather conservative bourgeois taste, which is a little at odds with the presence of modern art and the striking modernity of the wall-sized window. White surfaces, lightness, and transparency, the key words of architectural modernism and the art deco penthouses of many 1930s Hollywood films, are absent. In a white and transparent modernist interior, the chest concealing the body of the murder victim would be too much out of place. Morbid secrets seem to need the dark. In the somber interior, bright or loud colors, consequently, indicate important details. The colorful dishes of food are displayed on the chest as if they serve a sacrificial meal. Red is prominently present as an index of blood in two scenes that mirror one another: when a character cuts his hand on a broken glass and when another is wounded by a gun.

Since the story of *Rope* is told in "real time," light, colors, hues, and shades help to evoke the passage of time from late afternoon to night, from light to darkness. *Rope* starts, however, the other way around, with the opening of curtains and the switching on of lights. The tension between darkness and light also recurs frequently in the dialogue. Paradoxically, colors become more prominent as its gets darker. The burning candles become more and more visible in the sequence in which the maid is on the verge of opening the chest. Meanwhile, the lights of the nocturnal city have become visible thanks to a "light organ," a device that allowed for the gradual activation of the skyline's thousands of lights and hundreds of neon signs – Hitchcock even played with the idea of giving one neon sign the shape of his silhouette thus allowing to intrude his infamous cameo appearance in the private space of the penthouse. In the end, the man at the light organ had played, in Hitchcock's words, "a nocturnal Manhattan symphony in light" (Hitchcock 1948: 278). A decade prior to *Vertigo*, Hitchcock experimented in *Rope* with the expressive possibilities of urban neon light. After sunset, unnatural colors intrude into the apartment and the confines of the single set through a full scale neon sign near the windows in the side wall. The garish neon sign – its proximity to such an elegant penthouse, no doubt, violating New York's zoning laws – begins flashing just at the climax of the movie, when the murderers are revealed. Its dominating colors are red and green – the colors of blood and mold, death and ghosts. It is as if *Marnie*, who is haunted by the color red, finds herself in the seedy San Francisco hotel room of *Vertigo*, which is filled by the eerie green of a neon light. Already in his first color film, Hitchcock demonstrates that "his expressive and symbolic employment of color is wholly congruent with the constraints of photographic realism" (Allen 2006: 132).

Self-evidently, the decision to shoot *Rope* in color brought many difficulties. The construction of the single set had to take into account the movements of the bulky Technicolor camera. Moreover, the first prints of Hitchcock's first color film proved unsatisfactory. According to screenwriter

Hume Cronyn, "it was like a Mexican fiesta on Olvera Street" (*Rope Unleashed* 2000). Hitchcock spent nine days refilming *Rope* in order to achieve the gradual darkening of the color scheme and to avoid the too glaring color tones in the shadows, which must have been the biggest challenge for the Technicolor dye-imbibition system.

under capricorn

A historical costume drama situated in early nineteenth-century Australia, Hitchcock's next film, by contrast, did fit perfectly in the generic traditions of Technicolor. Nonetheless, in *Under Capricorn*, Hitchcock continued his explorations of subdued colors. The film was made in collaboration with cinematographer Jack Cardiff (1949), who had already acquired a reputation for the sensual color photography on some of Powell and Pressburger's films.

Under Capricorn also deals with tensions in a marriage and its spatial expression, the home. The domestic drama occurs in a house with a name, "Minyago Yugilla," which means "Why Weepest Thou" in the aboriginal language. The architecture refers to several sources and their specific colors: the Anglo-Palladian tradition, which was very popular in the colonies; early Australian architectural design forms based on the English Georgian farmhouse and the Indian bungalow as interpreted by the British; the picturesque country houses designed by John Nash around 1800; and Samuel Sloan's country houses built in the United States in the 1850s and 1860s.

The exteriors are only represented by means of glass paintings that show, through the pictorial convention of framing trees, the building bathing in Claudean twilight or a nocturnal blue. Unmistakably, these pictorial light effects have to conceal the artificiality of the glass paintings but, at the same time, they contribute to both the exotic and uncanny atmosphere of the house. Its set, designed by Thomas Morahan, was another one of Hitchcock's sophisticated machines that enabled him to use impressive long takes that sometimes move from floor to floor, through lengthy corridors and several rooms. For that purpose, the set consisted of sections that could slide open electrically and pieces of furniture that could easily disintegrate. Apparently aimless camera movements enhance the claustrophobic atmosphere and the feeling of voyeuristic intrusion that accompanies the entire visualization of the mansion. In *Under Capricorn*, Hitchcock took the innovative single-take technique of *Rope* a step further and combined it with the dark psychology, Gothic romanticism, and huge mansions that were present in *Rebecca*, *Suspicion*, and *Notorious*. Light and color contribute to this to a great extent.

Faithful to British Palladianism, the interior is marked by shades of blue and white. Blue walls are combined with white decorations (moldings, mantle pieces) in most of the rooms: a hall, a small antechamber, an elegant semicircular drawing room containing a Claudean landscape – it is as if the picturesque setting of the house itself recurs in the paintings it contains – and an elegant dining room with burgundy draperies on the windows. The walls of the dining room are decorated with candleholders and several paintings such as a grisaille tondo, a picture of a horse, a portrait of a horseman, and several landscapes. The paintings show the combination of classical restraint and romantic and picturesque elements that also characterize the architecture – even a genuine Gainsborough landscape painting was used in the film. In short, the house became the perfect place to dream of the characters' mother country, which one of the characters identifies by its colors: "the greens and purples of Ireland."

Strikingly, most of the scenes are at night or at dusk as a result of which the entire house is dominated by a contrast between the cool blues of the interior and red glow produced by the sunset or candle lights. Milly, the housemaid, is identified with the house by the way she is dressed in grey and blue. She merges literally into the architectural background whereas Henrietta (Ingrid Bergman) takes care of the colorful accents. She is introduced as a drunk eccentric carrying flowers in her hair and later, she wears a showy, yellow dress – "the first work of art I have ever done," her admirer states. Ready for the governor's ball, she has to reject the red jewels presented by her husband – she shouldn't be "decorated like a Christmas tree." At the end of the film, she wears a heart shaped hat in pink and blue.

Strikingly, the only day light scenes at Minyago Yugilla, which are dominated by pastel tints, are scenes in which she is sane and self-confident. The dramatic scenes, by contrast, are dominated by deep reds and gold. This is for instance the case in the scene in which she gives the full facts about her husband (he took the blame of a murder she committed) in the dining room as well as in the scenes, bathing in yellows and oranges, that are situated in her elegant bedroom, typically a site of disturbance and the equivalent of the forbidden locked room in other Gothic Hitchcock stories.

dial m for murder

Hitchcock's third color film was *Dial M for Murder*, which tells another story about somebody trying to kill another resident of his own house. This time, the story is situated in the ground floor apartment of a London mansion. Its interior is marked by sober and elegant classical decorations. The living room has eggshell colored walls and is richly furnished with seats, armchairs, side-tables, and a writing desk. In addition, the apartment is richly decorated and the sophistication of its residents is expressed by the presence of some artworks. A Warner Brothers press release states that "because he is a man of taste and culture, Hitchcock hand-picked many of the props, including an original Rosa Bonheur oil painting, long hidden in

Warners' property gallery, and a pair of valuable Wedgewood vases" (Jacobs 2007: 107). Some of these art works, such as the Bonheur painting, fauve paintings, and a postimpressionist flower piece, render touches of color to the restricted palette of the interior, which is beautifully rendered by Robert Burks' Warnercolor photography.

Again, the subdued colors emphasize the feeling of an enclosed and confined space. Its boundaries are not only underlined by the motifs of the locked door and the latchkey but also by the closed large window curtain – its dark green called "oppressive" by Johnson (1966: 9–10). In addition, the boundaries of the confined space are marked by a series of high angle shots whereas the claustrophobic feeling is further elaborated by the 3-D process. Although Hitchcock refused to capitulate to the outrageous eccentricities of 3-D gimmickry (no objects are thrown in the face of the viewer), he favored compositions that place lamps, knickknacks, and pieces of furniture of diverging colors in the foreground, walls well in the background, and human subjects in a middle-ground. In addition, a subtle depth of field is created by the camera, favoring low positions and gliding fluently around the furniture. In so doing, Hitchcock used the 3-D process to create dramatic effects, emphasizing the ways in which the apartment serves as a trap for the characters.

Again, the contrast between light and darkness contributes to this effect. Crucial scenes such as the planning of the murder, the murder itself (actually an attempted murder that turns into the killing of the murderer), and the exposing of the criminal are shown in darkness – with the light of the fireplace, the light from an adjacent room coming under the door, or a flash light as dramatic elements. Against the quiet and almost monochrome background of harmonious colors of the interior, the changing colors of Margot's dresses are remarkable. Wearing a color perfectly in harmony with the background in the company of her husband in the opening scene, Margot (Grace Kelly) is dressed in sparkling red in the subsequent scene with her American lover. As Laurent Fiévet (1995: 72–73) has noted, Hitchcockian red is often associated with the red theater curtain. Since Hitchcock heroines tend to appear late in the film, they are often surrounded by red indicating that the plot truly begins. According to Fiévet, in Hitchcock, red is also the color of fake appearances and of lies and he mentions Margot as an example. Later in the film, she is shown with a blue night gown during the murder scene as if she has merged into her domestic setting. The day after the murder, she is dressed in dark blue and she wears a brown coat in the final scene blending with the background again. Like Milly, the housemaid in Under Capricorn, she repeatedly becomes part of the interior. Referring to Scottie in the hospital room in Vertigo, Marnie disappearing in the urban gray, and Roger Thornhill in the vast wasteland of North by Northwest, Allen (2006: 134) noted that "loss of identity or emotional vacuity is evoked in precise moments in Hitchcock films through the loss of color." Margot is also wearing dark clothes during the scene of the trial, which is in many ways remarkable in respect to color. Apart from some establishing shots of the apartment's exterior, a shot in a cab, a view of an arriving ship, and some shots in a restaurant, the courtroom scene is the only scene that does not take place in the apartment itself. It is a scene, however, without spatial coordinates or in which space is exclusively constructed by color and light. Only a medium close-up of Margot and the judge are visible and they are shown against a monochrome background, which changes from blue to red. It is as if this red reverberates the blood that intruded and destroyed the home, which in Hitchcock is never a site of domestic bliss. Years before Marnie's obsession with red, the blood stain on the carpet in this bourgeois apartment acts as an intriguingly strange object. It is not only a literal stain on the floor but also an uncanny detail in the mise-en-scène, a stain in the visual field or what Zizek (1999) has called a "Hitchcockian blot."

the restrained mode

In his three first color films (and, to a large extent, also in his next color film *Rear Window*), Hitchcock favored muted colors before he started to celebrate the exuberance of glorious Technicolor from the mid-1950s onwards. This line of approach was already announced by Hitchcock in 1937, ten years before his first color film:

> I should never want to fill the screen with color: it ought to be used economically – to put new words into the screen's visual language when there's a need for them. You could start to color film with a boardroom scene: somber paneling and furniture, the director's all in dark clothes and white collars. Then the chairman's wife comes in wearing a red hat. She takes the attention of the audience at once, just because of that one note of color. (Hitchcock 1937: 258)

In so doing, Hitchcock's early color experiments tally with what Higgins (2007: 76–136) terms the subdued or restrained mode of Technicolor filming which flourished in the late 1930s. As in films such as *The Trail of the Lonesome Pine* (1936), *Nothing Sacred* (1937), *Dodge City* (1939), and *A Star Is Born* (1937), Hitchcock's first color films are characterized by narrow palettes and tight harmonies although this restrained mode allows for an occasionally overt display of color, dramatic punctuation, and elegant decoration. This predilection for muted colors can also be linked to the generic conventions of the somber domestic melodrama and the crime thriller, which both in the 1940s and early 1950s reached their apex in the "black-and-white" and "low key" genres of the Gothic romance film and film noir.

Together with John Stahl's *Leave Her to Heaven* (1946), *Rope* was one of the first crime thrillers shot in color. In addition, Hitchcock's subdued palette contributes to the creation of a claustrophobic interior, which is central to the plot of these films. Consequently, color plays an important part in the integration of the characters in the surrounding interior. However, blending the characters with their environment entailed specific problems in color photography. On the set of his first color feature *Rope*, Hitchcock was surprised to see the extent to which actors were separated from the background through the use of backlights even though in color there was no need for this (unless the actor should be dressed in exactly the same color as the background). In his famous interview with François Truffaut (1984: 183), Hitchcock stated that he truly believed that "the problem of lighting in color film has not been solved. I tried for the first time to change the style of color lighting in *Torn Curtain*." Last but not least, in *Rope*, *Under Capricorn*, and *Dial M for Murder*, specific colors, color combinations, and pictorial light effects help to mark the difference between inside and outside, and hence often between on screen and off screen. In so doing, colors greatly add to the construction of the motif of intrusion.

references

Allen, R. (2006) "Hitchcock's Color Designs", in A. Dalle Vacche and B. Price (eds) *Color: The Film Reader*, New York: Routledge: 131–44.

Bellour, R. (1995) "La Couleur Marnie", in J. Aumont (ed.) *La Couleur en cinéma*, Paris: Cinémathèque française: 147–148.

Cardiff, J. (1949) "The Problems of Lighting and Photographing *Under Capricorn*", *American Cinematographer*, 30, 10 (October): 358–59, 382.

Doane, M. A. (1987) *The Desire to Desire: The Woman's Film of the 1940s*, Bloomington and Indianapolis, IN: Indiana University Press.

Fiévet, L. (1995) "Vertiges chromatiques, Alfred Hitchcock: *Vertigo*", in J. Aumont (ed.) *La Couleur en cinéma*, Paris: Cinémathèque française: 72–73.

Haines, R. W. (1993) *Technicolor Movies: The History of Dye Transfer Printing*, Jefferson, NC: McFarland.

Higgins, S. (2007) *Harnessing the Technicolor Rainbow: Color Design in the 1930s*, Austin, TX: University of Texas Press.

Hitchcock, A. (1937) "Direction", in S. Gottlieb (ed.) (1995) *Hitchcock on Hitchcock: Selected Writings and Interviews*, London: Faber & Faber: 253–261.

Hitchcock, A. (1948) "My Most Exciting Picture", in S. Gottlieb (ed.) (1995) *Hitchcock on Hitchcock: Selected Writings and Interviews*, London: Faber & Faber: 275–284.

Jacobs, S. (2007) *The Wrong House: The Architecture of Alfred Hitchcock*, Rotterdam: 010 Publishers.

Johnson, W. (1966) "Coming to Terms with Color", *Film Quarterly* 20, 1 (Autumn): 2–22.

Neale, S. (2006) "Technicolor", in A. Dalle Vacche and B. Price (eds) *Color: The Film Reader*, New York: Routledge: 13–23.

Rope Unleashed (2000) [DVD] Universal. (Making-of documentary on the DVD of *Rope*, 1948. Directed by Alfred Hitchcock. Transatlantic Pictures.)

Truffaut, F. (1984) *Hitchcock/Truffaut*, New York: Simon & Schuster.

Waldman, D. (1991) "Architectural Metaphor in the Gothic Romance Film", *Iris* 12: 55–70.

Zizek, S. (1999) "The Hitchcockian Blot", in R. Allen and S. I. Gonzalès (eds.) *Alfred Hitchcock: Centenary Essays*, London: BFI: 123–140.

color and meaning

in *marnie*

s e v e n t e e n

j o h n   b e l t o n

In narrative films the meaning of color is primarily contextual, arising from the association of a color with a character, event, object, or situation that gives it meaning. To some extent, this mirrors the status of color as an epistemological phenomenon. It takes its identity, in part, from the object possessing that particular color. As an attribute of the object, it has no object status in itself (in this way, it resembles sound which is always the sound of something; a color is always the color of something). Thus the yellow purse in the first shot of Alfred Hitchcock's *Marnie* (1964) represents the first in a series of yellow objects in the film, ranging from Mrs. Edgar's refrigerator, Mr. Rutland's yellow vest, Mark's golden yellow bathrobe (which he puts around Marnie just before raping her), and Marnie's yellow dress (which she wears when she rides Forio). As an attribute of the purse (and these other objects), yellow takes its meaning as a color from them and from its relation to other colors in the film. The chain of associations links yellow with money; Marnie's yellow purse in the first shot is full of stolen money. The color yellow is associated with the use of money to buy affection: as Bill Paul suggests, in the scene in Mrs. Edgar's kitchen, when Marnie talks about how she gets "the money to set you up," their exchange is shot in front of a pale yellow refrigerator which we assume Marnie has purchased for her mother (Paul 1970: 60). Yellow is used to signify the power that position and wealth gives to certain characters. Thus Mark's father, an icon of patriarchal privilege, is introduced wearing a dark gold vest. At the same time, it also designates the ability of certain characters to "take possession" of others: Mark wears a yellow bathrobe when he rapes Marnie on their honeymoon and Marnie wears a pale yellow dress when she rides off on Forio (after Mark has retrieved the horse for her).

The color red, however, behaves differently. Though initially attached to objects such as red gladioli, red ink spilt on a white blouse, red polka dots on a jockey's white jersey, and a scarlet red hunting jacket, red is repeatedly wrenched from these disparate and seemingly random objects and projected upon the face of the heroine herself in the form of red suffusions that fade in and out. When Marnie encounters red, the nature of the object that is red is less significant than the fact of its redness; she responds primarily to the color, not to the object. Of course, individual red objects may ultimately prove to have significance, but Marnie's red-tinted reaction shots make the color primary and the object secondary, reversing the normal relation between attribute and object. Take, for example, the first bright red object—the red gladioli. The gladioli are subsequently revealed to be the gift of Jesse's mother to Marnie's mother for taking care of Jesse. From this perspective, they represent Marnie's loss of her mother's love to another child, who has taken her place. In this sense, they can also be said to point to the theme of jealous rivalry embodied by the sailor in the flashback who was also Marnie's rival for her mother's love. However, Marnie reacts to the flowers *before* she knows of their association with Jesse and she clearly reacts not to the flowers but to the color red, a reaction made clear by the red suffusion over her reaction shot. The attribute of red functions independently of the as-yet unknown meaning of the flowers. The gladioli turn out to be an exception that proves the rule—the rule that red objects resist the obvious chain of associations characterized by the color yellow. The red gladioli would seem to have no apparent connection to the red ink, the polka dots, or the hunting jacket.

In other words, unlike most color films, where color plays a secondary role as an adjectival property of an object (which is primary) and takes on the meaning of that object or chain of objects, the color red in *Marnie* enjoys an independent existence. Its relation to its object is often obscure. More precisely, the meaning of the color red functions as the film's central enigma. Alfred Hitchcock's *Marnie* was marketed as a "suspenseful sex mystery." At the core of its status as a mystery lies the color red. One of the film's central enigmas involves the meaning of the color red. *Marnie* may be a "suspenseful sex mystery" but the terms in which that mystery is framed focus on the solution of a mystery about the color red. This chapter thus argues that the color red in *Marnie* is *more* than any single object; it has a meaning that transcends the objects with which it is associated.

The mystery at the heart of the film is not that of a typical detective whodunit. Andrew Sarris famously described the first shot of the film in terms of Hitchcock's shot syntax. It was not "brunette with yellow handbag walk[ing] on platform" but "yellow handbag with brunette walking on platform," pointing out that we are "cued to money before Marnie" (Sarris 1970: 143). The next two scenes make it clear that Marnie's yellow handbag is full of stolen money. It is not the nominal, outer identity of the criminal that is in question but her inner identity. The mystery is not who stole the money but why. The red suffusions embody this enigma by connecting the color red to Marnie's subjectivity. Because of Marnie's extreme reactions to the color red, we come to link its meaning with the source of her psychological problems. If we can discover why she responds so to red or what red means to her, perhaps we can uncover the source of those problems and solve the mystery.

The film's red suffusions function as expressionistic markers of subjectivity, as exteriorizations of Marnie's inner psychological state. As such, they are objectifications of it and of her trauma. They are signs that point to an experience that has been repressed. The red suffusions mark the return of that repressed. Detached and/or displaced from its original object, red, in the form of the suffusions, acquires the status of an object— of redness in and of itself. Initially an attribute of an object, red becomes, over the course of the film, an object in itself. In this sense, the red suffusions function as a fetish, as a displacement and disavowal of Marnie's original trauma. They not only stand in for Marnie's psychological trauma but a red suffusion—the blood pouring over the sailor's white tee shirt—is literally *the last thing* she sees the moment before her realization of what she has done.

But the meaning of the color red is blocked—both for Marnie who is unable to understand her traumatic responses to the color and for the audience who, though in no way traumatized as Marnie is, experience the red suffusions as incomprehensible barriers to any access to the character of Marnie herself. The meaning of the color red has been repressed by both Marnie and the film. It is only at the end, when the color red is reconnected with its object, that the blockage will be removed and the mystery of the color red resolved.

If color, like everything else in classical Hollywood cinema, is typically characterized by transparency, the color red in *Marnie* is non-transparent, opaque—at best, translucent. Of course, the color red, especially with the value and saturation that it has been given here by the Technicolor dye transfer process, enjoys a natural, eye-catching visibility. But the red suffusions necessarily differ from red colored objects in that they are inherently expressionistic, calling attention to themselves as intrusive markers of heightened subjectivity. They are symptomatic manifestations of the hysteria that erupts and momentarily paralyzes both the character Marnie and the normal operations of the film text itself. The red suffusions quite literally constitute a blockage that obscures meaning—they function like curtains that have been drawn at crucial points between the narrative as it unfolds and our access to it.

The red suffusions (with one notable exception) are presented primarily as subjective, traumatic affect in reaction shots. Though prompted by red objects or other traumatic stimuli, they exist independently of those off-screen sources. These red suffusions mark the transformation of a simple diegetic color—e.g., red gladioli—into an internal displaced diegetic color—the red suffusion over Marnie's face—that reflects her subjective response to seeing that particular value and saturation of the color red.

The mystery of the suffusions is complicated by the fact that they are not always responses to the presence of the color red. There are a total of seven suffusions. Four of these are prompted by a red stimulus. The other three are not, complicating any attempt to reduce Marnie's trauma to the color red alone. In these exceptions to the rule, Marnie responds to audio and audio-visual stimuli. There are red suffusions over shots of Marnie's face during two nightmares after she hears the sound of three taps at a window. The suffusions also occur during a thunder and lightning storm. During the storm, the red suffusions shift from reaction shots of her face (the norm for six of the seven suffusions) to a red suffusion over her point-of-view shot of a white curtain. This is the notable exception referred to earlier: the red suffusion shifts from her reaction shot to her point-of-view (pov) shot.

Marnie's nightmares rework crucial elements of her original, childhood trauma—the three taps, the sudden cold. The storm sequence does the same. It reproduces the lightning and thunder that terrified her as a child and that triggered the sailor's attempt to comfort her. Mark's movement across the room toward her resembles that of the sailor and the red suffusions over the white curtains recall the blood on the sailor's shirt. These various audio and visual motifs allude to a primal scene of sorts, to a traumatic event whose repression has left behind a disparate assortment of fragmentary pieces that remain illegible until the penultimate sequence of the film. They are clues to the mystery that Hitchcock and his screenwriter, Jay Presson Allen, have planted that will pay off in the final flashback. The common denominator that binds these motifs together into a single scenario is that of the red suffusions. Structurally, the pattern is remarkable in its order and overall symmetry. Hitchcock alternates between red and non-red stimuli (see italics). The two nightmares occupy the second and the penultimate positions in the pattern (see boldface). And the pov shot stands at its center (see boldface and italics).

Red Suffusions

1. *Red Gladioli*
2. **First Nightmare (three taps)**
3. *Red Ink*
4. ***Lightning Storm (red tinted pov shot)***
5. *Red Polka Dots on Jockey's Jersey*
6. **Second Nightmare (three taps)**
7. *Red Hunting Coat*

See Plate 25: Stimulus: red ink on Marnie's white blouse resembles blood.
See Plate 26: Response: a red suffusion conveys Marnie's traumatized reaction.

At the same time, the last three red stimuli constitute a clear progression that culminates in the final images of the flashback and that clarifies the interconnection of red and white introduced in the first instance of red gladioli against a white window curtain. At Rutland's, Marnie spills a drop of red ink on her white blouse, panics, and runs to the ladies room to wash it out. The drop resembles a drop of blood; even her co-workers think that Marnie has been injured, reinforcing the association between red and blood, which Marnie has repressed and which she, knowing that it is only red ink, denies.

At the race-track, Marnie visits the paddock to see Telepathy, a horse she once saw train as a two-year-old. Telepathy's jockey is, by coincidence, wearing a red polka dot jersey, which triggers another one of Marnie's spells. The red polka dots on a white field exaggerate, as it were, the earlier drop of blood on her blouse, getting us closer and closer to the sailor's bloodstained tee shirt.

At the hunt, the connection between red and blood is directly established. As the hounds tear at the captured fox and the other members of the hunt look on with amused smiles on their faces, Marnie reacts in horror. This time, she sees a scarlet riding jacket, which sets her off. In each instance, from one drop of red to several polka dots to the red drenched jacket, red has taken us closer and closer, through its tangle of associations, to the repressed killing of the sailor. Like the earlier game of free association, which works on a verbal level, this sequence of color associations involving red and shirts is anything but free—it is carefully calculated to get us and Marnie closer and closer to the truth.

The final flashback sequence, which reveals the source of Marnie's trauma, achieves a certain explanatory power because of the highly expressive way in which it is shot. The action is seen *through* stylizing devices which mark it as traumatic. It is initially shot with a fish-eye lens which distorts space; the color of the sequence seems deliberately "aged" or otherwise disturbed, that is, unlike colors seen in the film proper; and the entire color scheme is set up so as to de-naturalize events (by washing out flesh tones in faces). The color used here is desaturated. It looks faded, evoking the past.

193

This desaturated color makes the intensity of the climax all the more powerful when the frame fills with highly-saturated, bright red blood. Watching the sailor's white tee shirt gradually turn red with blood, we can almost feel the jolt in the intensity of color as the pure white of the tee shirt slowly suffuses with red blood.

Hitchcock's strategy over the course of the film is to detach, then re-attach the color red from red objects. By detaching red from red objects, Hitchcock explores the gap between color and object, extending it to create a color mystery. In detaching red from its objects, Hitchcock engages his audience in a game of detection in which the meaning of the color red is the goal.

Hitchcock's brilliance in his manipulation of color and meaning rests upon the obvious banalilty of its resolution. Red proves to mean blood. One might ask how the solution of the color mystery in *Marnie* can hinge on the rather trite revelation that red stands for blood. We all know that; it is one of the most common cultural associations that the color has. Does the film merely pretend that there is a mystery on the level of color, when all along there is no mystery? Is the mystery manufactured? Do we feel as if we've been had by the narrator who has duped us into trying to figure out something that was right in front of our noses the whole time? The point, I think, is that though the meaning of the color red is obvious, it is repressed—both by Marnie and by Hitchcock, who encourages us to continue to look for its meaning, who prolongs that whole process as part of a narrative strategy that links us ultimately with Marnie. We might say that by the end of the film, we, like her, can admit that we unconsciously "knew" that red stood for blood all along. Like her, we recover a meaning that we had repressed (because it was so obvious).

The color mystery moves through a variety of situations that gradually and associationally arrive at the meaning of red—a red spot of ink on a white blouse that looks like blood, red polka dots on a white jersey, an all-red hunting jacket, the sailor's white tee shirt turning red with blood. The slow disclosure of the meaning of red engages the spectator in a psychoanalytic process, as if red were an element of the recurrent nightmare that Marnie has. It isn't, however. There is no red in her nightmare. It is one major element of the original trauma that Marnie has repressed. She recalls the lightning storm, the three taps, being taken from a warm bed into the cold, and the men in the white suits. It is thus the crucial element that, when identified, will solve the mystery of her recurrent dream and lead hopefully to her cure.

In *Citizen Kane* (1941), Kane's first (and last) word, "rosebud," is a signifier detached from and waiting to be reattached to an object, person, or other entity for its meaning to become clear (and even when that occurs at the very end of the movie, its literal signified is made clear but its meaning to Kane is not). Like the word "rosebud" in *Kane*, red hovers over the diegesis of the film *Marnie* until it finally reconnects with its object. As in *Kane*, the banality of meaning associated with the reconnection of signifier and signified is belied by the complexity of that sign's relation to a larger signifier. The fact that Rosebud is a sled explains nothing about what Rosebud meant to Kane. The fact that as the word "Rosebud" is displayed on screen, finally identifying the object for us, the letters that identify it are consumed by flames, as is the sled itself, is as much a part of its meaning as anything else. If "Rosebud" is a sled and the signifier "rosebud" finally attaches itself to an object, this signifier/signified clearly becomes, in turn, a signifier of yet another signified—of the unattainability of desire. It stands in for everything that Kane desired but which eluded him; it stands in for a profound inaccessibility that thwarts desire. Red in *Marnie* means blood but it also stands in for a complex bundle of fears and desires that obsess Marnie and that constitute the fabric of her dreamwork—unreciprocated love for her mother, oedipal jealousy, a profound sense of guilt, fear of male sexuality, fear of death, and emotional and psychological paralysis, not to mention a child's more normal fear of lightning storms. In *Marnie*, the fact that "red" means blood satisfies only one strand of the larger mystery of red. The closure that results from the color red's reassignment to its proper object belies the web of complex connotations it has acquired over the course of the film as a whole. It is not just blood. Nor is it the sum total of the trauma depicted in the flashback. It is everything that the film says and leaves unsaid about its central character, her relationships with others, and her experience in the world.

references

Allen, R. (2007) *Hitchcock's Romantic Irony*, New York: Columbia.

Paul, W. (1970) "Perception and Meaning in Hitchcock's *Marnie*," in J. Belton (ed.) *Alfred Hitchcock in America*, Cambridge, MA: Harvard University.

Peucker, B. (2011) "Aesthetic Space in Hitchcock," in T. Leitch and L. Poague (eds) *A Companion to Alfred Hitchcock*, Malden, MA: Wiley-Blackwell.

Sarris, A. (1970) *"Marnie," Confessions of a Cultist: On the Cinema, 1955/1969*, New York: Simon and Schuster.

archive

are my eyes really

brown? the aesthetics

of colorization in

casablanca

j a s o n   g e n d l e r

Since its notoriety in the late 1980s, a wealth of material has been written about colorization. However, very little of this material assesses the aesthetics of specific colorized films.[1] The dearth of analytical material is unsurprising, given colorization's status as an abomination within many film circles, but a comparative analysis of a black-and-white film in relation to its colorized counterpart is nonetheless a worthwhile endeavor. Whatever one might think of colorization, at base it is simply another color process, potentially akin to other color processes that attempt to integrate color and film; it is complete with many of the accordant challenges such integration poses. A comparison of the aesthetics of the colorized *Casablanca* (Curtiz, broadcast 9 November 1988) with the original black and white version (Curtiz, 1942) reveals the way in which the colorization process alters and contributes to the film's organization of space and the salience of information, while a comparison of the colorization with the aesthetic principles of three-strip Technicolor makes the choices of the colorization more apparent by indicating how another color process from the time of *Casablanca*'s initial production likely would have handled color in the film.[2]

Colorization is a computer-based process used to create color video versions of black-and-white 35mm films. In moving beyond the broad arguments about colorization's virtues – or more commonly, vices – to offer a comparative analysis of a black-and-white film and its colorization, it is important to keep in mind that one of the guiding principles of the stylization of space in classical Hollywood cinema is its subordination to narrative. Cinematic space primarily functions as a vehicle for narrative and works to support viewer comprehension of information important to the story (Bordwell, Staiger and Thompson 1985: 3, 6, 12, 50). Color can be considered one of the many stylistic devices that can help organize cinematic space, and thus it is also subordinated to narrative causality in classical Hollywood cinema. Therefore, one of the most fruitful means of analyzing the aesthetics of the colorized *Casablanca* will be to examine the degree to which its use of color adheres to the aesthetic principles of classical Hollywood cinematic narration.

Colorization companies certainly had aesthetic concerns and aspirations regarding their products; it is, after all, to the advantage of any business to put time and effort into producing the highest quality and most cost-effective product possible. Indeed, the time and care devoted to the creation of the colorized *Casablanca* is one of the best reasons for using that film as an entry point for an inquiry into the aesthetics of colorization; in its time, *Casablanca*'s colorization was one of the most championed exemplars of the process (Matthews 1988: 18; Edgerton 2000: 24–32).[3] In a particularly insightful rebuttal of the aesthetic arguments against colorization, David James even allows for the possibility that colorized films could improve upon the black-and-white originals, writing that:

> In some cases colorized movies may be aesthetically better than the originals. Only careful, open-minded comparison will do here. In the end, it will probably turn out that most of the black-and-white versions are indeed better works of art. Yet keep in mind that few of the 17,000 black-and-white movies existing in English are "classics". Thousands are actually pretty terrible. Some of the worst are virtually unwatchable. … Colorization would surely benefit some of these awful disasters, since almost anything would be an improvement! (James 1989: 338)

Clearly, this does not necessarily apply to *Casablanca*, which is widely regarded as a classic. Nevertheless, it is in the spirit of open-mindedness that this article approaches colorization.

the saliency of information in colorization

Throughout *Casablanca*, the effects of colorization alter the saliency of information in various ways. While there is an overall attempt to pack the frame with diverse, saturated hues, especially in wider establishing shots that encompass background objects, sets, and minor characters, the film does not consistently employ a wide variety of colors. Instead, it often uses a much more restricted color scheme, creating some compositions that could be considered problematic from a perspective that values narrative clarity. In the following example, the patterning of the hues assigned to certain figures uses low-contrast harmonies that divert attention away from a pertinent piece of causal information, and toward that which is both redundant and less directly relevant.

Late in *Casablanca* the despondent Frenchwoman, Yvonne (Madeleine LeBeau), who has previously attempted to ingratiate herself to Rick (Humphrey Bogart), reappears and nearly incites a fight between the French patriots and the Nazis when she brazenly accompanies a German soldier to Rick's café. Yvonne's role in the incident contrasts sharply with her behavior later that evening, during the climax of the singing competition between the French patriots and the Nazis. In this scene, close-ups show a tear-streaked Yvonne passionately singing along to "La Marseillaise," and shouting "Vive la France!" at the song's conclusion. Between these seemingly contradictory moments, an important shot helps explain her change in behavior. (**See Plate 27.**) In this shot, the Nazis sing "Die Wacht am Rhein" in the center background while Yvonne, seated to the left of the frame in the foreground, stares at her table and nervously sips her drink, seemingly ashamed. In the black-and-white release of *Casablanca*, Yvonne occupies a comparatively large proportion of the frame in relation to the Nazis, which helps to offset her marginal position in the frame. In the colorized version, however, Yvonne's presence in this shot is slightly diminished because the hues applied to her costume and skin pigmentation provide easy passage to other less important objects. (**See Plate 28.**) "Passage" occurs in low contrast color harmonies in which adjacent colors are analogous enough that they blend into one another. For example, placed side by side, colors such as lemon yellow, amber, gold, tangerine orange, and pumpkin orange would create strong passage (Branigan 2008: 7).[4] In this example from the colorized *Casablanca*, Yvonne's white blouse, the white tablecloth, and the light sand colored pillar and beige walls behind her tan and brown head are roughly analogous hues, making it easy for Yvonne to blend into the scenery like the table lamp that occupies lower center frame. Conversely, the brightly lit, green and blue hued Nazis stand out much more in the colorization than they do in the black-and-white version.

Yvonne is the center of interest in this shot; she is the only part of the image that provides any new, causally relevant information. The singing Nazis have been well-established in four previous shots, three of which feature them as the most visually salient part of the image. Given the redundancy of what would be yet another shot of the Nazis without Yvonne's presence in it — as well as the causal link this shot provides between Yvonne's blithe accompaniment of a Nazi and her patriotism during "La Marseillaise" – this shot seems to be designed specifically to allow for the observation of her reaction.[5] In the black-and-white version, hue is not a factor in guiding attention toward or away from certain objects, heightening the importance of other stylistic variables, such as the relative size and position of objects, and thus Yvonne is easier to observe. However, colorization alters the salience of information in this shot, creating a visual gradient that undermines the juxtaposition of scale in the black-and-white film by helping Yvonne blend into the causally irrelevant objects around her. Combined with her decentered framing and lower-key lighting, the colorization serves to emphasize the heightened color contrast of the brightly lit Nazis, potentially obfuscating a small but important causal link in Yvonne's character trajectory. Consequently, if the spectator fails to notice Yvonne in the shot prior to Victor's ordering the band to play "La Marseillaise," then one will have missed an important step in Yvonne's progress from opportunism to patriotism.

The effect of color on the spectator's attention to certain details is not restricted to minor characters such as Yvonne, but is a recurring trait of the colorized *Casablanca*.[6] Ilsa's (Ingrid Bergman) colorization often creates strong passage between her and her surroundings. A striking example occurs during Ilsa's reunion with Sam (Dooley Wilson). **(See Plate 29)**. Her pearl-white blouse and jewelry exactly match the tablecloth and differ only slightly from the ivory white of the lampshade next to her head and the curtains behind her, while the tan hue assigned to her skin is only a slightly warmer variation of the beige colored walls. Framing, focus, and lighting, especially the rim light highlighting her hair and shoulder, assist in separating her from the different spatial planes. However, the passage between her colors and those of her surroundings do not draw attention to her as the most significant figure for the narrative in the frame. This color scheme and the passage it creates are not in keeping with three-strip Technicolor films of the period, in which color was based on a set of organizational principles that insured against such ambiguities of composition. To better understand just how a Technicolor film from the period would have treated this scene, it will be useful to briefly describe Technicolor's guiding principles.

202

the aesthetic principles of technicolor

Technicolor's approach was the most successful integration of color into the classical Hollywood cinematic mode of production for many technological, industrial, economic, and aesthetic reasons, not the least of which was the company's adherence to the principle that color should serve in support of a film's narrative. Narrative support is one of four key principles advocated by Natalie Kalmus, head of Technicolor's Color Control Department (1923–1948), as outlined in "Color Consciousness," which she presented at a meeting of the Technician's Branch of the Academy of Motion Picture Arts and Sciences in 1935.[7] Kalmus oversaw the training of Technicolor color directors, and frequently worked in collaboration with them, thus most Technicolor films of the period incorporate the principles she helped to develop.

According to Kalmus, the colors used in a film "must be in absolute accord with the story action," and should augment the film's mood, not overpower the story (Kalmus [1935] 2006: 28). This is especially the case for costumes. Kalmus commented about the importance of wardrobe design, writing, "We plan the colors of the actor's costumes with especial care. Whenever possible, we prefer to clothe the actor in colors that build up his or her screen personality" (Kalmus [1935] 2006: 28). Another principle Kalmus stressed is "color restraint," or the use of subdued color schemes in an attempt to imitate natural color and not overpower the senses (Kalmus [1935] 2006: 28). Color restraint involved balancing highlights such as blues, reds, and yellows with neutrals such as whites, blacks, browns so that they worked to draw the spectator's attention to certain aspects of the image. For example, in a colorful setting, important characters should be dressed in offsetting colors, and vice versa. Another of Kalmus's principles was that color should direct attention toward important information. Central to Kalmus's conception of this principle is the notion of color separation:

> The term "color separation" means that when one color is placed in front of or beside another color, there must be enough difference in their hues to separate one from the other photographically. For example, there must be enough difference in the colors of an actor's face or costume and the walls of the set to make him stand out from the colors back of him; otherwise, he will blend into the background and become indistinguishable, as does a polar bear in the snow. (Kalmus [1935] 2006: 28)

This principle often led to the use of cooler tones or shadows in the background to offset warmer flesh tones, as well as the hierarchical organization of costume colors by character importance, which is part of her "law of emphasis" (Kalmus [1935] 2006: 28). Finally, Kalmus also emphasized color juxtaposition, or the coordination of color movement in the frame over time. Side by side, some colors alter our perception of adjacent colors, thus color directors needed to consider how changes in blocking, camera movement, or editing could affect color compositions. What works for one composition might not work when a character leaves the scene.

the colorized casablanca compared to technicolor

The scene of Ilsa's exchange with Sam clearly illustrates how the colorized *Casablanca* differs from Kalmus's principles. Had the film been made in

Technicolor, Ilsa's costume would have been made to stand out from her surroundings through high – or low – contrast color harmonies or greater variations in a single hue. For example, the wall behind her face would potentially have been colored so as to throw her flesh tones into relief. Such color organization would have helped to make her the most salient object within the frame and support the narrative, as she is the most relevant figure in this shot and scene. A lack of such color organization is a reoccurring trait of the colorized *Casablanca*: often Ilsa is clad in white outfits and poorly separated from other planes, becoming one neutral among many others.[8] The colorized *Casablanca* also deviates from Kalmus's law of emphasis, as many background players at Rick's café are colorized in hues that draw attention to themselves.

The colorization also differs from Technicolor through its effect on the visual passage between elements in the composition, as well as through the degree to which perspectival planes are separated (the difference between passage and plane separation is that passage is based largely on hue, whereas plane separation is contingent on many other devices in addition to hue, such as framing, focus, and lighting). These differences between versions raise the question of how the separation of planes and the passage between compositional elements were managed in the black-and-white image, since in the original there is only a hue variety of white, gray, and black. When Ilsa reunites with Sam in the black-and-white version, the framing, focus, and lighting all serve to highlight her – especially the lighting, which combines with the brilliance of Ilsa's costume to further separate her from the background curtains and the majority of the tablecloth and lampshade, which are cast in darker grays. (**See Figure 18.1.**) However, when hue is added, color lowers the saliency of luminosity and light/dark contrast, thus reducing the distinction between Ilsa and the background. (Colorization necessitates a lower contrast; if the image is too dark, the color won't come through. This effect is most easily visible in close-ups of Ilsa in which she wears a shadow-casting brimmed hat, such as in the scene in the Blue Parrot, or at the airport during the end of the film). In the black-and-white film, Sam simply becomes another darkly shaded figure on the edge of the frame, roughly analogous to the objects behind Ilsa, whereas in the colorization, his yellow suit is much more prominent amongst the more neutral colors, which fuse together into an indistinct mass.

Problematic separation of planes and visual passage which misdirects the viewer's eye occurs throughout the colorization. The scene in which Rick first briefly converses with Strasser and Renault is colorized mostly with whites and browns in both the foreground and background. The ivory-white of Strasser's and Renault's formal uniforms is identical to the table lamp and very similar to the pearl-white tablecloth, Rick's jacket, the silver caviar dish, and other dining instruments on the table. As with

Figure 18.1
The framing, focus, and lighting all highlight Ilsa in the black-and-white version. *Casablanca.*

Ilsa and Yvonne, the hue used for Caucasian skin is analogous to the beige used for the wall in the background. This color scheme is rather antithetical not only to Kalmus's statements about color charting developments in the plot, but also to her ideas about color helping to accentuate the neutrals and vice versa.

Again, we can ask how the scene between Rick, Renault, and Strasser might have been handled had *Casablanca* been planned for Technicolor. Rather than matching colors between foreground and background, the color director likely would have insisted on contrasting colors to throw the major characters into relief. The color director would have been slightly restricted by the colors of the uniforms worn by Renault and Strasser, because the scene in which they sit down with Rick calls for their wearing their white uniforms. If the script could not be altered to change their outfits, our hypothetical color director could have distinguished them from Rick by dressing him in a different color dinner jacket. However, Rick's white jacket, combined with his black pants and bow tie, serves to create some thematic resonance regarding his neutrality. Thus let us restrict the color director further by keeping Rick in white as well. In this case, the color director would likely contrast the characters with their surroundings. At the very least, the tablecloth, lampshade, and dining implements would have been strongly colored in dark hues to help offset the whites. It is likely that the walls behind each of the characters' heads would have been colored to contrast with that of the flesh and costume hues, per Kalmus's color separation principles, instead of the analogous whites and beiges that provide such easy passage between the characters and less important details. Potentially the walls would be more darkly lit as well. A Technicolor design would also tend toward higher contrast color harmonies between the characters and the surrounding objects, whether between warm and cool tones, or the juxtaposition of light and dark. White is neutral, so any other hues in this particular sequence would prove acceptable by highlighting the characters and making them the most salient figures within the frame, although the color of the walls, table-cloths, and lampshades would be carefully considered so that they would provide just as effective contrasts and harmonies for other scenes, especially for those involving Ilsa.

Particular care was often given to the color design of the female lead's costume and make-up in classical Hollywood films, both because their resplendence was often considered crucial to a film's financial success, and because a beautifying color design could support a film's narrative. As David Bordwell notes, romance usually comprises at least one of the main plot lines in many films of the classical Hollywood cinema (Bordwell, Staiger and Thompson 1985: 16). As half of the romantic couple that invari-ably motivates a major line of action in a film, the female lead must appear to inhabit some desirable characteristics, not the least of which is physical beauty. Carefully designed color schemes for make-up and costume could aid immensely in enhancing her desirability, thus supporting a romantic plot. The colorized *Casablanca* exhibits some of the careful attention paid to the female lead in the classical Hollywood cinema, especially with regard to the colorization equivalent of make-up. Ilsa's lips, and the lips of most of the other young female characters, even extras, are colored in a pleasant chestnut shade of red, and the irises of their eyes are colored with browns, blues, or greens. Additionally, the pale sclera of Ilsa's eyes and her teeth both remain white, which was not always true of many early colorized films. For instance, Vincent Canby wrote of the color of Constance Bennett's and Donna Reed's lips as "being the same cadaverous, gray-brown color" as the rest of their faces in the respective colorizations of *Topper* (McLeod, 1937) and *It's a Wonderful Life* (Capra, 1947), and of Stan Laurel's "coal-black" eyes in the colorization of *Way Out West* (Horne, 1937) (Canby 1986b: H21).

There are occasions when the colorized *Casablanca* does seem to accord to the principles laid out by Kalmus, most notably in the scene where Ilsa confronts Rick in his apartment at night. **(See Plate 30.)** The colors in this scene are potentially analogous to how they might have appeared had *Casablanca* been filmed in Technicolor. Ilsa's warm, yellow blouse, red waist sash, and black pants contrast sharply with the cool blue of the large drapes behind her, combining to create a high contrast color harmony out of the three primaries of the painter's palette.[9] This color harmony supports the story by clearly separating Ilsa from the drapes behind her, limiting the

passage of the spectator's eye between Ilsa's colors and those of her surroundings, such as that found in the earlier scene between her and Sam.
The large difference in hue between Ilsa's costume and the background
helps focus attention on Ilsa, and the de-saturated quality of the blue makes
the more saturated yellow and red of Ilsa's costume stand out. Additionally,
the relatively consistent blue of the background solves the problem of
color juxtaposition in this scene; as yellow-red Ilsa moves through the
space, the background remains blue behind her. Thus she continually
stands out as an important object, separated from the background plane,
while maintaining the color harmony of the scene and not running up
against colors that would offset that harmony. This painter's triad is maintained even in close-up, where her yellow collar is still visible, while the red
of her lips replaces the sash tied to her waist.

One likely explanation for some of the choices made in the colorization
is that in an attempt to claim some authenticity for it, the company producing the colorization, American Film Technologies, researched the original wardrobe colors to inform its work. As others have noted, this attempt
was somewhat misguided, because the original wardrobe colors really have
no bearing on what the film would have looked like had it been shot in
color (Fantel 1988: H30; James 1989: 334). Moreover, although there are
some things that the colorization of *Casablanca* does well, striving for original wardrobe colors creates some aesthetic difficulties, especially from the
perspective of a color process such as Technicolor, which strove to function within the terms set by the classical Hollywood cinematic mode of
production. Given that the colorization of *Casablanca* is considered exemplary of the colorization process of the 1980s and early 1990s, it is clear that
success in the terms of classical Hollywood is indeed not easily achieved.

notes

1. One exception from the popular press is a critique by Vincent Canby of the
   colorized *Topper* (broadcast 1985, original black-and-white release 1937)
   (Canby 1986a: H1, 21).
2. My analysis of the Technicolor aesthetic is derived from Natalie Kalmus's
   1935 speech entitled "Color Consciousness" (Kalmus, [1935] 2006).
3. I do not claim to be making a broad argument about the aesthetics of all
   colorized films, because different colorization companies had different
   approaches to the process and used different technologies (Kohs 1988: 15).
   However, considering that *Casablanca* is supposedly a superior colorization,
   it can serve as a model for other possible colorizations of the period.
4. Passage can be explained biologically: for informational efficiency, human
   brains are wired to respond to contours rather than homogenous surfaces.
   Consistent hue and luminance implies a lack of contour and, thus, analogous colors create passage by downplaying contour and reducing the
   saliency of edges, causing analogously-colored objects to flow into one
   another (Livingstone 2002: 92, 176).
5. Why, one might ask, does this shot not feature her more prominently,
   if its purpose is to provide information about her reaction and motivation

for her change in behavior? One answer is that such a shot would not suit the needs of the narrative. Yvonne is a relatively minor character, disappearing from the film after shouting "Vive la France!" A more prominent reaction shot might stress her presence and reaction more than would be appropriate.

6. Color transition in this sense is not always problematic. There could easily be an instance in which the kind of obfuscating shift described above is the desired effect. Alternatively, passage could also be an effective stylistic and narrational device, creating thematic resonance by uniting characters with their surroundings.

7. The Color Control Department is sometimes referred to as the Color Advisory Service.

8. One exception is Ilsa's scene in the Blue Parrot, where her broad-brimmed, white hat creates a plane of resistance between the hues of her face and those of the background.

9. The Technicolor printing process was adept at producing variations of red, yellow, and blue, so this triad is quite common in many Technicolor films, including *Meet Me in St. Louis* (Minnelli, 1945), *She Wore a Yellow Ribbon* (Ford, 1949), and *Singin' in the Rain* (Donen, Kelly, 1952).

references

Bordwell, D., Staiger, J., and Thompson, K. (1985) *The Classical Hollywood Cinema: Film Style and Mode of Production to 1960*, New York: Columbia University Press.

Branigan, E. (2008) "Making it Colorful: Relations and Practices," unpublished manuscript, University of California, Santa Barbara.

Canby, V. (1986a) "'Colorization' is Defacing Black and White Film Classics," *New York Times*, 2 November: H1, 21.

Canby, V. (1986b) "Through a Tinted Glass, Darkly," *New York Times*, 30 November: H21.

Edgerton, G. R. (2000) "'The Germans Wore Gray, You Wore Blue': Frank Capra, 'Casablanca,' and the Colorization Controversy of the 1980s," *Journal of Popular Film and Television*, 27: 24–32.

Fantel, H. (1988) "Foes of Colorization See Red over Black and White," *New York Times*, 19 June: H30.

Higgins, S. (2007) *Harnessing the Technicolor Rainbow: Color Design in the 1930s*, Austin, TX: University of Texas Press.

James, D. (1989) "On Colorizing Films: A Venture into Applied Aesthetics," *Metaphilosophy*, 20: 332–340.

Kalmus, N. (1935) "Color Consciousness," reprinted in A. Dalle Vacche and B. Price (eds) (2006) *Color, the Film Reader*, New York: Routledge.

Klawans, S. (1990) "Colorization: Seeing Through Rose-Tinted Spectacles," in M. C. Miller (ed.) *Seeing Through Movies*, New York: Pantheon Books.

Kohs, D. J. (1988) "When Art and Commerce Collide: Colorization and the Moral Right," *Journal of Arts Management and Law* 18, 1: 13–43.

Livingstone, M. (2002) *Vision and Art: The Biology of Seeing*, New York: Harry N. Abrams.

Matthews, J. (1988) "Colorization: Beginning to See Possibilities, as Time Goes By," *Los Angeles Times*, 9 November: 18.

"those men are

not white!"

neuroscience, digital

imagery and color in

o brother, where art thou?

w i l l i a m   b r o w n

In this chapter, I shall use discoveries from neuroscience to argue that color as much as movement is a source of pleasure in cinema. Pleasure here is defined in neuroscientific terms not simply as enjoyment but also as that which attracts our attention, and furthermore derives from the evolutionary reward for overcoming challenges in the visual field, such as recognising predators, prey, or mates (see Ramachandran and Hirstein 1999: 31). According to recent neuroscientific work on color perception, it appears that we perceive color *before* we perceive movement (Viviani and Aymoz 2001), and as a result of this I shall suggest that cinema is as much a medium of spectacle (beholding color) as it is a medium of narrative (which has at its core in-frame movement). This foregrounding of color is made clearer still through the practice of color manipulation in digital cinema, a phenomenon that has similarly been analyzed (e.g. by Scott Higgins 2003) for the effect that it has in downplaying narrative in favor of spectacle. The Coen Brothers' film, *O Brother, Where Art Thou?* (USA/UK, 2000), will then serve as a template for a cinema that self-consciously explores how color can diminish cinema as a narrative form in both "natural" (i.e. scientific) and artificial (i.e. through the digital manipulation of color) ways.

neuroscience and color

Neuroscientist Vilyanur S. Ramachandran and philosopher William Hirstein have controversially defined eight laws of aesthetic experience, the three most prominent of which are the peak shift effect, grouping, and artistic appeal through the heightened activity of a single dimension (Ramachandran and Hirstein 1999).

The peak shift effect suggests that creatures, including humans, find exaggerated forms more pleasurable than "normal" ones, especially if there is a reward involved. If rats are taught to discriminate between squares and rectangles, and are rewarded for choosing the rectangle, without further coaching they respond even more to longer and thinner rectangles. Furthermore, seagulls that recognize their mothers' beak as a yellow-brown rod with a red dot on the end respond with greater vigour to merely a long stick with a red dot on it, and even more so to a long stick with three red dots on it, even though to the human eye this looks nothing like a seagull beak. From this, Ramachandran and Hirstein extrapolate that human viewing pleasure might also rely upon responding strongly to "exaggerated" forms as found in artworks.

Grouping is the process by which humans will find patterns in otherwise disparate phenomena. That is, thanks to our prior understanding of what a Dalmatian looks like, we will pick one out from a collection of dots and splotches on a white page. This happens not only with forms but with colors as well: we find aesthetically pleasing designs that have patterns of color, as fashion designers know well (22).

The third principle that Ramachandran and Hirstein describe is "the need to *isolate* a single visual modality before you amplify the signal in that modality ... Isolating a single area (such as 'form' or 'depth'...) allows one to direct attention more effectively to this one source of information, thereby allowing you to notice the 'enhancements' introduced by the artist" (24).

In other words, seeing exaggeration, grouping, and drawing attention to a single aspect of a work of art induce pleasure in the viewer. This pleasure is the reward for diverting our attention, whether consciously or not, to these phenomena, which from an evolutionary perspective we seek to recognize in order to find out their nature (whether they are predator, prey, or mate).

Ramachandran and Hirstein have been heavily criticized for obvious reasons: seagulls and rats are not humans, they (the authors) do not take into account the artist, and one cannot box art into a system of such rules.

While I am sympathetic to these criticisms, I am also persuaded in part by their argument, not as a definition of art per se, but as a reason for a visual phenomenon to attract our attention and to be pleasing. It makes sense that we should direct our attention to objects, forms and colors that we associate with pleasure and reward, no matter how material or abstract these may be.

With regard to film, one might be tempted to dismiss Ramachandran and Hirstein's theory as irrelevant. André Bazin (1967) has argued that film is a transparent recording of reality, and while he has been criticized for taking this position (e.g. by Kendall Walton 1984), his theory of indexicality continues to hold sway in certain quarters, with D. N. Rodowick (2007) recently defending analogue cinema precisely for its indexical nature as opposed to the simulated realism of digital cinema. An acceptance of Bazinian transparency might lead us to conclude that, *contra* Ramachandran and Hirstein, cinema involves no "exaggeration" of the world. However, whether or not analogue cinema is an index of what was before the camera, through every material choice that occurs during filmmaking it is also an exaggeration/distortion of the reality that it supposedly captures in a "neutral" manner (Walton 1984: 249). Choice of camera, film stock and lens, development processes, camera position, mise-en-scène and editing techniques all distort reality, arguably making cinema a pleasurable exaggeration of reality, whether or not it qualifies as art. As we shall see, with digital filmmaking techniques, cinema's distortion/exaggeration of reality is even more apparent.

However, before discussing digital technology's role in cinema, I shall further consider color from the perspective of neuroscience. Beyond Ramachandran and Hirstein, other neuroscientific discoveries would seem to suggest that color perception has a privileged role to play in the film experience. Semir Zeki, another prominent neuroscientist, has written about how "[c]olour is a biological signalling mechanism that exemplifies very well the brain's quest for knowledge under continually changing conditions" (1999: 93). Color plays a key role in our being able to distinguish form (sorting different objects from each other) as well as depth (how far away those objects are) and movement. Zeki and colleagues (see also Zeki and Marini 1998) have found, however, that different areas of the brain respond to color when it is viewed in association with forms to when color is viewed "in the abstract," i.e. when an artist tries to divorce color from form, as in works by Piet Mondrian and fauvism: "their [the fauvists'] art used pathways [in the brain] that are quite distinct from the ones used by representational art that portrays objects in normal colors" (Zeki 1999: 94). Therefore even though color is helpful in allowing us to perceive form, we do not in fact perceive color and form with the same parts of the brain, and exaggerated colors in cinema might similarly stimulate different neurons to "normal" viewing conditions.

Furthermore, we do not perceive color, form, and motion at the same time. Instead of seeing "whole," different areas of our brains sort raw data from the external world for different bits of information; we have what Bartels and Zeki (2003) term separate but integrated "microconsciousnesses" that are themselves spatially and temporally distributed throughout the brain. One microconsciousness measures color, while another measures motion. These microconsciousnesses work in parallel and we do not perceive everything all at once, but over time, suggesting that consciousness is asynchronous and that the human brain has a time-based anatomy, or "chronoarchitecture" (Bartels and Zeki 2004).

This spatial distribution of processors for color, form and movement in the brain leads to a temporal difference between these three phenomena. As Viviani and Aymoz explain, "color and form are processed simultaneously ... [but] movement perception is delayed by about 50 milliseconds" (2001: 2909). If color and form are perceived more or less simultaneously, but before motion, which is etymologically speaking the very stuff of cinema (κίνημα/kínima means movement in Greek), it would seem that color is the stuff of cinema as much as movement and that we take pleasure in onscreen colors as much as we do in onscreen movement/action.

Another noted neuroscientist, Robert Solso, has written about how there is a difference in depth between colors. That is to say:

> In the real world of daily visual perception and processing of information, we experience the natural shift in colors of objects of varying closeness, and an object's color is an additional component of knowing where the object is. In keeping with the effects of atmospheric perspective, warm colors seem to advance while cold colors recede. For example, an orange or yellow object (warm colors) placed on a blue or green background (cold colors) seems to stand closer to the observer. This generalisation is likely related to the way we see these colors in the real world, in which atmospheric distortion has a cooling effect on colors proportional to their distance from the viewer (largely due to the refracting effect of water vapour in the atmosphere). (Solso 1994: 172–173)

212

Philosopher C. L. Hardin has argued that the "temperature" of color is as much a cultural phenomenon as it is a "natural" one, in particular pointing out that blue, normally associated with coolness, is in fact also the color of the hottest flames. However, while the association of color with temperature is of course a matter of acculturation, it is also perhaps the "natural expression of neural coding" (Hardin 2000: 121), since "warm" colors and "cool" colors provoke different responses. If, according to Solso, warm colors advance, while cool colors recede, then warm colors arouse us, while cool colors calm us. This stands to reason: as daylight comes, we become aroused by the approaching light, while the recession of light that is the blueness of evening calms us and prepares us for sleep – not least because light inhibits our production of melatonin, which in turn induces drowsiness in humans, especially under blue light (see Dawson and Encel 1993). In fact, monkeys have been shown to express high levels of anxiety when exposed to red light, while they themselves will always choose blue light if given a choice (explained in Hardin 2000: 121).

Therefore in cinema warm colors arouse us and make us more alert (with reds more arousing than yellows or greens) and are perhaps more pleasurable (in the sense of demanding attention) than cool colors. Not only is color processed before movement in the brain, but warm colors also give the impression of advancing towards us, of seeming closer than cooler colors. Psychologists Steven Franconeri and Daniel Simons (2003) argue that approaching or "looming" phenomena more readily attract our attention than receding phenomena: from this perspective, approaching and warm colors would be more "pleasurable" or "arousing" than cold, receding ones.

digital color

If color "naturally" appeals to us before motion, then this appeal is only heightened through the enhanced artifice of digital color manipulation. Lev Manovich has defined digital cinema as *colors changing in time*.

> Since a computer breaks down every frame into pixels, a complete film can be defined as a function that, given the horizontal, vertical, and time location of each pixel, returns its color ... For a computer, a film is an abstract arrangement of colors changing in time, rather than something structured by "shots", "narrative", "actors", and so on. (Manovich 2001: 302)

The digital image has no material being. As it is made up entirely of code, it simply contains pixels programmed to change color (even if these pixels combine to form a shape that is recognizable to a human viewer).

In the age of color manipulation via the digital intermediate (DI), it has been argued that color might disrupt narrative. Evoking the advent of Technicolor, which provoked a similar response, Anna Everett has written that, with digital technology, there has been a "move from Technicolor to ... 'technocolor'" (2003: 11) and Scott Higgins has argued that *Pleasantville* (Gary Ross, USA, 1998) was a "novelty-based demonstration film" showing off the possibilities of digital color and the DI, making it a more spectacular than narrative movie.

Higgins goes on to argue that *O Brother, Where Art Thou?* sees "[d]igital color ... harnessed to narrative ... [its] restrained designs emphasize that the technology can recede from attention, not simply provide a distracting gimmick" (2003: 67–69). *O Brother...?* involves, for Higgins, the use of digital color "in the restrained mode" (2003: 71) and therefore is predominantly a narrative film. However, in order to illustrate the preceding sections, I shall now contend that *O Brother...?* displays an ambivalent relationship between spectacle and narrative, particularly when we consider the film's digital enhancement of color "neuroscientifically." Furthermore, I shall argue that the Coens are well aware of the key role that color plays in their film.

O Brother...? is a rambling story about three escaped convicts, Everett, Pete, and Delmar, who are trying to find some buried money (in fact nonexistent) before the valley in which it is supposedly hidden is flooded to make way for a hydroelectric plant. It is set in Depression-era Mississippi and the look of the film is enhanced by the adoption of browns and yellows added in post-production (see Bergan 2000: 212–213). These give the film a sepia tint, a warm and nostalgic feel that is reminiscent of the photos of contemporaneous artists like Eudora Welty.

The film not only gives pleasure on account of its nostalgic look and feel, but from the neuroscientific perspective, *O Brother...?* is also pleasurable because the color manipulation follows Ramachandran and Hirstein's "peak shift" effect and *exaggerates* the look of the film. This is seen explicitly in the opening shot, where the camera drifts over and around a group of prison inmates crushing stones for the railroad as armed guards look on. In this shot, the image slowly fades from black-and-white to sepia to a full "color" image (the inverted commas here signifying that the color has been heavily manipulated). In other words, the shot demonstrates awareness of its own transformations.

In accordance with Ramachandran and Hirstein's third principle concerning the emphasis on one aspect of the picture over the others, this shot would also suggest that color is emphasized over form and movement – an emphasis that extends into the rest of the film such that the color has even been described as a "character" (Starr 2000). Not only is color artificially/digitally emphasized by the filmmakers in this pleasurable way, but this effect is achieved through a natural phenomenon, color itself, which precedes movement for the human viewer, suggesting that the film is not so much about narrative/movement, but more about its look and feel. Furthermore, the filmmakers choose to employ warm colors (yellow in particular) that spectators will find arousing, not least because they "advance" towards them. Since these warm colors are digitally created, and exaggerated to the extent that they can be considered a "character" in the film, Manovich's prognosis that the digital film is constituted by colors changing in time, as opposed to by actors and narrative, would seem an appropriate framework through which to consider the film.

"those men are not white!"

O Brother…? has what David Bordwell (1985) would call a deadline, which is a/the staple element in narrative cinema: here, the trio must find the money before the valley is flooded. However, this deadline is in fact false, since there is no money. Furthermore, if the men are supposed to be getting from their prison to the money in a linear fashion, it would appear that really they are going around in circles, since two thirds into the film the trio are back at the prison from which they initially escaped (Pete has been arrested again). The film does, therefore, have a linear narrative of sorts, but it also seems as interested in evoking 1930s Mississippi, not least through the use of color, than it does in telling a story; the color seems to be the star, not Everett/George Clooney. This is reflected by the lack of closure for Everett in the film: Everett is all along trying to win back his wife, Penny, but the film seems to end with her rejecting his promises to change. Indeed, far more of the film's running time seems given to scenes that have little or nothing to do with this main plot, but which do provide opportunities to glimpse the film's beautiful and digitally-manipulated southern setting, for example when sirens lure the trio to a riverside oasis, or when the three attend a prolonged baptism scene also in the river. Indeed, the film is filled with period details and iconography, such as a heavily laden Depression-era truck driving its owner's worldly possessions down a sepia-tinted and tree-lined avenue. This is not a film about linear, narrative progression, therefore, but a film in which the digital color scheme emerges as the main attraction.

Furthermore, if digital images are simply colors changing in time, then in many ways, the characters in *O Brother…?* are like the film itself: they, too, are metaphorical "colors" changing in time. "Those men are not white!" are words spoken by gubernatorial candidate Homer Stokes as he tries to have the Soggy Bottom Boys (Everett, Pete and Delmar, together with guitarist Tommy Johnson, who actually is black) arrested. Stokes, a Grand Wizard fresh from a KKK meeting that the trio has disrupted to save Tommy from hanging, is convinced that they are all black, and that they should be arrested for defiling his precious ceremony.

Given the popularity of the Soggy Bottom Boys, Stokes' words are ignored and he is carried off, his election campaign in ruins after "outing" himself as a racist. However, Stokes' words are not far off the mark. Everett, Pete and Delmar all have white skin, but as far their places as citizens go, they do not conform to the white orthodoxy that we might assume was dominant in 1930s Mississippi. It is significant for example that Parchman Farm, the prison from which the trio escape, was, as pointed out by Content, Kreider and White,

> an almost all-black prison camp established in 1904 by
> James Kimble Vardaman, a notoriously racist Mississippi

governor who believed prison labour could provide young black men with proper discipline, work ethics, and an appropriately deferential attitude towards whites – and that these young blacks could in turn provide cheap labour for the state's business barons. (Content, Kreider and White 2001: 43)

Everett, Pete and Delmar are visibly the only whites among black inmates, and, as Content, Kreider and White note, they are continually mistaken for blacks, for example by Stokes. Furthermore, when they make a recording at a radio station (with Tommy on guitar), the three try to pass themselves off as blacks. They renounce this almost immediately following a frosty reception from the DJ, who nevertheless later recalls them as "colored fellas, I believe." Even before Stokes says that the Soggy Bottom Boys are black during their barnstorming concert, he proclaims that "the color guard is colored" when Klan member Big Dan Teague removes the trio's Klan disguise as they attempt to rescue Tommy. In addition, Everett starts a fight with Vernon T. Waldrip, his rival for Penny's hand, in Woolworths, only to be defeated and thrown out. "And stay out of Woolworths" is the shout from an irate storeowner. This, as has been noted, is reminiscent of the case in 1959, when four young black civil rights activists were thrown out of Woolworths in Greensboro, North Carolina, for defying the "'legiti-macy' of segregated lunch-counter seating" (Content, Kreider and White 2001: 43–44). Whilst amusing that the three are continually misidentified as black, this "mis"-identification is reinforced by their strong relationships with black characters. For example, they are friendly with a wizened black seer and not only do they come to rescue Tommy, but their very first encounter with him involves them giving him a ride in the car that they have stolen from Pete's cousin, Wash. This is more than they do for Wash's white son, Boy, who rescues the trio from almost certain death following Wash's denunciation of the three to the police, and yet they send Boy back to look after his father rather than help him.

It would seem, therefore, that *O Brother...?* is a film whose content in some respects matches its form, since the characters, like the digital/digi-tized image itself, constantly become other; like digital images from the perspective of the computer, the three main characters are metaphori-cally/politically "colors changing in time."

216

conclusion

O Brother...? is pleasing as a result of its exaggerated, digital use of color/its "peak shift effect." Its use of warm and advancing colors especially makes the film pleasurable at the expense of (or neurologically "before") move-ment and narrative. This color-based move away from narrative is reflected in the digital construction of the images: if digital films are colors changing in time, then the human and narrative elements of the film are down-played in favor of these appealing colors. The film knows this, too: what narrative there is in *O Brother...?* is a MacGuffin, and the film prefers to glory in its colors in a self-conscious manner, as seen in the opening shot which slowly changes from black-and-white to color as it progresses. Finally, the film is also about color in a political sense: the main characters change color metaphorically throughout the film, such that they are defined not so much by a fixed psychology (a fixed psychology that we might deem typical of narrative cinema), but instead as people "changing color in time." In this sense, the film's form matches its content. *O Brother...?* uses artificial devices (digitally manipulated colors) to appeal to natural processes (human perception, pleasure via the peak shift effect and warm colors) to create a film that is metaphorically, politically, and also literally a film about color more than about narrative.

references

Bartels, A. and Zeki, S. (2003) "Functional Brain Mapping During Free Viewing of Natural Scenes," *Human Brain Mapping*, 21, 2: 75–85.

Bartels, A. and Zeki, S. (2004) "The Chronoarchitecture of the Human Brain – Natural Viewing Conditions Reveal a Time-based Anatomy of the Brain," *NeuroImage*, 22, 1: 419–433.

Bazin, A. (1967) *What is Cinema? Volume 1*, trans. Hugh Gray, Berkeley, CA: University of California Press.

Bergan, R. (2000) *The Coen Brothers*, London: Orion.

Bordwell, D. (1985) *Narration in the Fiction Film*, London/New York: Routledge.

Content, R., Kreider, T., and White, B. (2001) "*O Brother, Where Art Thou?*" *Film Quarterly*, 55, 1: 41–48.

Dawson, D. and Encel, N. (1993) "Melatonin and Sleep in Humans," *Journal of Pineal Research*, 15: 1–12.

Everett, A. (2003) "Digitextuality and Click Theory. Theses on Convergence Media in the Digital Age," in A. Everett and J. T. Caldwell (eds.), *New Media: Theories and Practices of Digitextuality*, New York: Routledge: 3–28.

Franconeri, S. L. and Simons, D. J. (2003) "Moving and Looming Stimuli Capture Attention," *Perception and Psychophysics*, 65, 7: 999–1010.

Hardin, C. L. (2000) "Red and Yellow, Green and Blue, Warm and Cool," *Journal of Consciousness Studies*, 7, 8–9: 113–122.

Higgins, S. (2003) "A New Color Consciousness: Color in the Digital Age," *Convergence*, 9: 60–76.

Higgins, S. (2007) "Technicolor Confections," *Journal of Visual Culture*, 6: 274–282.

Manovich, L. (2000) *The Language of New Media*, Cambridge, MA: MIT Press.

Ramachandran, V. S. and Hirstein, W. (1999) "The Science of Art: A Neurological Theory of Aesthetic Experience," *Journal of Consciousness Studies*, 6, 6–7: 15–51.

Rodowick, D. N. (2007) *The Virtual Life of Film*, Cambridge, MA/London: Harvard University Press.

Solso, R. L. (1994) *Cognition and the Visual Arts*, Cambridge, MA/London: MIT Press.

Starr, R. (2000) Interview on the *O Brother, Where Art Thou?* UK DVD, Momentum Pictures.

Viviani, P. and Aymoz, C. (2001) "Color, Form, and Movement Are Not Perceived Simultaneously," *Vision Research*, 41: 2909–2918.

Walton, K. L. (1984) "Transparent Pictures: On the Nature of Photographic Realism," *Critical Inquiry*, 11, 2 (December): 246–277.

Zeki, S. (1999) "Art and the Brain," *Journal of Consciousness Studies*, 6, 6–7: 76–96.

Zeki, S. and Marini, L. (1998) "Three Cortical Stages of Color Processing in the Human Brain," *Brain*, 121: 1669–1685.

william brown

towards a more accurate preservation of color

t w e n t y

heritage, research and the film

restoration laboratory

u l r i c h   r u e d e l ,   d a n i e l a   c u r r ò ,   a n d   c l a u d y   o p   d e n   k a m p

In his film *Dreams* (USA/Japan, 1990) director Akira Kurosawa cast fellow filmmaker Martin Scorsese as Vincent van Gogh. This ingenious choice was generally understood as a tribute to the latter's efforts to promote and advance the preservation of color films, an issue that had in particular come to the fore with the fast fading of color film stocks dating from the 1970s onwards (Stern 1995: 155). Using the master painter to evoke the film artist and his conscious color choices, Kurosawa and Scorsese created an image that, perhaps unintentionally, offers a metaphor that extends well beyond the color film art and technology of the past century's later decades.

Van Gogh was a master of color in the nineteenth century, during which new pigments and dyes were invented that came to characterize that century's changes in color technologies and aesthetics. The characteristic sunflower yellow, that of toxic chrome yellow pigments, however, has now darkened to a mere shadow of its original color, as recently confirmed with original van Gogh paint samples (Monico et al. 2011). The problem of "authentic" color is far from unique to modern color film: the earliest colors of cinema, the so-called "unnatural" applied colors, are much more akin to painting or lithography in their aesthetics and application than the later "natural" color film stocks.[1]

Far from being an easily defined or measurable characteristic of a painting, a film or any other object, color can be a very elusive quality to translate from one medium to another. Not only is it impossible to faithfully capture the hue and saturation of many natural and artificial dyes and pigments of, for instance, Van Gogh's paintings on conventional color photographic materials (such as, ironically, the Eastmancolor used for *Dreams*); the same problem of reproduction also extends to preservation of early applied color on modern film stock. In order to take the quest for faithful color restoration initiated by Scorsese back to motion picture's varicolored infancy, this essay is particularly concerned with the preservation of the dazzling variety of colors in early cinema (see Cherchi Usai 2000; Read 2009).

The methods of "applied color" comprise tinting (the immersion of the film in a dye bath, coloring the entire emulsion), toning (the transformation of the neutral silver image into one consisting of colored metal salts), combinations of tinting and toning, as well as the techniques of hand- or stencil coloring.[2] Preservation of these early colors has come a long way. The approach to consider applied colors mere "bells and whistles" has given way to methods of honoring and trying to approximate the original colors (Hertogs and De Klerk 1996: 18).

The "Desmet-method," originally developed by and named after Noël Desmet of the Cinémathèque Royale in Brussels, Belgium, was designed to recreate the dramatic effects of tinting and/or toning in particular and has been widely employed in Europe since the 1990s (Desmet and Read 1998: 147).[3] In this method, special printing values and procedures are applied in printing a black-and-white negative onto color positive stock to obtain a visual appearance similar in color to a tinted and/or toned reference print. The contribution of Desmet's technique to the restoration and study of early color cannot be overstated: replication of a film's original tinting and toning scheme – where available – is now commonly considered good archival procedure as part of the original film's appearance.[4] Hand- and stencil-colored films, where different colors were selectively applied to specific image areas, cannot be recreated with Desmet's method, and are now commonly preserved on color intermediate or negative material, using photochemical or sometimes digital intermediate routes. For tinted, toned, hand- or stencil-colored films, "color restorations" have thus become commonly accepted, even expected.

But might something still be missing? Much as previous generations of archivists chose to ignore the applied colors entirely – just preserving a film's "content" as black-and-white images – is there a danger of ignoring

220

some visual characteristics of early color out of ignorance, negligence or necessity? By reviewing the progress in the restoration of early color, focusing on the work of Haghefilm Conservation B.V. with the Nederlands Filmmuseum, now EYE Film Institute Netherlands, and George Eastman House (GEH), this essay tries to map out historic, current and future techniques in order to start answering these questions. First, a case study of a tinted and toned sequence from a famous example of the EYE collections will be discussed. The colors of this two-color combination can be captured photographically all at once, or alternatively, one at a time, and recreated by different photographic and chemical preservation routes. Then, photographic and chemical investigations will be discussed, which confirm and help to understand the remaining visual differences to the original Desmet method. Subsequently, the approach of the principles of archeometry to film preservation will be considered, as recently demonstrated for metal tones at George Eastman House. In conclusion, the future opportunities for color film preservation will be mapped, which emerge and offer the possibility to elevate the technical approaches to the scientific sophistication of those in archeology and fine arts.

tinting: the return of (an) applied color, a short history and current shortcomings

The situation in the Netherlands provides an instructive case study. The EYE Film Institute Netherlands has been a key player in both color film preservation and its academic discussion and theorization, organizing for example the seminal 1995 workshop "Disorderly Order – Colours in Silent Film."[5] For their preservation efforts, the institution has been working closely with Haghefilm Conservation B.V. for more than twenty years, and this shared history and the evolving approaches to preservation reflect general trends.

In its early years as a preservation laboratory in the 1980s, Haghefilm focused on preservation of black-and-white and "special" film formats (such as 22 mm and 28 mm), before venturing into color and ultimately, from the early 1990s onwards, by trial and error, adapted the Desmet approach.[6] In the late 1980s, applied color was usually preserved on internegative material, a color stock specifically made for creating color negatives from positive prints. What seemed a faithful approach to capture a film element's original colors, however, actually introduced its own problems, even in a case as straightforward as a monochrome colored tint. As Giovanna Fossati observed, a "reproduction of a tinted nitrate has the same 'white' whites as a toned nitrate, giving a substantial difference in appearance" (1996: 14). Ironically, with Desmet's approach, in which a black-and-white negative is used and photographic means are applied to re-generate the coloring effects on color print stock, rather than chemically treating a black-and-white positive, a more faithful representation of the original is yielded than with the color internegative route.

In the Desmet method, starting from a tinted and/or toned nitrate print, a black-and-white preservation negative is created, which is then used to print a new projection copy on modern color positive stock. When printing the color positive, two passes in the printer are normally required if the images to reproduce are tinted (or tinted and toned), one if the images are toned only. In one pass, the images carried by the negative can be printed with white light, in order to simulate the silver images of the tinted original on the positive, or with colored light, in order to obtain an image in which the dark parts are colored in a selected hue, similar to a chemically created tone. In another printer pass, necessary in order to simulate the effect of a tint, the positive stock is evenly exposed, without any negative, to colored light (a procedure known as flashing), resulting in a complementary effect that colors predominantly the highlights, which produces a visual impression not unlike chemical tinting. Using reference samples with different settings of printing and flashing values can help in better approximating the original. The printing values can then be refined after one or more so-called "correction prints." The nitrate original and the modern color positive are inspected side-by-side on an inspection bench until a close match is achieved.

Due to the lower price of black-and-white stock, Desmet's method utilizing a black-and-white preservation negative was developed as an economically advantageous route over the color internegative one. More importantly, concern over the archival stability of color materials makes the use of black-and-white masters archivally preferable.[7]

Other differences remain, however. Tests, in which black-and-white sensitometric control wedges (strips with different known exposure that allow technicians to measure the photographic behavior of film stocks and printing and developing methods) were tinted and compared to wedges printed on pre-flashed material (like in the Desmet method) to match the tint's hue, confirmed and quantified the main difference rooted in the nature of flashing. Basically, as the image's overall density increases, the color shifts (eventually reaching neutrality in the maximum density the film material allows) in the Desmet method, whereas it remains evenly strong in the chemical tint. Flashing mostly affects highlights; while in a chemically tinted film the amount of dye attached to the gelatin is unrelated to the image density. This does not matter much for the shadow areas, since they appear black to the eye in either method, but, compared to a chemical tint, a Desmet-print can visibly show a certain "muddiness" and a change or lack of color in the grays.

It is sometimes noted that an overall loss in contrast accompanies the Desmet method; indeed, flashing originated as a means for contrast control. However, it should be noted that chemical tinting also decreases a film image's contrast and was sometimes deliberately employed towards this end, as discussed by Anke Wilkening (2009: 98) for the tinting of *Die Nibelungen* (Fritz Lang, 1924). Also, the structural difference between black-and-white and color film stock itself may account for visual differences. Black-and-white film contains silver grains (randomly arranged, invisibly small curled up filaments, or threads, of silver). Color film on the other hand contains layers of yellow, cyan and magenta dyes in a less defined random arrangement of more diffuse, so-called dye clouds. These three dye layers may allow for matching the color of a particular, different dye, but often fall short of matching its saturation. In addition, since the black-and-white image component in a Desmet print is also comprised of dye clouds rather than silver particles, it may appear less crisp and less neutral than the image of black-and-white material made up of silver grains. It is these phenomena that account for the visual shortcomings of the Desmet method – minor to some, substantial to others, even to the point that some viewers voice a preference for black-and-white *tout court* over Desmet prints. A last point, affecting the original experience of applied colors and the projection of modern prints, is unrelated to film materials and dye chemistries, but should not go unmentioned in this discourse. Light sources for motion picture projection have changed, and consequently the same chemical tint will look somewhat different projected on carbon arc versus modern xenon light, and to make matters worse, this change might be slightly different for the chemical tint and for its Desmet match. Like the shortcomings of the Desmet process, this aspect raises the inevitable ethical restoration question: how closely approximated is close enough?

two colors: tint and tone, by means of discrete restoration routes including vintage chemical recipes

One of the gems of the EYE Film Institute Netherlands collections showcased in the 1995 Disorderly Order workshop was the 1912 Pathé film *De molens die juichen en weenen*, original title *L'âme des moulins,* directed by Alfred Machin.[8] Featuring stencil colors in different sequences as well as tints and tones, the film can serve as a showcase of the whole gamut of Pathé's applied colors in the pre-WWI era. **Plate 31** shows a reproduction of a frame from an especially beautiful scene, a *chiaroscuro* night shot of a man walking towards a mill from *De molens die juichen en weenen*.[9] The shot is toned blue and tinted pink. Even in the printed reproduction, the color is recognizable as a blue typically resulting from an Iron Blue tone.[10] The pink is similar to the color obtained with eosin or amaranth, dyes historically commonly used for tinting (Read 2009: 34; Read and Meyer 2000: plate 8.2). EYE Film Institute Netherlands kindly made the nitrate available to the authors for a restoration comparison of selected scenes on different stocks and through different routes.

In addition to these discrete restoration routes, a black-and-white print of a selected scene was chosen to tint and tone "by hand," using chemical recipes.

One might think that carefully inspecting the original and recognizing the chemistry of a tint or tone might give a definite answer regarding the make-up of the colors, but this is not straightforward or practically possible. Eosin, for instance, was historically used for pink tinting (Löbel 1912: 281). Chemically speaking, however, it is a slightly unusual dye. Commonly, tinting dyes are acidic, and oftentimes an addition of citric or acetic acid is recommended in historic recipes to aid the tinting process. However, in this case the acid dye eosin actually changes color to orange, different from the pink tint obtained when just dissolving the salt of the dye without added acid in water. Interestingly, a similar color is observed at the edge of the frame in an irregular shape, suggesting decomposition and/or fading. Has acid released from nitrate decomposition locally affected a color change from pink to orange? To make matters more complex, a similar orange is observed in the area of the image where the evening sun is seen – potentially suggesting a deliberate stencil color effect, which can only clearly be observed when projecting preservation copies on the screen, rather than the ravages of time and acid.

Lastly, while the color of Iron Blue is fairly easy to identify for the trained eye when inspecting the original film material, it is far from unambiguously defined. Paul Read has reported on the amazing color of Iron Blue but also on its fading by projection and ageing (Read and Meyer 2000: 272). Indeed, the vibrant color of "new" Iron Blue, made by following the Eastman recipe, is never seen in vintage originals, presumably due to ageing (Eastman Kodak 1922). A preliminary experiment following a recipe from Pathé's 1926 manual *Le Film vierge Pathé: Manuel de développement et de triage* (Didiée 1926: 129) resulted in a somewhat duller blue upon testing with modern stock. Such variations are not necessarily a surprise to those familiar with the traditional pigment chemistry of Iron Blue compounds that predate moving images. As with the variety of traditional pigments (Prussian Blue, Turnbull's Blue, Berlin Blue, Antwerp Blue, etc.) known for what is essentially the same chemical component, the exact color of the Iron Blue tone might well depend on the exact way of its preparation, the size of its particles, and thus perhaps even on the microstructure of the silver it is derived from.

towards an archeometry and chemistry of motion picture color

Film preservation is a relatively young discipline. Efforts to set up ethical and methodical guidelines have been informed by the first decades of film restoration, and have often been pursued independently by archives or even individuals seeking parallels between film restoration and the ethical principles set up in the classical disciplines of restoring art, archeological finds and other artifacts (Edmondson 2004). While some principles have indeed been generally accepted for film preservation – such as the reversibility of any action taken – others are harder to transfer, based on the fact that film restoration is restoration by duplication – creating a new object of what is often (perhaps uncritically) seen as an inherently reproductive art. Yet this "restored" object is not only different from its original by virtue of being a copy, but also by practical and technical limitations. Today it is impossible to create, for example, a Technicolor dye transfer print, or a black-and-white print on nitrate base. And, for tinted and toned originals, only very few laboratories routinely or even commercially engage in chemical tinting and toning of modern restoration copies.

Perhaps the latter limitation makes it even more important to follow the lead of classical restoration disciplines. In the scientific arena, the restoration of art and archeological artifacts is supported by various branches of conservation science and of archeometry, i.e., the use of scientific means to study archeological artifacts (Wagner 2007). Similar studies have been, arguably for the first time, conducted on motion picture film samples in 2008/2010 at George Eastman House's Kay R. Whitmore Conservation Center, using the technique of so-called X-Ray Fluorescence (Ruedel and Podsiki 2013 [forthcoming]).

Chemical approaches, however, should not be limited to the scientific study of the historic material itself. Indeed, the issues discussed above regarding tinting, including eosin and its comparison to the nitrate original with its decomposition patterns, can be regarded as a form of experimental archeology, as pioneered by Paul Read (1998). Such experiments can encourage a closer look into the analog and digital methods of simulating tints on modern film stock, and thus further the understanding of both materials. They have also proven very valuable in teaching and outreach, as in experimental archeology. Even if they fail to encourage a more widespread revival of the craft (for a variety of reasons, including practical and budget-related ones), they are worthwhile in their own right for the study of color history and technology.

There is, however, one other discipline of science that is even more rarely considered for application in film preservation than conservation chemistry and archeometry: Imaging Science (Saxby 2002). A comparatively young formal interdisciplinary field, it explores the physical, chemical, optical, but also the neurological and psychological factors concerning the perception of what we call color. Thus, it is the only field that scientifically considers the entire process relevant for film preservation, from understanding a historic color technology, to matching it as closely as possible using modern techniques, and, finally, the viewing of the result by a modern audience. In current practice, Imaging Science is often concerned with the proper reproduction of an original's colors (often of historic and art objects) and includes study of the color and chemistry of different colored materials, as for instance, in the "art-si" project at the University of Rochester which has explored spectral imaging for more faithful capturing of the colors of painting (RIT 2005). Given that film restoration employs reproduction of colors, often using chemistries different from the original, this is clearly another discipline that has much to offer the field of film preservation, perhaps presenting possibilities to devise specific capturing and reproduction routes for more faithful rendition of particular historic color systems.

future opportunities

With a new generation of film preservationists entering into the field and specializing in various aspects of the discipline, future enriching and transdisciplinary opportunities arise, in which new experiments and approaches will be inspired by fields as diverse as art conservation, archeometry and imaging science. Those film preservationists open to – or, even better, trained in – relevant technologies and fields may find (especially under the threat of the "death" of analog, carrier based photographic film) an opportunity to further preservation technologies and routes, while engaging in a constant dialogue with archives, academics from both the arts and the sciences, and the restoration laboratories.

acknowledgements

Like every study of the historic chemistries and current restoration techniques, this paper would not have been possible without the seminal research done by Paul Read (who has also been very gracious in discussing his insights), and the restoration routes established by Noël Desmet and other pioneers of the field. The authors would further like to thank Bert Hulshof, Leo Kuyper, Herman Laman, Peter Limburg, Menno Revers, Leen Treuren, Juan Vrijs (Cineco / Haghefilm Conservation B.V.); Giovanna Fossati (EYE Film Institute Netherlands); Ed Stratmann (George Eastman House, Motion Picture Department); Taina Meller, Patrick Ravines and Cheryl Podsiki (George Eastman House, Photography Conservation Department); and Paolo Cherchi Usai (Haghefilm Foundation).

226

notes

1. Eastmancolor (established in the United States) and Agfacolor (Europe) are examples of *chromogenic* film, which is characterized by the use of dye couplers in layered photographic emulsions. Unlike "unnatural" color systems, these systems aim at photographically capturing a scene's original colors and reproducing them in the photographic film by means of dyes generated during development. The chromogenic systems were preceded

by the famous Technicolor system, which shares characteristics of both systems: original colors are captured (albeit on three separate black-and-white film strips), but the positive prints are produced in a process that is essentially lithographic rather than photographic. Generally speaking, these colors are more stable than those of chromogenic film, and can share the saturation and vibrancy otherwise unique to the earlier applied colors.

2. As the color is not noticeable in the darkest areas of the images, tinted films display a tonality ranging from black to the chosen tinting color; in other words, highlights (including the areas between the perforations) look colored while the underlying image appears neutral. The coloring agent is usually an acid dye. Examples include the textile dye Orange G and the food dye tartrazine. As the colored component is formed from the image's silver, toned films rather display a tonality ranging from the deep color of the tone to white; in other words, highlights (including the areas between the perforations) ideally appear neutral, while the image itself is colored. The colored component can be an inorganic, colored metal compound (metal toning), or a more or less colorless metal salt (e.g., silver iodide) subsequently dyed with a basic dye (mordant or dye tone). Examples for metal toning include Prussian Blue (Iron Blue) and silver sulphide (sepia).

3. Similar methods were concurrently developed elsewhere; see for example Case (1987).

4. In an ideal scenario, a tinted and toned copy from the film's original country and time of release would be available. Foreign prints need to be treated with caution as "texts" as their tinting might well be different from the original release. Tinting instructions can be found in "cutting continuities" (basically, protocols of the final edited version of a film) or in "slugs" (short pieces of leader which might contain hand-written instructions) in the original negatives, although in that case the exact hue of a certain color might still be somewhat ambiguous. Often, original negatives might also be arranged by tints, rather than in their narrative chronology, which can help in establishing their original colors. Interesting exceptions are tinted titles in otherwise black-and-white films. In some cases, these are considered of too little relevance to compromise the quality of the photographic images by printing on color stock, or to justify the extra effort of positive splicing in preservation prints.

5. A transcript of the workshop is printed in Hertogs and De Klerk (1996).

6. After having been bought by contemporary film laboratory Cineco in 1995, the synergy of the two companies led to a newly found creative experimentation: Johan Prijs (one of the Haghefilm founders) started experimenting with original camera negative Fuji 64D as a preservation internegative. Originally a highly unusual duplicate material, currently, films with stenciled colors are photographically reproduced almost exclusively with the help of this stock, due to its generally better reproduction of the hues and saturation of the original.

7. This advantage is considered so substantial that, for instance, in the recent digital restoration of the originally tinted and toned Abel Gance 1919 masterpiece *J'Accuse!* (EYE Film Institute and Lobster Film in collaboration with Haghefilm Conservation B.V.), the digital files were written out to black-and-white duplicate negative for subsequent Desmet color grading, rather than applying the colors digitally and recording to color intermediate. Employing a black-and-white negative has the further advantage of largely

227

eliminating discolorations that are considered to be age and decomposition related, and thus not part of the original. The Desmet printing route on color stock then allows the re-application, photographically rather than chemically, of the colors in a way that somewhat resembles the original tints and tones. Indeed, while the saturations of particular color dyes cannot be achieved on modern film stocks, careful timing allows quite close matching of the original hues.

8. The film is also known under the English title *Windmills that Cheer and Weep.*
9. Reproduced courtesy of the EYE Film Institute Netherlands.
10. Blue dye tones are well documented. See for instance Read (2009).

references

Case, D. (1987) "Producing Tints and Tones in Monochrome Films Using Modern Color Techniques", *SMPTE Journal*, 96: 186–190.

Cherchi Usai, P. (2000) *Silent Cinema: an Introduction*, London: British Film Institute.

Desmet, N. and Read, P. (1998) "The Desmetcolor Method for Restoring Tinted and Toned Films", in L. Berriatua (ed.) *Tutti i colori del mondo: il colore nei mass media tra 1900 e 1930*, Reggio Emilia: Diabasis: 67–70.

Didiée, L. (1926) *Le Film vierge Pathé: Manuel de développement et de tirage*, Paris: Établissements Pathé-Cinema.

Eastman Kodak (1922) *Tinting and Toning of Eastman Positive Motion Picture Film*. Rochester: Eastman Kodak Co. Third, revised edition. Available at http://www.brianpritchard.com/tinting_and_toning_of_eastman_po.htm (accessed 22 March 2009).

Edmondson, R. (2004) *Audiovisual Archiving: Philosophy and Principles, Commemorating the 25th anniversary of the UNESCO Recommendation for the Safeguarding and Preservation of Moving Images*, Paris: United Nations Educational, Scientific and Cultural Organization.

Fossati, G. (1996) "Coloured Images Today: How to Live with Simulated Colours (and Be Happy)", in D. Hertogs and N. De Klerk (eds.) *Disorderly Order: Colours in Silent Film, The 1995 Amsterdam Workshop*, Amsterdam: Stichting Nederlands Filmmuseum: 83–89.

Hertogs, D. and De Klerk, N. (eds.) (1996) *Disorderly Order: Colours in Silent Film, The 1995 Amsterdam Workshop*, Amsterdam: Stichting Nederlands Filmmuseum.

Löbel, L. (1912) *La Technique Cinematographique*, Paris: H. Dunod et E. Pinat.

Monico, L., Van Der Snickt, G., Janssens, K., De Nolf, W., Miliani, C., Dik, J., Radepont, M., Hendriks, E., Geldof, M., and Cotte, M. (2011) "Degradation Process of Lead Chromate in Paintings by Vincent van Gogh Studied by Means of Synchrotron X-ray Spectromicroscopy and Related Methods. 2. Original Paint Layer Samples", *Analytical Chemistry*, 83, 4: 1224–1231.

Peres, C., Hoyle, M. and Van Tilborgh, L. (1991) *A Closer Look: Technical and Art-Historical Studies on Works by Van Gogh and Gauguin: Cahier Vincent 3*, Zwolle: Waanders.

Read, P. (1998) "Tinting and Toning Techniques and their Adaption for the Restoration of Archive Film", in L. Berriatua (ed.) *Tutti i colori del mondo: il colore nei mass media tra 1900 e 1930*, Reggio Emilia: Diabasis: 77–88.

Read, P. (2009) "Unnatural Colors: An Introduction to Colouring Techniques in Silent Era Movies", *Film History* 21, 1: 9–46.

Read, P. and Meyer, M. P. (2000) *Restoration of Motion Picture Film*, Oxford: Butterworth-Heinemann.

RIT, Art-Sci.Org. (2005) Online. Available at http://www.art-si.org (accessed 16 May 2011).

Ruedel, U. and Podsiki, C. (2013) XRF Studies of Toned Motion Picture Clippings at George Eastman House. [forthcoming]

Saxby, G. (2002) *The Science of Imaging, An Introduction*, Bristol: Institute of Physics Publishing.

Stern, L. (1995) *The Scorsese Connection*, Bloomington, IN: Indiana University Press.

Wagner, G. (2007) *Einführung in die Archäometrie*, Berlin: Springer.

Wilkening, A. (2009) "Fritz Lang's *Die Nibelungen* / A Restoration and Preservation Project by Friedrich-Wilhelm-Murnau-Stiftung", *Journal of Film Preservation*, 79/80: 86–98.

herbert g. ponting's

materials and texts

t w e n t y   o n e

liz   w a t k i n s

> *For as long as celluloid can last, the filmed record of Captain*
> *Scott's last tragic journey to the Pole is at last completed. It has*
> *taken years of work, and now posterity can look on it, just as we*
> *do, for as long a time as discovered science can ensure (Ponting,*
> *11 August 1924: 8)*

The 2010 digital restoration of *The Great White Silence* (Ponting, 1924) com-
memorates the centenary of the departure of the British Antarctic
Expedition (1910–13). Herbert G. Ponting's photographic record of the
expedition has been integral to the narratives that have emerged around
the loss of the polar party. The stills and cine-photography formed a
strand of the expedition's scientific research by offering a visual record
of the region. A study of the provenance of the 2010 restoration discerns
a supplementary layer of information (residual marks of production
and decay) beneath the fascia of image and narrative. The interpretation
of instructions that are scratched into the film and attributed to
Ponting have informed the "return" of color in the 2010 release of *Silence*.

The restoration refers to and incorporates sections of film from diverse archives and pasts elaborating a historiographic process that embeds ideas of authorship and authenticity in a narrative of irresoluble loss.

Herbert G. Ponting, camera artist to Captain R. F. Scott's fated polar expedition (1910–1913), re-edited his film footage across an initial twenty-year period in response to the technological and cultural contexts of each release. The material and textual alterations that can be tracked across the different versions reveal a tension between the film as scientific document, historical record and the continuing development of a narrative that underlies its remobilisation as a commercial enterprise in the film market. A study of the polar film footage necessarily encounters the materiality of these revisions as the shifting configurations of Ponting's images and texts. The theoretical implications of these various versions extends to an analysis of the layering of materials and digital manipulation of color in the 2010 restoration of *The Great White Silence* (H. G. Ponting, 1924) as a process which echoes Ponting's filmmaking practice.

Fossati's concept of "the archival life of film" (2009) facilitates an analysis of the ontology of the film material and photographic index that constitute the "authentically poetic" of documentary film (Bazin 1967: 154). These elements persist in the "convergence-divergence" (Fossati 2009: 137) of analog and digital in the 2010 color restoration of *The Great White Silence*. This discourse, of authenticity and authorship, in which the return of color is keyed to Ponting's instructions scratched into sections of leader, is invoked in the digital simulation of tinting and toning as applied color processes. These technical alterations open a space in which to address the impact of the digital on the film object and text. It is in this sense that the reconstruction (Busche 2006: 3) of the color scheme operates as a facet of historiography, imagination and memory.

The camera negatives were initially processed by Ponting in the Antarctic and returned to the UK in two consignments to be screened in two parts under the title *With Captain Scott R.N., to the South Pole* (1911 and 1912). Ponting, who held the rights to the expedition stills photography, subsequently purchased those for the cinematograph films from the Gaumont Company in 1914 for £5,100. Following the Great War, Ponting moved to re-circulate the film, but found it met with poor receipts. Bazin's suggestion (1967: 154) of the 1919 release as a pretext for interest in *Nanook of the North* (Robert Flaherty, 1922) differs from Ponting's rationalisation of his decision to edit the footage into *The Great White Silence* [*Silence*]. For Ponting, Flaherty's film was indicative of continuing public interest in exploration documentaries. Work on editing *Silence* began after the 1921 publication of his written account of the expedition, *The Great White South*.

Ponting's work "perfecting [the] film record of the expedition" included the insertion of intertitles to facilitate the circulation of the films in regional theatres without the need to deputise lecturers (Ponting, 21 March 1924). Although initially optimistic, by April 1926 Ponting commented that his proportion of the receipts for *Silence* stood at £22 per week compared to the production cost of prints at £100 each. Following the emergence of synchronised sound film in the late 1920s Ponting undertook further revisions to incorporate this technology into *90° South* (1933) at an estimated cost of £10,000 (Ponting, 22 October 1932). During this period Ponting's correspondence with Frank Debenham who, with his assistant Miss Winifred M. Drake, advised on the accuracy of the film's illustrations, indicates the difficulties of revitalising the film in keeping with the full breadth of technological developments that would position his "ancient results equal to modern panchromatic photography" (Ponting, 22 October 1932; 15 August 1933).[1] Adaptations to the technique required to produce *90° South* included the transfer of material to film stock with different perforations and the alteration from the speed of filming at 16 fps to that of the 24 fps of synchronised sound projection. The residual effects of these technical manipulations are visualised in the instabilities of the image in relation to the frame (Ponting, 12 January 1933). Ponting's revision incorporates additional material including the commissioning of new maps, a 25-foot painting of the landscape, a diorama and an amended animated line and map sequence, each of which was filmed and inter-cut with still photographs to further illustrate the journey of Scott, Wilson, Oates, Bowers and Evans to the South Pole (Ponting, 15 August 1933). This practice is in keeping with his advocacy of the film's educational value, in seeking to effectively convey the details of the expedition, its scientific work and the fate of the polar party.

Ponting's correspondence with Debenham indicates the exaggeration of certain aspects of the landscape, such as Mount Erebus, to facilitate the dramatic appeal of the film, while other information that is "only of interest to scientists" is omitted or remains without denotation (Ponting, 15 August 1933; 20 May 1933). Ponting notes that these exaggerations when on the screen "give a remarkable idea of the kind of terrain in which the expedition operated" (Ponting, 30 October 1931). This indicates a continuing tension between the film negatives as both a mode of scientific exploration and historical record, and the demands of producing a coherent and captivating narrative as the footage is re-edited toward its broadly educative potential.[2]

Ponting held the rights to all of the still photographs taken on the expedition, including those few images taken by Bowers and Scott at the South Pole; a fraction of these appear in *Silence*. The cinematography of the polar party was staged prior to their departure to the South Pole so the interleaving of still-photographs assists in the representation of the final journey that Ponting did not film. Incorporation of these images offered new material to a film that had been widely circulated by the time of his purchase of copyright in 1914. Following the initial disputes over the right to give lectures accompanying the photographic and cinematographic records, this practice enabled him to revitalise the film beyond the scope and period of the Gaumont Company's ownership.

In reformulating the film footage to the shifting interests of its anticipated reception the visual appeal of the image and the drama of the story are emphasised. The tension between the film as commodity and expedition record lies in the accumulation of information and its erasure and of the materials and detritus that invoke a direct relationship between the photographic imprint and the cinematic illusion projected of light. While the re-editing of the film footage is responsive to different innovations, indicating its potential to be deciphered as a tract of film history, such alterations in technique also affect the film as a text.

Ponting's awareness of the photographic records of the expedition as a commodity is reflected in his earlier comment that "it is only the pictorial prints that pay" (Ponting, 17 December 1913). Ponting voiced a plan to "secure good color effects of the Antarctic icescape by means of new autochrome cameras" (*Daily Mail*, 31 May 1910), an intention that was reflected in a report published prior to the departure of the expedition that "a large stock of plates […] for securing the effects of the Antarctic in true natural colors" was to form part of the documentation of the expedition (*The Times*, 28 May 1910: 8). Similarly the handwritten notes on the paper sleeves used to protect the photographic plates indicate that Ponting recorded different light conditions and natural phenomena including that of the Australis Borealis. By detailing the geographical orientation, date and time that the negatives were exposed the images offer co-ordinates both of the inhabitation of the region and of the expedition as an epistemological object.

Ponting's references to the use of color for his still photography primarily concern the selection of hues that enhance the subject: "Ice Blink" is printed "in the green [carbon] tissue" and another "in a very fine blue tissue, which seems to suit the subject exactly" (Ponting, 15 June 1926). In *Silence*, however, the fourteen different combinations of tinting, toning and hand coloring that are detailed by instructions scratched into sections of film indicate a color design that is also significant to its themes and narrative.

Cherchi Usai tracks the significance of certain colors in the silent period to suggest thematic associations, such as a shift to amber which could signal "when a table lamp was turned on in a room" (1991: 29–38). In *Silence* the thematic use of color, perhaps unintentionally, maps territory, both by delineating between areas associated with the ship and those inhabited by the Antarctic wildlife. In this context a shift from amber in the record of the expedition member's daily work to the sepia tone and green tint of zoological studies indicates that of a different realm, whilst combinations of a blue tone and pink tint are associated with the effects of light refracted by the ice. Ponting's use of color contributes to narrative progression through a historiographic practice of editing and commissioning new material.

The initially black-and-white film footage and selected photographs of the Terra Nova seen through an ice cave can be linked to his written account of the expedition, which is particularly attentive to color:

> During this first and subsequent visits, I found the coloring
> of the grotto changed with the position of the sun; thus
> sometimes green would predominate, then blue, and then
> again it was a delicate lilac. (Ponting [1921] 2000: 68)

The still photographs edited into *Silence* signal a temporal elapse that formulates a narrative surrounding the transient morphology of icebergs. (**See Plate 32.**) His literary articulation indicates a "myriad of crystals" that "decomposed the rays into lovely prismatic hues, so the walls appeared to be studded with gems" (Ponting [1921] 2000: 68). Descriptions of ice vary from "rainbow-hued flashes of light, mirrored by the dancing lapping wavelets" to the ice formed like "lily-leaves" that "took on autumn tints of orange with russet-shadows and their upturned edges were topaz" in the light of the midnight sun (Ponting [1921] 2000: 30, 54). Such descriptions suggest what was not immediately recorded by the cinematography. The movement of the ice floe is evoked in *Silence* through inter-cut still and moving images of the grotto taken a year apart, each shot colored in jewel-like tones to be found in tinting and toning catalogues. The addition of color to these images offers the cinematographer's perspective as a layer of interpretation over the "subtle shadows of the snow and [...] wonderful transparent texture" that Scott notes of his black-and-white photography (Scott [1921] 2000: xv).

The significance of color to the narrative is established in the opening section of the film. The initial black-and-white images of Captain Scott and Ponting position them as auteurs of both the expedition and the diegesis before the color scheme is instigated as the Terra Nova sets sail. The changes in color that are contiguous with those of the film's themes are reduced in the section detailing the final journey to the Pole. This also gives an inflection of coherence across a section that is assembled from a significant number of technical revisions including animation, still-photographs and drawings, to avoid distraction from the tale. A shift in color to a blue tint denotes their imminent demise in the "fateful tent" which persists across the memorial portrait photographs of the five men. The still images screened are the work of duplication across a strip of 35 mm film. This contrasts with the transcendent blue tone and amber tint that transfigures the remaining images: drawings of an angel reaching down to Captain Scott and a cairn of rocks surmounted by a cross that marks the graves of the expedition members. Notably the remaining inter-titles of *Silence* are dominated by a quote from Scott's diary and marked by the imaged authorisation of his handwritten signature which forecloses the film.

The 2010 restoration of *Silence*, which sees the return of the chromatic schema, is drawn into a discourse of authenticity and authorship through reference to the color instructions scratched into sections of leader that accompany the film negatives. **(See Figures 21.1 and 21.2.)** For *Silence*, as with many examples from the 1920s, the instructions do not consistently distinguish between tinting, toning and hand painting as possible methods of coloring the film. Luciano Berriatúa notes "the variety of these tints and their intensity from year to year. And also from laboratory to laboratory", indicating potential points of divergence from the color instructions (Berriatúa 1998: 135–139).[3] Both Paul Read and Nicola Mazzanti indicate material inconsistencies that occur between prints of what is ostensibly the same film due to differences in the concentration of dye solution and the duration of the submergence of each strip of film (Mazzanti 2009: 67–93; Read 2009: 9–46; *BJP* 1924: 611–614). For example, the recurrence of a color instruction could incur a variation in color intensity. It is in this sense that the salience of color in the study of *Silence* encounters numerous factors affecting the variations in hue, transparency and intensity that result from different dyes and processing methods.

Figure 21.1
Ponting's color instructions scratched into sections of film leader.

Figure 21.2
Ponting's color instructions scratched into sections of film leader.

Mazzanti states that the chromatic score of a film could also alter accord-ing to the national and cultural context of its distribution (Mazzanti 2009: 67–93). *Silence* was circulated in countries including Britain and Germany and, as *Expeditie naar de zuidpool 1910–1913* (1925/1940), in the Netherlands. A copy of the tinted and toned print that is held at the EYE Film Institute in Amsterdam was used as a point of reference for the BFI National Film and Television Archive's 2010 color restoration. In the 1990s Angelo Lucatello's comparative work, which contributed to the later digital resto-ration, identified several differences between the 1923 nitrate soft print of *Silence* and the EYE Film Institute's holdings which include additional material such as a still-photograph of Dr Atkinson's frost bitten hand. Such combinations of elements also extend to the duplication of fragments of leader and instructions in the fine grain contact print assembled in the 1990s by the NFTVA. The diversity of materials that informed the recon-struction (see workflow chart in **Figure 21.3** at the end of this chapter) indicates the potential for the film image and text to alter.

These sections are dated according to later releases and so pertain to different configurations of the film footage. The restoration also referenced a print accessioned as *L'Eternel Silence* (1922) at La Cinémathèque de Toulouse which echoes the color scheme of the Dutch and BFI NFTVA variants.

This print pre-dates *Silence* and can be distinguished from the other holdings by its form and content: the images of light conditions differ and the sequence detailing the fate of the polar party is conveyed through intertitles rather than duplicated still photographs, sequences of stop-motion animation and imaged paintings of the 1924 version. For Mazzanti the collation of different versions and generations of prints toward what Busche calls a reconstruction (2006: 3) can elicit shifts in the film text by decomposition or design to constitute a "variant" rather than new "version" of a film (Mazzanti 2009: 76–77). While Ponting's re-editing constructs new versions, the trajectory of the digital reconstruction forms a variant within the cultural context of its production. The "return of color" through digital grading encounters inconsistencies in the filmic elements sourced. The inflection of color across the configuration of assembled materials (see the workflow chart) noted in the exhibition of the 2010 print contributes to the discourse of authorship and authenticity. The sequence edited from *Silence* that forms a trailer for the NFTVA plays on this discourse as the final image shows the visual erosion of four explorers from one of Ponting's staged sequences as they are gradually encompassed by the expanse of the landscape. The figure of the dissolve and the erasure of the visible are entwined with a configuration of the fascinatingly irresolute details that surround the loss of the polar party. Through the dissolved image the interplay of historiography, technology and memory traces a scenography of loss.

In evaluating the concepts of "authorship" and "variants", Ponting's correspondence with Debenham is significant in its recognition of the involvement of four assistants. The assistants include Mr Gent, who had been the Gaumont Company's representative in Australasia and acted as their signatory on the agreement with the expedition. Gent was in Ponting's employment from 1918 until at least 1930 on a wage of £400 per annum. Ponting states that in addition to his work on the cinematographic films Gent was responsible for the care "of the negatives and everything appertaining to them" (Ponting, 29 July 1929; 8 January 1930). Color instructions relating to *Silence* and editing instructions for *90° South* were incorporated into the NFTVA's fine grain duplicating positive. In particular, the instructions that are dated as contemporary to the production of *90° South* are attributed to Ponting, but are written in the third person, indicating the work of both Ponting and his assistants which informed the digital reconstruction.

The concept of a variant is immured in the materiality of the film. Materiality evokes the economies of production and circulation, but also the shifting technology and text of each re-edit and re-release. The assembled images of each film are never entirely contained by the narrative, but as they are interpreted by the spectator, they participate in its mapping. Interpretation lies in tension with the anomalies of deterioration that reveal the material base of the cinematic illusion: each film element sourced bears the marks and scratches specific to its storage and use, so sustaining its own temporality. For Rosen it is preservation that affirms authenticity, allowing the spectator to invest in the visible traces of damage that betray the age of the film's edifice (Rosen 2001: 52). The complex temporality and achronology of the film material underlies that of its narrative form and the salient marks that Rosen addresses.

In a sense, the process of reconstruction resonates with Ponting's own practice. The assembled materials therefore map the path of the digital reconstruction to formulate an image of the film elements and a digital simulation of the applied color processes of tinting and toning. Each transfer to a new medium signals a shift in the image and text. The assembled "film" accumulates the characteristics of each medium and process; alterations remain visible through the details that they add or erode from the image. It is in this sense that charting the provenance of the reconstruction (see the workflow chart) indicates the significance of film as a cinematographic document. Variations in the physical characteristics and temporalities of the film materials and texts, which are integral to a study of the broader context of Ponting's work, signal a problematic familiar to color film restoration. The materiality of the film, which evokes both the technological and cultural context of each release and its circulation as commodity, plays on the "authentically poetic quality" that Bazin invokes through the indexicality of the photographic and authorial perspective (1967: 154). However the imbrication of image and narrative in a historiographic practice emphasises the myths surrounding the expedition and distracts from Bazin's sense of the photographic as an unmediated record which instead is drawn into a complicated staging of space and time (Galt 2006: 53–71).

Ponting states his revisions as a way "to keep the great story up-to-date in technique and fresh in the public mind" and to maintain them as "priceless historical records" (Ponting, 15 November 1932). His advocacy of a permanent record consistently reaffirms his loyalty to the expedition in a determination to revitalise memories of it. Ponting's correspondence with Debenham also indicates the visual record's continuing potential for commercial exploitation and a need to recuperate the expenditure of film production. Conversely the transfer of the film as document to a new medium incurs a loss of image resolution and instigates an index of each new stage of production. The subsequent image sustains a trace of previous generations of film material. The residual imprints of processing and the simulacra of marks specific to other film elements reveal fragments and images drawn from diverse pasts into a new narrative form. Such traces reside within a narrative which plays on the spectator's fascination with uncertainty and change. Doane's analysis of the paradox between contingency and rationalisation that infuses the emergence of narrative form suggests that the affectivity of cinema lies in the fear of disorder (Doane 2002: 140–141). Doane writes that whilst the transience of time reveals a "corruption [that is] 'proper' to it, its fixed representation [as photographic image] also poses a threat, [that] produces aesthetic and epistemological anxiety" (Doane 2002: 3). The frailties of representation are immured in the regulation and organisation of "time" between the photographic index, the film-still and the temporal ordering of narrative. Ponting's films, as document and narrative form, rely on the ontology of film material that is subsumed between actuality and historiography. In keeping with Rosen's *Change Mummified*, as a direct reference to Bazin, the construction of Ponting's documentary text can be said to belie "the referential ambitions" of historiography (Rosen 2001: xi). As Rosen notes, cinematography and historiography are "social and cultural operations as much as technological and epistemological structures" that similarly privilege narrative continuity over the achronology of the specific film elements drawn together in a reconstruction (2001: xii). A textual analysis of the 2010 variant of *Silence* necessarily addresses the residual traces of the diverse materials on which it relies.

For Latour, the production of a transfer or copy means that "we never see an image, but one element in a cascade of transformations" (Latour 2010: 183). The image as point of access to the cinematic archive offers a fascia that is itself susceptible to change through the effects of shifting configurations of materials and media. The complex edifice of the 2010 variant extends the discourse surrounding authenticity and historiography from *Silence* as the 1924 version of Ponting's film footage of the British Antarctic Expedition (1910–1913). The "restoration trajectory" emphasises Latour's comment that without re-use the concept of the original is diminished (Latour 2010: 183). The concept of authenticity suggests a point of continuity within the material and textual practices of the historiographical process and narrative of the reconstruction.

The reconstruction reflects Memelsdorff's analogy of a written musical score, which requires an aesthetic choice in its implementation that is similar to the inflection that the restoration puts on Ponting's color instructions; each is read and interpreted as a set of actions to be taken (Memelsdorff 2010: 197). Although an assumption of objectivity underlies the subjective selections made, there are layers of interpretation from Ponting and his assistants, through to those of the reconstruction. The NFTVA's work documents a trajectory through previous generations of materials now detailed and in storage. A study of the restoration trajectory tracks alterations in design and the contingent marks that register the susceptibility of celluloid and photosensitive emulsion to the impact of the environment during filming and storage. Traces of the technologies of production and decay constitute data which can be read as a supplementary record of the expedition and form a strand of the historiography of its materials and texts. Ponting's photographic work is integral to the narratives that have emerged around the expedition. The restoration underscores and distances photography and detail as paradigmatic of authenticity. It also offers a new

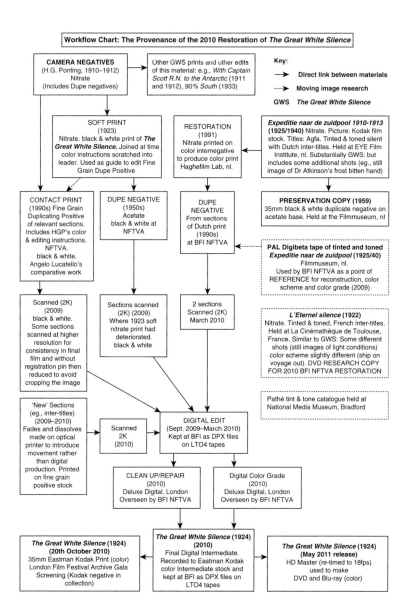

Workflow Chart: The Provenance of the 2010 Restoration of *The Great White Silence*

CAMERA NEGATIVES
(H.G. Ponting, 1910–1912)
Nitrate
(Includes Dupe negatives)

Other GWS prints and other edits of this material: e.g., *With Captain Scott R.N. to the Antarctic* (1911 and 1912), 90% *South* (1933)

Key:
→ Direct link between materials
⤏ Moving image research
GWS *The Great White Silence*

SOFT PRINT
(1923)
Nitrate. black & white print of *The Great White Silence*. Joined at time color instructions scratched into leader. Used as guide to edit Fine Grain Dupe Positive

RESTORATION
(1991)
Nitrate printed on color internegative to produce color print Haghefilm Lab, nl.

Expeditie naar de zuidpool 1910-1913
(1925/1940) Nitrate. Picture: Kodak film stock. Titles: Agfa. Tinted & toned silent with Dutch inter-titles. Held at EYE Film Institute, nl. Substantially GWS: but includes some additional shots (eg., still image of Dr Atkinson's frost bitten hand)

CONTACT PRINT
(1990s) Fine Grain Duplicating Positive of relevant sections. Includes HGP's color & editing instructions. NFTVA.
black & white.
Angelo Lucatello's comparative work

DUPE NEGATIVE
(1950s)
Acetate
black & white at NFTVA

DUPE NEGATIVE
From sections of Dutch print (1990s)
at BFI NFTVA

PRESERVATION COPY (1959)
35mm black & white duplicate negative on acetate base. Held at the Filmmuseum, nl

PAL Digibeta tape of tinted and toned *Expeditie naar de zuidpool* (1925/40) Filmmuseum, nl.
Used by BFI NFTVA as a point of REFERENCE for reconstruction, color scheme and color grade (2009)

Scanned (2K)
(2009)
black & white.
Some sections scanned at higher resolution for consistency in final film and without registration pin then reduced to avoid cropping the image

Sections scanned (2K) (2009)
Where 1923 soft nitrate print had deteriorated.
black & white

2 sections
Scanned (2K)
March 2010

***L'Eternel silence* (1922)**
Nitrate. Tinted & toned, French inter-titles. Held at La Cinémathèque de Toulouse, France. Similar to GWS: Some different shots (still images of light conditions) color scheme slightly different (ship on voyage out). DVD RESEARCH COPY FOR 2010 BFI NFTVA RESTORATION

Pathé tint & tone catalogue held at National Media Museum, Bradford

'New' Sections
(eg., inter-titles)
(2009–2010)
Fades and dissolves made on optical printer to introduce movement rather than digital production. Printed on fine grain positive stock

Scanned 2K
(2010)

DIGITAL EDIT
(Sept. 2009–March 2010)
Kept at BFI as DPX files on LTO4 tapes

CLEAN UP/REPAIR
(2010)
Deluxe Digital, London
Overseen by BFI NFTVA

Digital Color Grade
(2010)
Deluxe Digital, London
Overseen by BFI NFTVA

***The Great White Silence* (1924)**
(20th October 2010)
35mm Eastman Kodak Print (color) London Film Festival Archive Gala Screening (Kodak negative in collection)

***The Great White Silence* (1924)**
(2010)
Final Digital Intermediate. Recorded to Eastman Kodak color Intermediate stock and kept at BFI as DPX files on LTO4 tapes

***The Great White Silence* (1924)**
(May 2011 release)
HD Master (re-timed to 18fps) used to make DVD and Blu-ray (color)

Figure 21.3

Workflow chart of the British Film Institute National Archive's 2010 restoration of *The Great White Silence* (H.G. Ponting, 1924)..

point of access to *Silence* as film text and to a narrative that plays on imagination, memory and the historicity of the subject. For its historical, narrative and pictorial significance the chromatic scale of the film, like the deictic salience of marks and scratches, offers the illusion of the past in the present that allows the spectator to invest in the digitally colored image as an image of authenticity.

acknowledgements

My thanks to Kieron Webb and Angelo Lucatello at the British Film Institute National Film and Television Archive; Haghefilm Filmmuseum and EYE Film Institute, Amsterdam; La Cinémathèque de Toulouse; Scott Polar Research Institute; Deluxe Digital, London, and the AHRC.

notes

1. Debenham was a geographer on the *British Antarctic Expedition* (1910–13). He was later Director of the Scott Polar Research Institute.
2. Although the rights for *90° South* were vested in the nation Ponting was offered five years exploitation rights to recuperate this personal expenditure, the profits from which were incorporated into his estate following his death in 1935.
3. The NFTVA consulted a Pathé catalogue of tints and tones and additional individual frames that form part of the Kodak collection at the National Media Museum Bradford. These sources were used as a point of reference for the 2009–2010 restoration of *Silence*. Additional reference material included prints of *Silence* from the EYE Film Institute and La Cinémathèque de Toulouse, and a research screening of tinted and toned prints of *The Lodger* (Hitchcock, 1926) and *South* (Frank Hurley, 1919) for NFTVA restoration project members and technicians from Deluxe Digital, London.

references

Bazin, A. (1967) "Cinema and Exploration", trans. Hugh Gray, *What is Cinema? Volume 1*, Berkeley, CA: University of California.

Berriatúa, L. (1998) "Regarding a Catalogue of the Tints Used on the Silent Screen", *All the Colors of the World: Colors in Early Mass Media 1900–1930*, Reggio Emilia: Edizioni Diabasis: 135–139.

British Journal of Photography [BJP] (1924) "A Review of Dye Toning Processes", *British Journal of Photography [BJP]*, 71, 3360: 611–614.

Busche, A. (2006) "Just Another Ideology? Ethical and Methodological Principles in Film Restoration", *The Moving Image*, 1: 1–28.

Cherchi Usai, P. (1991) "The Color of Nitrate", *Image*, 34, 1–2: 29–38.

Daily Mail (1910) "Captain Scott's Men. Science with the Camera. Terra Nova's Start Tomorrow", *Daily Mail*, 31 May, MS1453/39/1-2 Scott Polar Research Institute, Cambridge.

Doane, M. A. (2009) *The Emergence of Cinematic Time: Modernity, Contingency, Archive*, Cambridge, MA: Harvard University Press.

Fossati, G. (2009) *From Grain to Pixel, The Archival Life of Film in Transition*, Amsterdam: Amsterdam University Press.

Galt, R. (2006) "'It's so cold in Alaska': Evoking Exploration between Bazin and *The Forbidden Quest*", *Discourse*, 28, 1: 53–71.

Latour, B. (2010) "Concluding Remarks: How to Inherit the Past at Best", in P. Gagliardi, B. Latour and P. Memelsdorff (eds), *Coping with the Past: Creative Perspectives on Conservation and Restoration*, Leo S. Olschiki: Civiltà Veneziana Studi 52.

Lucatello, A. (2010) "How Do They Do It? *The Great White Silence*", The Discovery Channel, 27 October. Online. Available at http//ww.yourdiscovery.com/video/how-they-do-it-how-they-do-it-the-great-white-silence/

Mazzanti, N. (2009) "Colors, Audiences and (Dis)continuity in the 'Cinema of the Second Period'", *Film History*, 21: 67–93.

Memelsdorff, P. (2010) "Concluding Remarks: How to Inherit the Past at Best", in P. Gagliardi, B. Latour and P. Memelsdorff (eds), *Coping with the Past: Creative Perspectives on Conservation and Restoration*, Leo S. Olschiki, Civiltà Veneziana Studi 52: 197.

Ponting, H. G. ([1921] 2000) *The Great White South*, New York: Cooper Square.

Ponting, H. G. (17 December 1913) Letter to Apsley Cherry Garrard, *British Antarctic Expedition 1910–1913*, MS559/102/2, Scott Polar Research Institute, Cambridge.

  – (3 February 1917) Letter to Lady Kathleen Scott, MS15/3, Scott Polar Research Institute, Cambridge.

  – (11 August 1924) "*The Great White Silence* Programme Notes", D.1500/1/1, Bournemouth Electric Theatre, Dorset History Centre: 3-10.

  – (30 October 1931) Letter to Debenham, MS 280/28/7a: ER, Scott Polar Research Institute, Cambridge.

  – (22 October 1932) Letter to Padre Hayes, MS964/7/22, Scott Polar Research Institute, Cambridge.

Ponting, H. G. *British Antarctic Expedition 1910–1913*, Volume 7, MS280/28/7, Scott Polar Research Institute, Cambridge.

  – (21 March 1924) Letter to Frank Debenham.

  – (15 June 1926) Letter to Frank Debenham.

  – (29 July 1929) Letter to Frank Debenham.

  – (8 January 1930) Letter to Frank Debenham.

  – (15 November 1932) Letter to Padre Hayes.

  – (12 January 1933) Letter to Frank Debenham.

  – (20 May 1933) Letter to Frank Debenham.

  – (15 August 1933) Letter to Frank Debenham.

Read, P. (2009) "'Unnatural Colors': An Introduction to Coloring Techniques in Silent Era Movies", *Film History*, 21, 1: 9–46.

Rosen, P. (2001) *Change Mummified, Cinema, Historicity, Theory*, Minneapolis, MN: University of Minnesota Press.

Scott, R. F. ([1921] 2000) "Kathleen Scott's Foreword", in H. G. Ponting, *The Great White South*, New York: Cooper Square: xv.

The Times (1910) Saturday 28 May: 8.

about the american

film institute

The American Film Institute (AFI) is America's promise to preserve the history of the motion picture, to honor the artists and their work and to educate the next generation of storytellers. AFI provides leadership in film, television and digital media and is dedicated to initiatives that engage the past, the present and the future of the motion picture arts. The *AFI Film Readers Series* is one of the many ways AFI supports the art of the moving image as part of our national activities.

AFI preserves the legacy of America's film heritage through the **AFI Archive**, comprised of rare footage from across the history of the moving image and the *AFI Catalog of Feature Films*, an authoritative record of American films from 1893 to the present. Both resources are available to the public via AFI's website.

AFI honors the artists and their work through a variety of annual programs and special events, including the **AFI Life Achievement Award**, **AFI Awards** and **AFI's 100 Years … 100 Movies** television specials. The **AFI Life Achievement Award** has remained the highest honor for a career in film since its inception in 1973; **AFI Awards**, the Institute's almanac for the 21st century, honors the most outstanding motion pictures and television programs of the year; and **AFI's 100 Years ... 100 Movies** television events and movie reference lists have introduced and reintroduced classic American movies to millions of film lovers. And as the largest nonprofit exhibitor in the United States, AFI offers film enthusiasts a variety of events throughout the year, including the longest running international film festival in Los Angeles and the largest documentary festival in the U.S., as well as year-round programming at the **AFI Silver Theatre** in the Washington, DC metro area.

AFI educates the next generation of storytellers at its world-renowned **AFI Conservatory** – named the #1 film school in the world by The Hollywood Reporter – offering a two-year Master of Fine Arts degree in six filmmaking disciplines: Cinematography, Directing, Editing, Producing, Production Design and Screenwriting.

Step into the spotlight and join other movie and television enthusiasts across the nation in supporting the American Film Institute's mission to preserve, to honor and to educate by becoming a member of AFI today at AFI.com.

American Film Institute

Robert S. Birchard
Editor, *AFI Catalog of Feature Films*

index

Note: Numbers in bold refer to a figure.